A History of Gwent

A HISTORY OF GWENT

RAYMOND HOWELL

GOMER PRESS
1988

First Impression - 1988
Second Impression - 1989
Third Impression - 1993

ISBN 0 86383 338 1

Printed at
Gomer Press, Llandysul, Dyfed

er cof am
Dr. T. J. Anthony

Contents

Preface

In this book, I have set out to provide a concise history of Gwent from the earliest times to the present. I hope that I have succeeded in offering an overview of the major historical traditions in the region which will be of interest to the general reader. An additional hope is that a framework has been provided which will prove useful to future researchers considering various topics in more detail. Recent research has already greatly expanded our knowledge of the development of Gwent. This is particularly true of the period between the withdrawal of the Romans and the arrival of the Normans. The excellent work by Professor Wendy Davies of University College, London, for example, has brought the kingdom of Gwent from the realm of informed speculation to that of hard historical fact. Similarly, recent excavations of Roman sites, most notably work in and near Caerleon undertaken by David Zienkiewicz of the National Museum of Wales, has greatly enhanced our understanding of Roman Gwent. More recent periods have also profited from important new re-interpretations. Particularly notable in this respect is work done on Chartism and the Newport rising, with books by David J. V. Jones, senior lecturer at University College, Swansea, and by Ivor Wilks, professor of history at Northwestern University, Illinois. Such new material has been incorporated into the present book. Inevitably, a concise general survey such as this must be drawn largely from secondary source material, but an effort has been made to utilize both new and standard references. All of this material has been footnoted in detail and it is hoped that the note sections of this book will provide a usefully thorough bibliography of the history of Gwent.

There is certainly scope for investigation of a wide range of topics concerning Gwent with considerable material available to the researcher. The Gwent County Record Office, for example, holds a wealth of material, much of it under utilized by historians. The Newport Library Reference Section is another useful repository and local libraries such as Chepstow also have original holdings of local interest. In many respects, the history of Gwent is uniquely important among the regions of Britain. A vital border location has made Gwent a centre of continuing conflict as well as a focus for strong cross culture contacts. Its central role in the industrial revolution has also made it a pace setter in social change. Nevertheless, the region has not attracted the historical interest which it deserves. It is true that good local studies have been produced. The prolific work of Ivor Waters in Chepstow and Keith Kissack's studies on Monmouth are cases in point. Nevertheless, since Bradney's monumental efforts of half a century ago, comprehensive works on the region as a whole, apart from Arthur Clark's study, have not followed. One factor which has contributed to this lack of interest is a reluctance by basically English historians to attempt to deal with Welsh material or to come to grips with Welsh traditions. Most Welsh historians, on the other hand, have preferred to concentrate on the North, West and Glamorgan. This is unfortunate in several respects, not least being that, as this book demonstrates, the Welsh dimension is crucial to the historical development of Gwent. As a consequence, the role of the Welsh language and culture has been examined in some depth in this book and notes point to useful Welsh material.

Throughout the preparation of this history, I have benefitted from suggestions offered by friends and colleagues. Of special help have been students in a series of adult education classes which I have taught concerning aspects of the history of Gwent. Their interest and enthusiasm as well as probing questions, have contributed in no small measure to this book. I am also grateful to the library staff at the Gwent College of Higher Education who have been helpful throughout in mobilizing resources. My colleagues at Caerleon, Alwyn Lewis, head of history, and Alun Worthington, senior lecturer in geography, have read the text and offered helpful suggestions. Particular thanks also go to David Zienkiewicz who has kindly read the Roman sections, offering expert advice. He has also counselled caution on contentious pre-Roman matters and I hope that such sections, where interpretative questions are difficult, have been clearly identified in the notes. Any failure to do so, or other errors or omissions, reflect only on the author. A final word of thanks goes to my wife who has provided not only moral support but also the important substantive assistance of typing the final draft of this book.

A Map of MONMOUTHSHIRE.

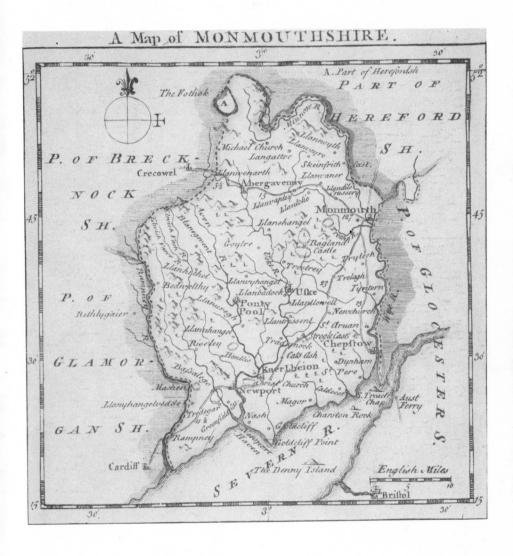

The Earliest Inhabitants

When the first men arrived in Gwent, they found themselves moving through terrain bearing little resemblance to the region today. The last phase of glaciation in Britain, the Devensian, lasted from about 70,000 to 8300 B.C. In phases, a great ice sheet pushed south to a line running roughly from Abergavenny to Hereford. Naturally, areas near to the glacier, including the whole of the remainder of Gwent, would have been bitterly cold tundra. Paleolithic hunters moving along the ridge above Chepstow would have looked north to see the ice sheet in the distance with only the tops of the Black Mountains rising above the glacier. There were also other dramatically different features. With so much water caught up in the glaciers, sea level fell by at least 200 feet and coastlines advanced. A land bridge linked Britain to the continent and much of the Bristol channel was dry land with the Severn being simply a broad river valley. Land bridges enabled early hunters to pass easily, but the conditions could not have recommended Gwent to many of them. A more benign climate and a ready supply of flints for tools in the southeastern chalk regions of England made those areas more attractive to the hunting bands. Despite the difficulties, however, hunters did follow their prey, including reindeer, mammoth, bison, cave lions and the woolly rhinocerus, into Gwent.[1]

Given the influence of glaciation, it is not surprising that there are few examples of Lower or Middle Paleolithic tools from the region, although isolated finds from places including Chepstow confirm an early presence. Upper Paleolithic activities, however, are somewhat more clear since key cave sites have been excavated. One of the most famous of these was west of Gwent, on the Gower peninsula, where the 'Red Lady of Paviland' was discovered. The 'Lady', actually a young Cro-Magnon man, had been buried ceremoniously with a necklace of animal teeth and ornaments of ivory and sea shells some 20,000 years ago. The body was covered with red ochre which stained the bones and provided the skeleton with its name. Even more relevant for early Gwent are the finds from King Arthur's Cave, Whitchurch, which overlooks the Wye. An upper Paleolithic hearth, flints and animal bones confirm that the cave was a camp site for the early hunters who represent the beginning of the story of man in Gwent.[2]

By about 7500 B.C., there was a marked improvement in the climate. As temperatures rose and the ice retreated, the forests began to grow with willow, aspen, birch, hazel, and pine making their appearance. As tundra gave way to woodland, the animal life took on a more modern appearance. Red deer, wild oxen and wild pig became the prey of Mesolithic hunters. The arrival of new peoples in the region during the Mesolithic saw the introduction of innovative stone tools. Notable among these were the microliths, small flints, which could be used to tip weapons. Despite such changes, however, there was also a strong measure of continuity which is demonstrated at King Arthur's Cave where there was almost continuous occupation and the Paleolithic tradition flowed easily into the Mesolithic.[3] The most important point which should be stressed is that men continued to support themselves as hunter-gatherers. Even favoured camp sites would be occupied for only portions of the year as the hunting groups had to allow for migration of their prey and changing weather. This long-established life style did not change until about 4000 B.C., the beginning of the Neolithic period in Britain.

The Neolithic brought a fundamental change in lifestyle resulting from the rise of agriculture, with permanent settlement in small farming communities. Food supplies increased and surpluses were produced for the first time, permitting a measure of specialization of function. Among the developments associated with the change in many parts of Europe was an increasing production of pottery. Such changes reached Gwent through the arrival of settlers probably coming in small groups rather than in a mass migration. There is an important point to be made concerning these new arrivals with their revolutionary ideas. For many years, there has been a tendency to think of prehistoric Britain as being easily divided into a highland and a lowland zone, assigning the whole of Wales to the former. The model suggests that new immigrants and ideas came first to the lowland zone where they were quickly established and then only slowly and partially spread to highland regions. There is, however, good reason to be sceptical about this model quite apart from the obvious fact that an area like Gwent has clearly defined highland and lowland zones of its own. It is important to remember that Wales, along with Cornwall, extends into the Irish sea and offers safe havens for seafarers as well as good routes into the interior. The Irish sea can be seen as a natural magnet for the seaborne population movements from Western

Europe which have been demonstrated to have been a continuing phenomenon.[4] These seaborne influences were significant at several stages and impacted directly on Gwent even in the early Neolithic. A related fact which should be kept in mind is that while the sea level had risen opening Gwent to seafarers, the coastline was still different from today. The greater extent of the Caldicot levels is confirmed by a Neolithic skull and animal bones found some twenty feet below present sea level at the Alexandra South Dock in Newport.[5]

One of the most striking features about early Neolithic farming communities is the chambered tombs which they built. These tombs, the cromlechau, remain as impressive monuments to the first agricultural settlers in Gwent. The idea of the chambered tomb seems to have come from areas including Britanny and the Iberian peninsula and the seaborne transmission of their culture has led to somewhat fanciful descriptions of 'missionaries' spreading a new megalithic religion along the western coasts of Britain. It is certainly clear that Neolithic settlers moved up the Bristol channel with the Severn estuary providing entry into the interior. These settlers, clearing land with their polished stone axes, introduced farming and stock raising with cattle being particularly important. Pottery was introduced and eventually the new arrivals merged with earlier inhabitants to produce a new cultural synthesis. The most obvious legacy of this culture is the chambered tomb. Large stone slabs, or capstones, were placed on top of upright stone supports, with drystone walling sometimes filling any gaps, to form a burial chamber. A cairn of stone or barrow of earth was then placed over the chamber. There were variations in the design of the tombs with the long barrow consisting of a chamber at one end of a forecourt, apparently being the earliest form. A particularly striking example of the type is Pentre Ifan in West Wales. A later variation is seen in Tŷ Isaf, an example of a transepted gallery tomb associated with the Severn-Cotswold tradition, which is located in the southern foothills of the Black Mountains. At Tŷ Isaf, a funnel shaped forecourt led to a wedge-shaped cairn with a false entrance. The burial chambers, which when excavated revealed the bones of 33 people, were actually approached by passages from the sides of the cairn. This tomb is important because it is typical of a cluster of no fewer than 16 similar tombs at the foot of the Black Mountains.[6]

Over the millenia, the mound covering many of these cromlechau has weathered away leaving the skeleton of the tomb, sometimes with the capstone still in position, as a particularly evocative ancient monument. Those in the Black Mountains are important indicators of the pattern of Neolithic settlement in the region. Two Gwent tombs are particularly significant in this respect. The chambered tomb at Heston Brake near Portskewett, with a chamber of some 20 feet by 5 feet in a now greatly reduced mound once approximately 70 feet by 40 feet, is only about a mile inland from Sudbrook which would have been an obvious landfall for migrants moving up the Bristol channel. To the northwest, near Devauden, is Y Gaer Llwyd, still impressive despite the fact that its capstone has partially collapsed. It is possible that these tombs mark the path of Neolithic settlers slowly moving through Gwent in the direction of the Black Mountains. Movements in other directions also seem likely as is suggested by the related tomb at Gwern y Clepa near Tredegar Park in Newport.[7] Inevitably, many inferences must be drawn from these tombs, since we have no examples of actual settlement sites in the region. Nevertheless, there are other indications of the presence of these earliest Gwent farmers. Among the most important of their tools were the polished stone axes which allowed them to clear their lands. These axes were significant over a long period, and a thriving trade in them developed. Local examples have been found near Usk and Chepstow.[8]

The Neolithic period lasted for some 2,000 years. By about 2500 B.C., however, new influences resulting from the arrival of the Beaker people began to change the old synthesis.[9] Copper technology was among the most important early innovations associated with these people, who buried their dead singly accompanied by the distinctive bell beakers which have given them their name. They clearly used bows and arrows as archers' wrist guards have been found as well as distinctive tanged arrowheads with two barbs. The Beaker influence was particularly significant because the early stone circles and other standing stones seem to date from this period. The famous bluestones from the Preseli Mountains, for example, were originally set in a double circle at Stonehenge during the Beaker phase. Similarly, in Gwent, the three great standing stones of Trelech were probably also erected at this time.[10] There is another interesting possibility concerning the Beaker people. It has been suggested that they should be viewed as proto-Celtic and that a form of Celtic speech in Gwent dates from their arrival.[11]

Obviously the Beaker people brought significant changes to the region. The pace of change soon began to accelerate and by about 2000 B.C., copper technology gave way to bronze. It was found that adding one part of tin to nine of copper produced a harder and more durable metal which was useful for both tools and weapons. There are numerous examples of Bronze Age sites in Gwent including the mound at Langstone. In addition, the heavily rimmed urns which were adapted for the newly adopted cremation burials of this period have been found at Usk. Of special interest is the emergence of a bronze industry in south Wales which specialized in socketed axes with distinctive decorative ribs running along the blade. Gwent and Glamorgan were centres of this industry and examples of the axes have been found at several locations including sites in and near Usk, Llanarth, Trelech, Llanddewi Rhydderch, and Tintern. Particularly important was a hoard of seven looped socketed axes found on Livox Farm, St. Arvans.[12]

The St. Arvans hoard could imply a smith settled near a population concentration. On the other hand, it could also suggest stock buried at a time of danger. There is certainly evidence to suggest that times were unsettled. One contributory factor may have been the arrival of iron-using Celts from the continent. Certainly people were moving along the western seaways again and the Llyn Fawr lake offerings from Glamorgan suggest the arrival of a Celtic war leader there in the late seventh or early sixth century B.C. This has led some experts to suggest that defensive considerations began to dominate and that the beginning of hill fort construction may date from the late Bronze Age.[13] To most minds, however, hill forts suggest the Iron Age and the classical Celts. At this stage, the difficult prehistoric picture becomes somewhat more certain as we find Gwent at the heart of the territory of the Silures, the dominant Celtic tribe in South Wales.[14]

NOTES

[1] Stanford, S. C., *The Archaeology of the Welsh Marches* (London: 1980) pp. 34-35; and Houlder, C. and Manning W. H., *South Wales, Regional Archaeology* (London: 1966), pp. 11-13.

[2] Stanford, pp. 35-39; and Houlder and Manning, pp. 13-14.

[3] Evans, John, *The Environment of Early Man in the British Isles* (London: 1975), pp. 77-83; and Stanford, pp. 41-43. The six skeletons found at Ifton quarry may date from this period.

[4] See especially Alcock L., 'Celtic Archaeology and Art' in Davies, Elwyn (ed.), *Celtic Studies in Wales, A Survey* (Cardiff: 1963), pp. 4-7 and Bowen, E. G., *Saints Seaways and Settlement* (Cardiff: 1977), pp. 1-27.

[5] Stanford, p. 45. The remains were found in 1911 during an extension of the dock.

[6] Briand, Jacques, *The Bronze Age in Barbarian Europe* (London: 1979), pp. 30-31 and 69-70; Stanford, pp. 44-54; Houlder and Manning, pp. 27-28; and Houlder, C., *Wales: An Archaeological Guide* (London: 1974), pp. 132-133. See also Daniel, Glyn, *The Megalith Builders of Western Europe* (London: 1958).

[7] Stanford, pp. 46-48. The Tinkinswood tomb near Cardiff seems to demonstrate features of both the Pentre Ifan and Severn-Cotswold traditions. For details of locations of tombs and possible routes of movements see Roese, H. E., 'Some Aspects of Topographical Locations of Neolithic and Bronze Age Monuments in Wales: IV Chambered Tombs and Burial Chambers' in *The Bulletin of the Board of Celtic Studies*, XXIX, IV, 1982, pp. 763-775.

[8] Ibid, p. 48. For more details of the axe industry, see Clough, T. H. and Cummins, W. A. (eds.) *Stone Axe Studies: Archaeological, Petrological, Experimental and Ethnographic.* (Council for British Archaeology: 1979).

[9] The 2500 B.C. date marks the arrival of the Beaker people in Ireland. Their influence in Gwent began somewhat later.

[10] Briand, p. 18; Stanford, pp. 55-60; and Houlder and Manning, pp. 35-41. The Trelech stones continue to be known in some quarters as Harold's Stones. This unfortunate and confusing description is based on nothing more than the possibility that Harold Godwinson may have looked at them in 1065. The Beaker people were brachycephalic, round headed, in contrast to the dolichocephalic, long headed, Neolithic peoples. It is important to remember that the henge monuments which sometimes preceded stone circles were Neolithic.

[11] For a discussion of the question, see Dillon, M. and Chadwick, N., *The Celtic Realms* (London: 1973), pp. 16-19 and 265. While some will question this interpretation, the alternative seems to be assigning the origin of Celtic speech to Halstatt arrivals in the late 7th or early 6th century B.C. If this is the case, their linguistic influence was immense—greater even than that of the Latin which followed—and this lends weight to the proto-Celtic Beaker argument.

[12] Stanford, pp. 61-64. Details of beaker finds, including a complete example of a distinctive barbed and tanged arrowhead, at St. Brides Netherwent are in Buckley, 'The Excavation of a Bronze Age Barrow Mound St. Brides Netherwent' in *Archaeologia Cambrensis*, CXXIV, 1975, pp. 36-51.

[13] Ibid, and Alcock, pp. 9-11.

[14] The problems of attempting to present a comprehensible model for the prehistoric development of the region are immense. The situation is well explained by Peter Salway, an expert on Roman Britain. In discussing the present state of flux in interpreting the British Iron Age, he suggests that, 'specialist opinion on this period is at present so fluid that anything more than a bare outline is likely to be obsolete as soon as it is written, and certainly by the time it is published.' It should be noted that experts disagree, at times dramatically, about dating of prehistoric material. A particularly exciting recent discovery is of prehistoric trackways on the Caldicot levels. Discovered by coastal warden Derek Upton, the tracks have recently been announced by Bob Trett, curator of the Newport Museum. Hurdles of coppiced hazel formed trackways some 6-7 feet wide which have been dated to about 400 B.C. The trackways open exciting new avenues for investigation on the levels and may impact on the structure of society dominated by the strongpoints of Sudbrook and Wilcrick below Llanmelin.

The Silures

Our view of the lifestyle of prehistoric peoples in Gwent must inevitably be highly speculative. When we come to the Celts, however, the picture is clarified by more extensive archaeological evidence supplemented by classical references which bring the Celts onto the stage of history. It should be stressed that observations by Roman writers must be viewed with some caution since there was always a measure of self justification for campaigns against 'barbarian' foes. Critical classical views emphasising unsavoury elements like the cult of the head must be balanced against such sophisticated Celtic innovations as soap, the wheeled chariot, and primitive reaping machines. Nevertheless, classical references are useful. From disapproving Roman observers, for example, we find that a drooping moustache was an almost mandatory feature among Celtic tribesmen. We also have sufficient descriptions of the 'Celtic thirst' to leave little doubt that they enjoyed their ale. When Diodorus Siculus describes the two features, writing that 'drink passes as through a strainer', we can begin to visualize the tribesmen themselves. [1]

Archaeologically, too, there is considerable material to help complete a mental image of the Celts. The classical Celts, who once controlled some 800,000 square miles of Europe, traditionally define the European Iron Age. The early phase on the continent, c. 800-450 B.C., is identified as Halstatt, named after a site in Austria. The late Iron Age, with its distinctive art forms, is styled La Téne from a site in Switzerland. It has long been common practice for British archaeologists to identify Celtic material as Iron A, relating to the continental Halstatt; Iron B, derived from La Téne; and Iron C, which was Belgic. Gwent hillfort sites demonstrate all three, with the Iron C influences possibly being associated with Caradog and the resistance to Roman invaders. There is, however, now some reluctance to rely too strongly on this classification system with its implied suggestion of waves of invasion. The modern tendency is to view Iron A and B traditions as resulting more from a diffusion of ideas and techniques than of large scale movements of peoples. [2] Nevertheless, it is clear that iron age population movements did take place.

There is a reference in Tacitus, our best classical source on the Silures, to 'Iberian' characteristics among curly haired warriors. [3] This has given rise to suggestions, which must be viewed with some caution, that an

Iberian stock were ruled over by a conquering warrior class of fair, continental Celts. There is certainly no doubt that there were arrivals of bands from Europe along the western seaways. The Llyn Fawr site discussed in the previous chapter suggests a Celtic band carving out territory to establish a new dynasty at about the beginning of the sixth century B.C. The new arrivals were unquestionably Celts; among the artefacts recovered is the only known British example of an iron Halstatt long sword. Other sites demonstrate similar arrivals from the continent. There is, however, an important observation to be stressed about these finds. At Llyn Fawr, in addition to classical Iron A implements, there was also an iron sickle which was a copy of an insular design in bronze. Elsewhere insular axes were also copied and it does not strain the imagination to visualize newly arrived continental iron smiths producing implements for established populations demanding the older Bronze Age designs. If this is the case, it suggests a fairly rapid and complete assimilation which may have been aided by linguistic similarities between the new arrivals and Bronze Age populations. We can be confident that the Silures, in common with other southern British tribes, emerged as Brythonic, or P Celtic, in speech. In other words, they used a language which was to evolve into modern Welsh. [4]

As has already been seen, the most obvious diagnostic feature of the Iron Age is the hill fort and there were several distinctive elements in the hill forts of the Silures. One feature was that the Silurian forts tended to be quite small in comparison with examples in England or on the continent. Many would be better visualized as enclosed farms rather than major fortifications. In addition, there was a preference for turning the ends of the fort's ramparts inwards to form a funnel leading to a gate. As the funnel was narrow, attackers approaching the gate would be easy prey to slings and spears of defenders on the ramparts. Multiple ramparts were also common although in some forts these were set closely together in an obviously military plan while in others the ramparts were widely spaced, apparently to allow cattle to be driven into the defences of the fort. [5]

Distinctive hill fort design helps to establish the tribal boundaries of the Silures which can be done with a fair degree of confidence. Gwent and Glamorgan were the homeland of the tribe which was concentrated in lands bordered by the Bristol channel to the south, the Wye on the east and the Tywi on the west. The aggressive Silures at times pursued an expansionistic policy which took them beyond these borders. It is probably not insignificant that the largest Silurian hill forts are on the borders—Y Gaer Fawr in the Tywi valley and Spital Meend on the east bank of the Wye. There is also strong evidence for Silurian expansion toward the northeast. The region between the Monnow and the Troddi rivers seems to mark the early border between the Silures and the tribe which Stanford identifies as the Decangi of Herefordshire. A particularly significant site, however, is the Twyn y Gaer hill fort near Symonds Yat. The site began as a Decangian fort but it was later modified to the Silurian pattern, as the size of the fort was reduced and the gateway ramparts were rebuilt to create the Silurian funnel effect. It is likely that Twyn y Gaer demonstrates Silurian expansion at the expense of the Decangi.[6]

The nature of Silurian hill fort construction allows some suggestions to be made about lifestyle of the tribe. The small, widespread fortifications have led some authorities to suggest that the tribe was loosely knit and that kinship and clan loyalties were dominant among the Silures.[7] There was almost certainly scope for inter, as well as intra, tribal conflict. For example, in a barter economy with cattle having special significance, it would not be surprising for rustling raids to occur. There must also have been considerable local insularity. Nevertheless, there was sufficient tribal cohesion and organization to allow the Silures to exert widespread influence. As will be seen, this was especially true when tribal lands were threatened by invaders. In addition, we know that the Silurian aristocracy was well versed in the 'duties and pleasures of hospitality', traditionally an important feature of Celtic society. Ornamented domestic equipment has survived to present a picture of this phase of Silurian life. The hearth was obviously a social focus and elaborately designed wrought iron fire dogs have survived. So too have tankards for the beer or mead which was vital in the provision of hospitality. The best of the British iron age tankards comes from Trawsfynydd in north Wales, but several Silurian examples survive, notably in a group from Seven Sisters.[8]

The nature of Silurian society has led to a reluctance to accept the concept of a tribal capital, preferring to visualize an oligarchical approach to tribal organization. One site, however, recommends itself as a particular focus of Silurian authority. Llanmelin hill fort, one of the few Silurian forts to be excavated, is located on the spur of a hill about one mile north of Caerwent commanding impressive vistas across the Caldicot levels to the Bristol channel. On three sides the hill itself provides steep natural defences and two lines of banks and ditches were originally thought sufficient to protect the three acre fort. At a later date, however, the entrance was rebuilt on the classical inturned pattern and three rectangular enclosures were added to one side of the fort. These enclosures were clearly intended for cattle.[9] Llanmelin was probably the tribal capital of the Silures, an argument strengthened by the Roman decision to build Caerwent nearby as a civitas to relocate the tribal leadership. It is true that the first reaction to Llanmelin as the principal tribal centre is one of scepticism, not least because the site is far from the geographical centre of Silurian territory. The location and role of Llanmelin becomes more comprehensible, however, when Sudbrook camp is examined. The Silures were clearly influenced by the south-western tribes across the Severn and significant numbers of 'Glastonbury culture' artefacts have been found on Silurian sites. Sudbrook was in the perfect position to control this trade and its defences, still impressive today, attest to its importance. A massive rampart, once over 16 feet high, and three parallel ditches protected the camp. The site is difficult to interpret due to later Roman influence and to coastal erosion which has destroyed part of the fort. Nevertheless, it seems clear that Sudbrook was the principal port of the Silures.[10] This is important in assessing the key role of Llanmelin which was an easily defensible position between the Usk and the Wye which controlled the approaches to Sudbrook.

Trade influences through Sudbrook helped to shape Silurian society. It is clear that borrowed Celtic cultural traditions also affected the religion of the tribe. It is likely, for example, that the Druids were influential, acting as both arbitrators and priests, since the Celtic priesthood was widespread in Britain as well as on the continent. Much of the extensive literature describing Druidical beliefs is pure fantasy but some elements are known including the fact that they taught continuity of life beyond the grave. One consequence of this was that it encouraged warriors to acts of bravery in battle with fear of death doing little to restrain tribesmen.[11] Worship of a warrior god was important to most Celtic tribes and the Silures were no exception. Thanks to the Roman practice of incorporating local deities into their own pantheon, we know something of Silurian gods. Important among them was Ocelus who was linked to the Gaulish war god, Lenus. Worshipped at Caerwent, Ocelus was twinned with Mars, the Roman god of war. The base of a statue inscribed 'Deo Marti Leno s(ive) Ocelo Vellaun(o)' has been found at Caerwent although only the feet of the god, accompanied by a web footed bird survive. The bird was probably a goose which was associated with warfare in Celtic mythology. [12] Worship of Ocelus confirms that some Silurian traditions were in keeping with continental Celtic practices. Other elements, however, seem unique to the tribe. The Celts had a pantheon of deities, many of them local in character and evidence of at least one Silurian cult has survived, again through Roman borrowing. Antefixa were Roman tiles attached to the eaves of buildings to avert evil and an important group survives from Caerleon, the legionary fortress built to control the Silures. The tiles themselves were Roman but the themes portrayed were completely native, reflecting an attempt by superstitious soldiers to propitiate local deities. On no fewer than seven surviving antefixa, the central focus is a male head with clearly defined cat ears. Some have short strokes suggesting cat fur. The unique representations probably reflect a tradition among the Silures of a local deity, manifesting himself in feline form. There is a useful parallel in Irish mythology with Cairbre Cinn-cait, Cairbre of the Cat Head. There were two cat's ears upon him, according to the poet who tells us that:

Thus was Cairbre the cruel
who seized Ireland south and north
two cat's ears on his fair head
a cat's fur through his ears.

It is conceivable that there was a common tradition linking this tale with the cat cult of the Silures. Even more relevant, however, is the deep impression of the cult which survived into post-Roman times to re-emerge in the Welsh triads as the monster cath Palug. The descriptions in the triads give us a clearer picture of the Silurian cat which was a particularly ferocious beast. The speckled monster cat was a destroyer of men. According to a triad, 'nine score men fell for its food, nine score warriors.' [13]

A final feature of Silurian religious belief is that the Celts worshipped in sacred groves and at wells with water worship being a feature of their belief. This also seems to have been the case with the Silures and may have been a factor in the comparatively late Romano British temple at

Lydney built within the enclosure of an existing hill fort on the banks of the Severn. The temple was dedicated to Nodens who was associated both with healing qualities and with water. Nodens in his Welsh form is Lludd Llaw-ereint, Lludd of the Silver Hand, or perhaps more traditionally Lludd of the Silver Arm. There is a suggestion that the silver waters of the Severn may have been seen as the arm of the god, retaining the earlier forms of water worship of the pre-Roman Silures.[14]

Worship of the warrior god Ocelus and the cult of the ferocious cath Palug are in keeping with the traditional view of the Silures. One point upon which all sources agree is the reputation for ferocity enjoyed by the Silures which was confirmed as the Romans approached Gwent. When resistance to the Romans collapsed in the south-east of England, Caradog, son of the Catuvellaunian king Cunobelinus, turned west to the Silures.[15] The war leader found the Silures receptive and the acceptance of Caradog by the tribe has led some to suggest a possible family link with the Silurian aristocracy. An alternative suggestion is that the strongly anti-Roman Druids smoothed his entry into Gwent.[16] Whatever his means of introduction, Caradog found the war-like Silures anxious to resist the Romans. In the early stages, the influence of Caradog was significant in organizing that resistance since he seems to have had a wide reputation which allowed him to exercise authority over all the remaining independent British tribes. The last stand of Caradog, in 52 A.D., occurred after he had moved north to join the north Welsh Ordovices. Defeated attempting to defend an elevated position on the upper Severn, Caradog fled to the Brigantes only to be surrendered by their pro-Roman queen Cartimandua. His capture was greeted as a great victory in Rome where the captives were displayed in front of the Praetorian Camp by Claudius. It was here that, according to Tacitus, Caradog made his famous speech saying:

> I had horses, men, arms, wealth. Are you surprised I am sorry to lose them? If you want to rule the world, does it follow that everyone else welcomes enslavement? If I had surrendered without a blow before being brought before you, neither my downfall nor your victory would have become famous.

The speech has the ring of a 'set piece' of Roman literature and must be regarded with some scepticism. On the other hand, whatever Caradog said impressed his captors. The dignity and character of the British chief led to a pardon for Caradog and his family.[17] There is, however, an even more important sequel to the story. The defeat and capture of Caradog seems to have had no impact on the resistance of the Silures at all.

Legionary fortresses had been established on the periphery of Silurian territory and soon a successful anti-Roman guerilla war was taking a surprising toll. As Tacitus put it, 'the Silures were exceptionally stubborn'. A large force of legionaries sent to build a fort near Silurian territory was attacked and cut off, probably at Clyro in Powys. A Roman relief force managed to rescue them but not before the commander, a prefect or praefectus castrorum, and eight centurions had been killed. Soon another foraging party was beaten back from tribal lands. Cavalry and auxiliary infantry units were sent to quell the Silures and they too were forced to flee. Even more serious reverses followed. Ostorius Scapula, the governor of Britain, had found it necessary to commit the legions against the Silures only to see two auxiliary cohorts lured into a Silurian trap and captured. The Silures distributed the prisoners to other tribes and appeared to be emerging as the centre of an anti-Roman British confederation. Roman cavalry trappings in the Seven Sisters hoard probably represent booty from one of the skirmishes during this period. It was at this stage that the strain became too great and Ostorius died. Tacitus was sure that the reason was that the governor was 'worn out with care' from the strain of the protracted campaign against the Silures. A new governor, Aulus Didius Gallus, was appointed rapidly but by the time he arrived an even greater disaster had befallen the Romans. Remarkably, the Silures actually met and defeated a legion, probably the Twentieth. The struggle continued and it was not until the late 70s that the Silures were finally subdued.[18] It is striking that within five years of the beginning of the Roman conquest, south-eastern England was under effective control. It required 35 years for a similar degree of control to be established in Silurian territory and even then a massive military presence, perhaps some 30,000 men in Wales in 78 A.D., was required. There can be no doubt that the ferocity of the Silures presented the Romans with one of the most intractable challenges they faced in the whole of the western empire.

NOTES

[1] A wide range of popular works on the Celts is available. Among the better ones are Dillon, M. and Chadwick, N., *The Celtic Realms* (London: 1967) and Chadwick, N., *The Celts* (London: 1970).

[2] Dillon and Chadwick, pp. 15-16; Alcock, pp. 11-14; and Adkins, L. and Adkins, R., *A Thesaurus of British Archaeology* (London: 1982), p. 74.

[3] Tacitus, *Agricola*, 11. The most easily obtained version is the Penguin classic, translated by H. Mattingly: *Tacitus, The Agricola and the Germania*, p. 61. The well-known Iberian description must be treated with caution, especially in view of Tacitus' idiosyncratic view of the geographical relationship between Spain and Britain. The description generally translated as swarthy can be rendered ruddy.

[4] Alcock, pp. 9-11; and Dillon and Chadwick, pp. 257-294. The latter source offers a good discussion of Celtic language and literature, including P Celtic and Q Celtic variations.

[5] Stanford, pp. 112-116; Alcock, pp. 16-20; and Houlder and Manning, pp. 54-59. It is impossible to be confident about the nature of occupation in the larger forts with some experts suggesting substantial permanent occupation and others seeing the forts as refuges only in times of danger. At present, insufficient Silurian sites have been excavated to be sure.

[6] Stanford, pp. 112-123. The identification of the Herefordshire tribe as Decangi is not universally accepted. Many archaeologists adopt a cautious approach to matters such as hill fort styles and tribal boundaries. For a thorough, if technical, summary of the pre-history of the region, see Taylor, A. J., (ed.), *Culture and Environment in Prehistoric Wales* (Oxford: 1980).

[7] Alcock, pp. 16-20; and Houlder and Manning, pp. 58-62.

[8] Alcock, pp. 26-27. An important point to be borne in mind is that the Silures tended to produce little pottery, using instead more perishable wood and leather utensils. This practice, also common in Ireland, makes interpretation of Silurian sites particularly difficult. There was, however, local Silurian pottery production, notably simple straight sided jars with slightly thickened rims. For a description of this Llanmelin type, see Spencer, B., 'Limestone-Tempered Pottery from South Wales in the Late Iron Age and Early Roman Period' in *The Bulletin of the Board of Celtic Studies*, XXX, III & IV, 1983, pp. 405-419.

[9] Houlder and Manning, pp. 58-59; and Stanford, p. 114.

[10] Stanford, pp. 112-116; and Nash Williams, V. E., 'An Early Iron Age Coastal Camp at Sudbrook near the Severn Tunnel', *Archaeologia Cambrensis*, 1939, pp. 42-79.

[11] A good study of the Druids, fact and fiction, is found in Piggot, S., *The Druids* (London: 1968).

[12] Ross, Anne, *Pagan Celtic Britain* (London: 1968), p. 173.

[13] Ross, pp. 99-101 and 301-302; and Bromwich, Rachel, *Trioedd Ynys Prydein* (Cardiff: 1961), pp. 484-487. There are alternative interpretations, see Boon, George, *Laterarium Iscanum: The Antifixes, Brick and Tile Stamps of the Second Augustine Legion* (Cardiff: 1984), pp. 1-12. The strong feline characteristics and later Welsh material, however, are persuasive.

[14] Ross, p. 176-179.

[15] The Celtic Caradog is preferred to the classical form, Caratacus. The invasion took place in 43 A.D.

[16] Houlder and Manning, pp. 62-63; and Webster, G., *Rome Against Caratacus* (London: 1981), p. 15.

[17] Tacitus, *The Annals of Imperial Rome*, II, 10., Salway, Peter, *Roman Britain* (Oxford: 1981), pp. 105-106; and Webster, pp. 30-39. The Penguin translation of Tacitus is by Michael Grant.

[18] Salway, pp. 106-107; Houlder and Manning, p. 63; and Tacitus, *Annals*, II, 10.

Roman Gwent

Effective Roman military control in Gwent was finally achieved under the direction of Sextus Julius Frontinus, governor of Britain from c. 74-78 A.D. Frontinus was credited with having 'conquered the powerful and warlike nation of the Silures, overcoming both the valour of his enemies and the difficulty of the terrain.'[1] From early outposts north of the Silures, the main Roman thrust into Gwent followed the river Usk with forts at Abergavenny (Gobannium) and Usk (Burrium). Usk was especially significant since a timber fortress was built there, possibly for the Twentieth Legion, perhaps as early as 55 A.D. Finally, in about 75 A.D. the final step was taken with the establishment of the fortress at Caerleon, under the abandoned Lodge Hill fort of the Silures, on the banks of the Usk. The location was a good one, free from the dangers of flooding which plagued Usk and positioned to allow receipt of supplies coming up-river from the Bristol channel. Caerleon, or Isca as it was known to the Romans, immediately became the centre of military control in south Wales. The fortress served the same role for the south that Chester did for north Wales and between them, the two legionary fortresses controlled at least 30 auxiliary garrisons positioned throughout the country. The headquarters of the Second Augustan legion, Caerleon functioned as the administrative base for the network of forts which maintained Roman control over the Silurian tribesmen who had proved so intractable.[2]

It appears that there were three stages of construction at Caerleon. At the outset, a bank and ditch with timber pallisades, towers and gateways were built, creating the traditional rectilinear plan of the fortress. Originally the buildings were of timber, with the exception of the large masonry baths; gradually from the end of the first century the barracks and other buildings were rebuilt in stone. The presence of the massive baths and of stone lined sewers beneath the main streets shows clearly that the fortress was intended as a permanent one from the outset.[3]

The permanency and significance of Caerleon is reflected in the range of buildings erected. Important among them was the headquarters building, a portion of which lies under the parish church today. A paved piazza was surrounded on three sides by porticoed ranges of offices. On the fourth side was the basilica, the great hall, with yet another range of offices behind. An obvious social focus was the imposing fortress baths which have revealed a wealth of information concerning daily life in the fortress. There was also a substantial hospital within the defences. Inevitably, considerable space was given over to barracks which were long, narrow blocks with a veranda running down one side. Pairs of rooms opened onto the veranda with the inner ones serving as dormitories, accommodating eight men, and the outer rooms being used for storage of arms and other equipment. Approximately one third of each barrack block was widened to accommodate the centurion and his staff. The extra space was in part administrative since there was generally a central corridor in this section with a number of rooms providing offices opening onto it. The additional space, however, also reflected the gulf between the commissioned centurion and the common soldiers. The relative status is clearly reflected in rates of pay since in about 100 A.D. the annual pay of the centurion was 5000 denarii when the legionary soldier received 300.[4]

One of the most striking constructions at Caerleon was the amphitheatre built just outside the fortress defences in about 80 A.D. The arena was an oval 184 feet long and 136½ feet wide. It was surrounded by an earthen bank supported, internally and externally, by stone walls rising to a height of some 32 feet. There were eight entrances with barrel vaults. The scale was impressive as tiers of seating could accommodate the entire legion, approximately 5200 men. It is considered likely that the amphitheatre was never finished in stone, and that the upper part was of a timber framed construction.[5]

It is clear from the nature of construction that Caerleon was an imposing centre of Roman power in south Wales generally and Gwent in particular. Not surprisingly, substantial civil settlement developed around the fortress. Recent excavation at Great Bulmore has demonstrated that a separate, but extensive settlement also spread along the east bank of the Usk. If, as seems likely, a colony of retired soldiers developed with settlement north along the river in the direction of Usk, the river valley between Caerleon and Usk must be seen as the main island of Roman culture in what was potentially still a hostile region.[6] In the general historical development of Gwent, however, the decisive formulative influence was less the lifestyle in this Romanized zone than the Roman approach to, and relations with, the Silures. Frontinus had a considerable reputation as a lawyer and administrator and it was undoubtedly he who decided to embark on a pacification programme for the Silures. This represented a radically different, and more considered, approach than the vindictive demand for the extermination of the tribe by Ostorius. The first step in the pacification process, which followed a well-established pattern already employed effectively in Gaul and other parts of Britain, was to remove the tribal leadership from Llanmelin and relocate it in the newly constructed Roman town of Caerwent or Venta Silurum, the market town of the Silures. [7]

Caerwent was laid out, on the traditional rectangular Roman pattern. A main street running east to west was flanked by two other east-west streets and these were crossed by four running north to south, dividing the town into twenty neat blocks or insulae. The usual range of public buildings included a forum enclosed on three sides by colonnaded shops and administrative buildings. The basilica, which served as the town hall, formed the fourth side of the square. To the east of the forum was a Romano-Celtic temple, a rectangular building surrounded by a veranda. The principal bath building stood to the south of the forum. Near the south gate was a large building with some twenty rooms around a courtyard which is generally identified as an inn or mansion. Those insulae not occupied by public buildings were given over to houses; most of those facing the main street were 'strip houses' designed as shops. Elsewhere, there were larger, impressive quadrangular houses built around a courtyard on a pattern common in Italy. The size of the latter houses was such that three or four filled an insula. It is difficult to be certain about the population living in the town, but it is probable that at its peak in the fourth century, between 2,000 and 3,000 people were resident there. [8]

In view of the massive military presence in Gwent and the success of programmes of Romanization in other regions, rapid assimilation of the local population might have seemed likely. The ferocious tenacity of the Silures, however, meant that the process was a slow one. Caerwent was originally built largely without defences, reflecting the confidence of the army that it could quickly subdue any lingering native hostility. The necessity of erecting an earth rampart around the town in about 130 A.D. indicates that this confidence was misplaced. Even more striking were developments in the 190s. After the assassination of the emperor Commodus in 192 A.D., the governor of Britain, Clodius Albinus, withdrew a large proportion of the troops in Britain, despite reports of unrest in Wales, in an attempt to seize the imperial throne. In the event, Albinus was defeated at Lyon in 197 A.D. Significantly, the removal of the troops may have led to open revolt in Gwent where there was significant reconstruction and repair at Caerleon between 198-209 A.D. Despite euphemisms in explaining the need for repairs, it is not unreasonable to think that the damage resulted from 'destruction at native hands during the absence of the garrison'. Similarly, the late second century saw the earth rampart at Caerwent strengthened by the stone walls, portions of which are still so imposing today.[9] If this model is correct, it suggests a remarkably single-minded hostility by some tribesmen. Clearly, Roman cultural influences would have spread more slowly to isolated highland regions where the language remained exclusively Celtic and the pattern of social organization continued along tribal lines. It is reasonable to assume that highland tribesmen were as hostile as circumstances would permit and that Roman influences reached more remote parts of Gwent only slowly.

Nevertheless, slow assimilation did occur and the new Romano-British cultural synthesis was eventually established among all the Silures. We have already seen the example of the fusion of religious practices including the twinning of Ocelus with Mars and the adoption of the fierce cath Palug by the Romans. The key to this fusion of culture was, of course, Caerwent. Because the town was established as a civitas of the Silures it is likely that the tribal aristocracy, re-located in the new town, adapted to Roman practices fairly quickly. Certainly from the early third century there are surviving inscriptions which confirm the existence of a tribal senate of the 'Respublica Civitatis Silurum'. This body, consisting of some 100 men meeting in Caerwent, would have had responsibility for matters like public works, registering various transactions and raising taxes. There are two particularly important points to be made about this development. One is that the senate clearly maintained a Silurian identity. The second is that the tribal organizational hierarchy was modified and sustained only through the adoption of Roman practices. Given a degree of continuing rural hostility and the relative wealth of the houses in the town, in the early stages, the leadership may well have encountered a measure of alienation and estrangement from far-flung rural communities.[10] Slowly, however, as communication and transport improved, even remote regions embraced the new structure of society. A key factor in spreading the new usages was the road system. Originally constructed for military purposes, the roads soon came to have a decisive role in expanding trade and spreading new cultural innovations. One important road connected Caerleon with Chester passing through Usk and Abergavenny; it also extended west through Cardiff on to Neath (Nidum) and Carmarthen (Moridunum). A branch road connected Usk with Monmouth (Blestium). A major east-west route through Gwent came from Bath, crossing the Severn by ferry to Sudbrook, and then passed to Caerwent and on to Caerleon by way of Penhow and Catsash, in part following today's A48; another route connected Caerwent with Gloucester (Glevum). Originally this road crossed the Wye by a ford at Tintern; a bridge was built later about one mile north of the present bridge at Chepstow. The road forked at Crossway Green, Chepstow, with the southern route passing through Pwllmeyric to join the main east-west road to Caerwent. The northern fork ran roughly down the middle of today's Chepstow race course towards Monmouth. There were many minor roads in the area, most still waiting to be traced today.[11]

As the road system developed and commerce increased, new cultural influences spread from the urban centres into the countryside, where the economic base continued to be agricultural. The vast majority of residents of Roman Britain were engaged in agriculture, many providing for the insatiable grain demands of the army. In the early period, meeting this demand was difficult as is seen from the discovery of imported Mediterranean grain at Caerleon. Nevertheless, an obvious restructuring of agricultural production meant that by the fourth century Britain was not only self sufficient in grain but was also a net exporter to the continent. Changes in farming practices resulted from the development of a villa system in the countryside. There are, however, difficulties in identifying, or even defining, villa sites. To the Romans, a villa was simply a house in the country, and as a consequence it is difficult to define where native farmsteads end and Romano-British villas begin. Nevertheless, there are rural sites with distinctive features, including pottery and architectural remains, which clearly qualify as villas. One such was at Caldicot. In addition to concentrating on food production, it is also clear that the Romans exploited natural resources to such an extent that local industry emerged in Gwent. An iron furnace at Usk, for example, confirms local smelting and quantities of iron slag have also been found near Trelech and Monmouth. There was iron mining in the

Forest of Dean and possibly at Porthcaseg on the west side of the Wye. The iron workings in the surrounding region undoubtedly account for Abergavenny's Roman name-Gobannium, which can be translated as the place of the blacksmiths. Abergavenny may have been a particularly important industrial site since it is known that coal was also dug in the region. A final important area of economic exploitation was use of the extensive forests which became centres of charcoal production.[12] The extent of this economic development inevitably accelerated social change and contributed to the eventual acceptance of the Romano-British synthesis throughout Gwent. There continued to be a strong Celtic flavour in local society but more and more it was tempered by Roman traditions.

NOTES

[1] Tacitus, Agricola, 17.

[2] Boon, George, Isca (Cardiff, 1972) especially pp. 18-23. For Usk, see Manning, W. H., Report on the Excavations at Usk 1965-1976, University of Wales Press.

[3] Ibid, pp. 23-24 and 37. See also Zienkiewicz, D., The Legionary Fortress Baths at Caerleon (Cardiff: 1986).

[4] Ibid, pp. 71-89. A concise history of the fortress for schools is Moore, Donald, Caerleon, Fortress of the Legion (Cardiff: 1979). Details of army organization are discussed in Webster, Graham, The Roman Imperial Army (London: 1974). A more localized treatment is Holder, P. A., The Roman Army in Britain (London: 1982).

[5] Wheeler, Sir Mortimer and Nash Williams, V. E., Caerleon Roman Amphitheatre (Cardiff, 1970); and Boon, pp. 89-101.

[6] See for example, Salway, p. 586. The 1984 Bulmore excavation was directed by David Zienkiewicz of the National Museum of Wales.

[7] Salway, p. 138. The town was built shortly after Caerleon itself.

[8] Craster, O. E., Caerwent, Roman City (Cardiff: 1951), especially pp. 3-5; Stanford, pp. 162-163; and Frere, Sheppard, Britannia (London: 1974), p. 296. Excavation of the basilica at Caerwent is being conducted by Richard Brewer of the National Museum of Wales.

[9] Boon, pp. 47-48; Stanford p. 164; and Craster, p. 6.

[10] Salway, p. 138 and 590-591; Stanford, p. 164; and Craster, pp. 5-7.

[11] Rivet, A. L. F., and Smith, Colin, The Place-Names of Roman Britain (Cambridge: 1979) pp. 173-178; Bradney, Sir Joseph, A History of Monmouthshire, Part I, Vol. IV, (London: 1929), pp. 1-2 and 36; and Boon, p. 19.

[12] Stanford, pp. 160-161; and Rivet and Smith, p. 369. For a detailed discussion of villa development, see Percival, John, The Roman Villa (London: 1976); and Rivet, A. L. F. (ed.), The Roman Villa in Britain (London: 1969). There is considerable scope for investigation and identification of villa sites in Gwent. If the Book of Llandaff's references to villas implies the continuation of Roman farmsteads into the post Roman period, these could provide fertile starting points for a survey. An example of the numerous Llandaff references is Villa Guidcon which is identified as Trelech Grange. At least one Romano British farmstead enclosed by palisades has recently emerged from an investigation of crop marks at Llanmartin. See Vyner, B. E. 'Cropmarks at Llanmartin, Gwent' in The Bulletin of the Board of Celtic Studies, XXVIII, II, 1979, pp. 343-346. Mike Fulford of Reading University has recently suggested that the Wentlwg, and possibly the Caldicot, levels were drained and reclaimed in the second century. This reclamation was probably done by the legion, to supplement their farming territory.

A Neolithic farming community of about 4,000 B.C.
(National Museum of Wales)

An aerial view of Llanmelin hillfort, a principal tribal centre of the Silures
(National Museum of Wales)

The great Roman baths at Caerleon

The amphitheatre in Caerleon during excavations 1926-27
(National Museum of Wales)

One of a series of antifixa from Caerleon
thought by some experts to represent a
diety of the Silures
(National Museum of Wales)

A first century A.D. flagon from Caerleon
(National Museum of Wales)

Above, the south wall at Caerwent, the civitas capital of the Silures. Left, a bastion added to the defences at Caerwent in about 340 A.D.

Two fourth century bronze penannular brooches from Caerwent

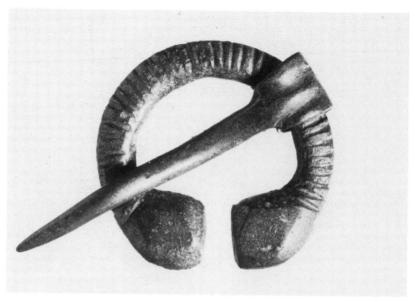

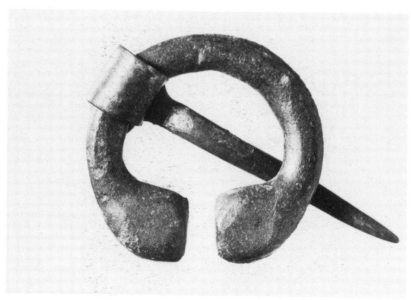

A brooch from the post-Roman cemetery at Caerwent, probably associated with the monastic community of Tathan

(National Museum of Wales)

The Celtic cross from St. Arvans

(National Museum of Wales)

Fragments of crosses from Caerleon and (below) Great Bulmore near Caerleon

Native Revival and the Celtic Church

As has been seen, legionary occupation at Caerleon fluctuated. Between 122 and 135 A.D., for example, part of the legion was committed to construction of Hadrian's Wall. Similarly, in the 190s many troops were on the continent with Albinus and their absence may have intensified unrest in Gwent. In the early third century, however, most of the Second Augustan Legion was at Caerleon engaged in the major reconstruction effort described in the previous chapter. It was at the end of the third century that the legion appears to have been withdrawn, probably in about 290 A.D. as a result of the upheavals associated with the establishment of a rebel regime in Britain by Carausius. Occupation at Caerleon did continue through the fourth century; coin sequences extend as far as Arcadius, c. 388-95. Presumably, however, there were only civilian residents during this period. This does not suggest the withdrawal of the army from south Wales, but does demonstrate a re-orientation of forces. From about 270 A.D. the activities of Saxon pirates were on the increase in the channel and Irish raiders posed an additional danger to western coasts. Partially in response to this threat, and probably also for internal reasons in an increasingly turbulent empire, the 'Saxon Shore' forts were established. As a part of this process, in about 300 A.D. the old fort at Cardiff was rebuilt, becoming the new Roman military centre for south Wales.[1]

During the late fourth century, however, Roman control became increasingly tenuous. The weakening of the military presence was accelerated in 383 A.D. by the removal of most of the army by Magnus Maximus, Macsen Wledig in its Welsh form, in his attempt to establish himself as emperor. Troop strengths seem not to have been renewed and local authorities were forced to provide defence as best they could. By 410 A.D. when the Emperor Honorius, in response to an appeal for assistance, told British authorities to look after their own affairs, many were already doing so. Caerwent offers the perfect example. The fort at Cardiff was well-placed to guard against raids up the Bristol channel. It is obvious, however, that residents of Caerwent, which was vulnerable to seaborne raids, did not consider that it offered protection enough. As a result, in about 340 A.D. the town's defences were strengthened by the addition of the polygonal bastions which can still be seen fronting the south wall. These bastions were copies of similar fortifications which had been erected at Cardiff and were designed to provide flanking fire and platforms for ballistae, machines which could hurl heavy stones for distances of up to 400 yards. Moreover, the town gates were modified with the south gate being completely blocked by a regularly coursed stone wall. The north gate too was re-built with entry being reduced to a narrow gap in what had previously been a spacious arched gateway.[2] It has been suggested that at this time, 'the civitas Silurum was given teeth' by the creation of a para military force at Caerwent. One of the most remarkable features of this period is that as native administration was re-established, Celtic aesthetic tastes reasserted themselves. La Téne artistic forms, for example, re-emerged in south Wales and some hill forts were re-occupied.[3] Occupation of Caerwent clearly continued into the post-Roman period. There are, for example, coins from Arcadius and Honorius, c. 393-423. While the authenticity of Byzantine coins of the sixth to ninth centuries is now regarded as questionable, there are artefacts confirming continuing occupation including, most notably, a double spiral-headed pin which has been dated as sixth or seventh century.[4] Even more significant are radio carbon dates from a cemetery just outside the walls of Caerwent which indicate burials in the fifth, sixth, eighth and ninth centuries.[5]

An assertion of native leadership at Caerwent reflected developments in Britain as a whole. With growing external threats and rapidly declining Roman authority, a new British leadership emerged. By about 425, this leadership seems to have been exercised by Gwrtheyrn who was in turn opposed by a pro-Roman faction led by Ambrosius Aurelianus. Fear of an attempt to re-assert Roman control by forces from the continent may have been a factor in leading Gwrtheyrn to recruit Saxon mercenaries who revolted in the 440s. While the background to this period is highly uncertain, at some stage Ambrosius seems to have displaced Gwrtheyrn and attempts to re-forge Roman links were not abandoned at least until the death of Aetius in 454.[6] The actual nature of authority and degree of control exercised by Gwrtheyrn and Ambrosius is impossible to determine as is what, if any, influence they had on Gwent. Nevertheless, the view of Ambrosius as the leader of a pro-Roman faction supports a model of modified Romano-British society continuing into the fifth century. Despite a reassertion of Celtic culture, it is reasonable to assume that some Roman influences remained strong in the west of Britain even after the Saxon incursion had destroyed them in the east. It is clear that at least one inheritance from the Roman period which flourished was Christianity.

The turning point for Christianity in the empire was Constantine's victory at the Milvian Bridge in 312 A.D. From the following year, his enthusiastic support produced the 'Peace of the Church' and Christianity became legal in the empire. British bishops appeared almost immediately, participating in Councils on the continent. The Christian tradition in Gwent, however, was even older than this since two of Britain's earliest martyrs, Julius and Aaron, were executed for their faith at Caerleon, probably in the persecutions of 249-51 or those of 257-259.[7] By the fifth century, Christianity was well established in Gwent. This does not suggest that there was a uniform or unchallenged Christian tradition. Pagan Romano-British practices certainly continued into the fifth century.[8] Also significant is the widespread acceptance of the Pelagian heresy in Britain. In about 384 A.D. the British monk Pelagius, then in Rome, began to challenge Augustine's pessimistic view of human nature and the assumption that man could not avoid sin. Instead, Pelagius taught a system of free will and individual responsibility for salvation. It was for every man to decide for himself whether to act wrongly or rightly. Following from this basic premise, Pelagius argued against original sin asking how God, who forgives men their own sins, could blame them for someone else's.[9] There is little doubt that the doctrine gained support in Gwent; there is even a tradition that Pelagius was born in Usk.[10] Pelagianism was certainly strong enough to have been the cause of the visit to Britain by Germanus in 429 and it has been suggested that Gwrtheyrn himself was a Pelagian.[11] The emphasis on free will had an obvious appeal to a re-emerging native leadership and opposition to the orthodoxy of the church in Rome could have political as well as religious implications.

Whatever the extent of Pelagian or pagan beliefs, however, a largely traditional form of Christianity seems to have triumphed in Gwent by the beginning of the sixth century. The threat of an expanding Saxon menace may have been a factor encouraging people to put aside religious differences. Probably even more significant was the influence of religious leaders associated with the age of the Celtic saints. Among the earliest of the Welsh saints was Dyfrig, or Dubricius in its Latin form. Probably born sometime in the mid to late fifth century, Dyfrig is described as a Roman priest and his influence demonstrates a continuing acceptance of some Roman usages. The centre of Dyfrig's influence was Ergyng, the area beyond the Monnow which today has been largely incorporated into Herefordshire. His principal house, possibly at Welsh Bicknor, was one of two bishoprics in south Wales in the early post-Roman period; the second may have been Llandeilo Fawr. Most of Dyfrig's influence was concentrated in Ergyng, but there is evidence including a dedication at St. Cynmarch near Chepstow, to suggest that he was also active along the lower Wye.[12]

It is important in attempting to form an image of post-Roman Gwent to note that Dyfrig emerged from the local Romano-British population and shaped a church to serve that community which retained still-recognizable Roman traditions. In the region of St. Cynmarch, however, the home-grown Christianity of Dyfrig had to reach an accommodation with another tradition. The Irish, after having accepted Christianity, became great early evangelists and a typical example was Tathan, or Tatheus, who founded a church at Caerwent. Despite his name and Irish ancestry, it is possible that Tathan arrived from Gwynedd where a large Irish community faced increasing pressure from Cunedda who had imposed his authority on north Wales. Arriving by sea, probably at St. Pierre, Tathan founded his monastic church at Caerwent. His establishment not only encouraged the growth of Christianity in Gwent, but also assured that Caerwent would continue to be a focus of local society. It is impossible to walk along the great south wall at Caerwent today without being struck by the scale and grandeur of the place. For fifth century visitors, unused to any large-scale stone construction, the impact must have been even greater. The description attributed to Tathan of 'the good, fertile, lofty, noble city of Caerwent' must have seemed particularly apt.[13] There can be no doubt that Caerwent continued to be an important ecclesiastical centre in the post-Roman period. Archaeological evidence is at present patchy and the apsidal building discovered overlaying the baths at Caerwent may or may not have been Tathan's church. The literary evidence, however, is conclusive for the continuing significance of the town at least as a monastic settlement. Also important is the fact that Caerwent gave its name to the emerging kingdom in the region—Gwent.[14]

The early saints produced a thriving Christian community which was able to groom its own natural successors. A notable example was Cadog, traditionally the son of the Gwent king Gwynllyw and Gwladys, whose influence in Gwent is reflected in a series of dedications including the Llangattocks and in churches in Monmouth, Raglan and Caerleon. Cadog, educated at Tathan's community in Caerwent, went on to become a noted educator in his own right, rivalling even Illtud. The educational role of monastic communities is highly significant because it provided cultural continuity in this region during the darkest of what is improperly described as the dark ages. In addition, it stresses an important distinction between the church emerging in this part of Britain and the main stream of Roman Catholicism. Wales was a centre of the Celtic church, an institution which differed in many respects from that on the continent. For example, the method of determining the date of Easter, a test of the educated man during this period, was different. So was the tonsure of the monks. The Celtic church also showed a marked reluctance to accept the concept of celibate clergy—to such an extent that many monastic offices were hereditary. Another significant feature of the Celtic church was that larger foundations were 'clas' churches, with a body of resident monks. The cells of these members of the clas were located within the enclosed yard of the church called the 'llan' which has given the name to so many villages through Gwent and the rest of Wales. One role of the clas church was education and sons of noble families travelled considerable distances to these educational centres. In the early development of the church in Gwent, two important clas churches were Caerwent and Llandogo. It was inevitable that this distinctive Celtic system would be challenged by traditional Roman Catholicism and when Augustine arrived, he attempted to reconcile the Celtic churchmen to Rome, probably in 604. The often told story of this episode suggests that Celtic representatives met Augustine at Aust after having decided upon a simple test of his Christian principles. They decided that if, when they arrived, Augustine rose to his feet and greeted them as brothers in Christ, they would accept his message. If, on the other hand, he remained seated and greeted them haughtily they would reject his call. Augustine kept his seat and the Celtic church retained its independence, refusing to conform until 768 and retaining differences even then.[15]

As a consequence, it was the tradition of the Celtic church which shaped religious usages in Wales, including Gwent. As has been seen, important Celtic saints included men from Gwent. By the same token, saints from other parts of Wales, enjoyed considerable status in Gwent.

There are, for example. several dedications to St. David, Dewi Sant. Obvious examples are Llanddewi Fach, Llanddewi Rhydderch, and Llanddewi Skirrid. There are other dedications at Dewstone near Caldicot, Trostrey, Llanthony, Llangyfyw, and Bettws. Teilo also has several dedications including Llantilio Crossenny, Llantilio Pertholey and at Llanarth.[16] The main point about all these developments, however, is that they demonstrate a strong early Christian tradition flourishing in the region. Places like Caerwent, for example, have a good claim to unbroken Christian worship from Roman times to the present. Particularly important in this context were the larger monastic foundations, especially those for which documentary evidence in the Book of Llandaff, Liber Landavensis, suggests a long period of influence. Foundations from Gwent, Ergyng and Glamorgan which are notable in this respect include Welsh Bicknor, c.575-866; Llandogo, c.625-942; Llancarfan, c.650-1075; Llandough, c.650-1075; Llantwit, c.650-1075; Rhosili, c.650-925; Bishopston, c.650-925; Llangors, c.720-925; Llangwm, c.860-1075; St. Maughan's, c.860-1072; Llandaff, from c.860; and Caerwent, c.950-1075.[17]

There was clearly a widespread and early Christian tradition throughout Gwent. Numerous smaller churches were established giving parishes through the region an ancient religious inheritance. The example of a limited survey of churches in southeast Gwent demonstrates the point clearly. Charter references show that near Chepstow, churches were abundant. Examples, and earliest references, include: Mathern, 620; Llandogo, 625; Porthcaseg, 693; Cynmarch, 625; Llansoy, 725; Monmouth, 733; St. Arvans, 955; Penterry, 955; Trelech Grange, 960; Pwllmeurig, 970; Llanishen, 980; and Crick, 1022. There were probably also foundations at Howick in 660 and at Mounton in 730.[18] It should be noted that while parish churches stand on the sites of most of these churches, there are no surviving structures. Even the large monastic foundations, with the possible exception of Caerwent, were made of wood. There is, for example, a description of the timber built Llancarfan with roofs visible at a great distance. While obviously imposing at the time, these timber structures have left no trace.[19]

NOTES

[1] Boon, especially pp. 62-67; Craster, p. 8; and Salway, pp. 288-290.

[2] Craster, pp. 8, 14-15, 19-20; and Salway, pp. 299-301, 320-321. See also Thomas, G. 'O Maximus i Maxen' and Jarret, M., 'Magnus Maximus and the end of Roman Britain' in *Transactions of the Honourable Society of Cymmrodorion*, 1983, pp. 7-35.

[3] Alcock, pp. 35-37.

[4] Stanford, p. 171; and Lang, Lloyd, *The Archaeology of Late Celtic Britain and Ireland* (London: 1975), p. 111.

[5] Davies, Wendy, *Wales in the Early Middle Ages* (Leicester: 1982), p. 24.

[6] Salway, pp. 466-478. Gwrtheyrn is more commonly known as Vortigern. The speculative question of Arthur and possible Arthurian links with Gwent is examined in the appendices.

[7] Salway, pp. 340-341, 720-721; and Davies, E. T., *An Ecclesiastical History of Monmouthshire* (Risca: 1953) pp. 19-23.

[8] Ross, pp. 4-6.

[9] For a concise explanation of Pelagian doctrine, see Kelly, J. N. D., *Early Christian Doctrines* (London: 1977) pp. 357-361.

[10] Davies, E. T., p. 24.

[11] Salway, pp. 443, 462-466.

[12] Bowen, E. G., *The Settlement of the Celtic Saints in Wales* (Cardiff: 1956) pp. 36-37; Davies, E. T., p. 28; Davies, W., *The Llandaff Charters* (Aberystwyth: 1979) p. 91; and Evans, G. and Rhys, J., *The Text of the Book of Llan Dav* (Aberystwyth: 1979), pp. 79-86. Evans' version of Llyfer Llandaf remains the only available full text despite the fact that it first appeared in 1893, and the medieval Latin text is difficult. Fortunately, however, Wendy Davies has provided an extremely valuable assessment of the charter material. Both sources will be cited below, Llyfer Llandaf as Ll and Davies' book as Charters. Assigning dates to matters like the life of Dyfrig present immense difficulties. See, e.g. Doble, G. H. *Lives of the Welsh Saints* (Cardiff: 1971) n. 8, p. 59. All Llandaf dates are approximate.

[13] Davies, E. T., pp. 28-33. Reference to Irish Christianity requires some consideration of Patrick. A Romano-Briton who was kidnapped in an Irish raid at the age of 16, probably between 405 and 409, his grandfather Potitus and his father Calpornius were members of the local decurionate. While the evidence is minimal, the location of the family home has still been the subject of considerable debate. As plausible a case can be made for placing the home in Gwent as for the other suggested possibilities.

[14] Rivet and Smith, p. 493. The evolution was from Cair Guent to Gwent.

[15] It is impossible to say how much of the story of the meeting with Augustine, which is drawn from Bede, is apocryphal. There are, however, good treatments of the Celtic church including Chadwick, N., *The Age of the Saints in the Early Celtic Church* (Oxford: 1961); Hardinge, L., *The Celtic Church in Britain* (London: 1972); Bowen, E. G., *Saints, Seaways and Settlements in the Celtic Lands* (Cardiff: 1977); and Doble.

[16] Davies, E. T., p. 37.

[17] Davies, Wendy, *An Early Welsh Microcosm* (London: 1978), pp. 123-124. These references do not show dates of foundation, but simply confirm that a church was in existence at a particular time. Other sources demonstrate, for example, the earlier monastic tradition at Caerwent.

[18] Ll. pp. 218-221; Charters, p. 120; and Howell, R. C., *Fedw Villages* (Cwmbran: 1985), p. 14.

[19] Davies, W., Middle Ages, p. 25.

The Kingdom of Gwent

The church was clearly an important stabilizing influence in the state of flux which existed in early medieval Gwent. With the collapse of Roman authority, however, secular demands required that a new political system should also emerge and soon regional kingship developed to provide a measure of stability. By the sixth century a number of small kingdoms had been established. One of these was Ergyng where Erb and his descendants ruled from about 525. Traditionally, Gwent proper was ruled by Glywys who passed an emerging kingdom to his son, Gwynllyw in the sixth century. There is, however, evidence to connect Glywys with the Gower peninsula and the original holdings of the family, styled the kingdom of Glywysing, may have been largely to the west of today's Gwent.[1] One feature about these early kingdoms is that they were very small and probably largely self-contained entities. With Celtic tastes re-emerging and some hill fort re-occupation it is easy to visualize the emergence of strong local leaders who were able to regularize their authority through some form of hereditary succession. The pattern, however, began to change in about 600 with the consolidation of the kingdom of Gwent, largely as a result of Saxon pressure. In the decade of the 570s, there were a series of Saxon victories in the west of England establishing control over places like Gloucester, Cirencester and Bath. The disequilibrium which resulted soon put Gwent itself under threat. The main Gwent dynasty emerged with Tewdrig in the second half of the sixth century. According to a tradition recorded in the Book of Llandaff, the aged Tewdrig retired to Tintern at about the time that the Saxons began to probe across the Wye. Given a reputation for bravery as a military leader, Tewdrig, was prevailed upon to return and lead the resistance to the Saxon advance. The decisive battle was fought at Pont y Saeson near Tintern and resulted in a sweeping victory for the men of Gwent who by this time can be described, both culturally and linguistically, as Welsh. The success, however, was achieved at a cost as Tewdrig was mortally wounded in the fighting. His son, Meurig, carried his father south and buried him where he died, at Mathern.[2]

There are two particularly significant consequences of this episode. One is that the Saxon advance towards southeast Wales seems to have been checked almost completely. The second is that Meurig ap Tewdrig was able to establish himself firmly as king of Gwent and his successors maintained the dominance of his dynasty. There is some evidence to suggest that Meurig made an early marriage into the family of Glywys which provided him with authority in the west. He certainly eventually married Onbraust the daughter of Gwrgan, king of Ergyng, bringing this northeastern region under his control. Thus dynastic marriage and military prowess allowed Meurig to secure himself in Gwent. In the early stages, sub kings, probably members of earlier dynasties, continued to exert some influence. Within four generations, however, these sub kings disappeared and the heirs of Meurig were, generally speaking, in full control.[3]

The kingdom ruled by Meurig and his successors was effectively modern Gwent and Glamorgan. From the tenth century, because of the dominance of Morgan ap Owain, Morgan Hen, the whole of this region became known as Morgannwg. Even then, the terms Gwent and Glywysing continued to be used although there does not seem to have been a precise territorial definition for either.[4] An inevitable observation which must be made is that the kingdom, extending from Wye to Tywi, was geographically the same as that of the Silures. There is certainly no reason to give any credibility at all to the genealogists of Morgan ap Owain who claimed on his behalf descent from, among others, Gwertheyrn. Nor is there any direct evidence to suggest political inheritance from the Roman period. Nevertheless, it is difficult to avoid the suspicion that some influence from the Romanized leadership in Caerwent survived into the emerging kingdom of Gwent. The possibility of a legacy from the civitas of the Silures certainly cannot be rejected out of hand.

Whatever the early influences may have been, however, the emergence of a strong dynasty under Meurig does not imply strong kingship on a late medieval pattern. Kingship in Gwent was always a question of personal property with little view of an organized or centralized state. The Welsh approach to inheritance, gavelkind, which provided for estates to be divided among sons inevitably led to fractionalization, or at least sharing, of the kingdom. It is clear that sons frequently did share the kingdom. For example, Meurig himself dominated Gwent from about 620 to c.665. Athrwys ap Meurig was also styled king, although he predeceased his father by some ten years. Morgan ap Athrwys was king until c.710, sharing the kingdom for a time with his brother Ithel. There were four sons of Ithel ap Morgan who were all described as king and who must have been exercising authority at the same time. There may have been some geographical differentiation with, for example, Rhys ap Ithel active largely in Glamorgan while his brother Ffernfael concentrated his interests in Gwent. This is by no means certain and overlapping jurisdiction is likely. This pattern of shared kingship certainly continued. In the tenth century, for example, we find Morgan and Cadwgan ap Owain sharing authority as king not only with each other but also with a first cousin, Cadell ap Arthfael.[5] This model was not universal. Morgan ap Owain eventually ruled as principal king in the region which people began to describe as Morgan's land, Morgannwg. This degree of dominance, however, was the exception rather than the rule.

The whole notion of kingship in Gwent raises a variety of interesting questions. There can be little doubt that courts or halls were important as centres of society; there are numerous examples from the tales of the Mabinogi, Heledd's lament for Cynddylan, and other early literary survivals which stress the central social role of the hall. Eating, drinking and singing around hearth and cauldron provided a focus which would not have been foreign to pre-Roman warriors. Despite this importance of the hall, it would be wrong to think of kings of Gwent holding court in a late medieval fashion. As Wendy Davies suggests, a better description would simply be one of public meetings at a royal residence. Unfortunately, there is only one clear reference to a royal residence which can be identified and that is the hall of Ffernfael at Cemais in 755.[6] Wherever halls were located, their existence does not suggest a static monarchy. On the contrary, kings clearly moved through their domains accompanied by a body of retainers called milites. These groups have been described as a war band, a military retinue, a royal bodyguard, and a band of thugs. The accuracy of the different descriptions depends on the observer's perspective and undoubtedly varied according to the circumstances and attitude of the king. One role of the milites was certainly to extract the rents and renders due to the king. Important among them was gwestfa, the right of the king to demand hospitality. Beer, bread, meat and honey were owed to the king. Gwestfa was received from the freemen of the region, being rendered annually. A similar render, dawnbwyd, was due from the bond peasants and in later law tracts, was collected twice annually.[7] This primitive process of taxation led to the emergence of an elaborate administrative structure to assure payment.

The basic social unit was the tref which today would be translated as town but which originally implied an estate or farm; hamlet might be the best working definition. The most important unit of royal administration, however, was the cymyd or commote which was notionally made up of 50 trefi. The largest unit was the cantref, literally 100 trefi. Traditionally, the cantrefi of Gwent included the western region, Gwynllwg, with Gwent Uwchcoed and Gwent Iscoed, Gwent above and below the Wentwood, in the east. Another distinction in the stratification of the social system was the cenedl or kindred, a concept important in the law codes. A significant role of the kindred was payment of compensation for injury. Privilege was based on the status, braint, of an individual. This braint could be effected by birth, land owned, or office held. A wife's status depended on the braint of her husband. Among payments authorized in the law codes, was sarhad, compensation for insult, which was assessed on the basis of the braint of the wronged party. Similarly, there were provisions for homicide payments, galanas. Responsibility for this 'life price' belonged to the kindred extending to the fifth cousin. Kindred for the purposes of inheritance reached only to second cousins.[8]

The role of the kindred was clearly significant. Even more important in Gwent, however, was the influence of the uchelwyr, the elders or gwyr dda (good men) of the region. In practice there were two types of uchelwyr with the milites of the king clearly qualifying as members of an aristocracy. Far more important, however, were the elders of the local landowning community. Retaining a recognizable regional group identity, they clearly exerted a substantial influence. This could even extend to the removal of a king as is demonstrated by the uchelwyr of Gwent, the 'chief men', acting as a body in arranging the murder of Einion ap Owain, king of Dyfed, in 984. Such an action was obviously drastic and unusual. Nevertheless, the significance of the uchelwyr in daily life seems to have been reasonably constant. Transactions were conducted before them and they exercised power in regulating a variety of social relationships. There is also evidence to suggest that the uchelwyr in Gwent were particularly important, exercising more authority than their counterparts in other Welsh kingdoms. They may, for example, routinely have met and taken decisions on their own authority without the presence of the king. These meetings have been described as an 'unsophisticated but functional assembly'. Their influence may actually have increased in the eighth century when charters in the Book of Llandaff demonstrate a spate of grants by non-royal landowners. The existence of powerful bodies of regional elders in Gwent is highly significant since it means that these uchelwyr could, along with the church, restrict abuses of royal authority.

Restrictions on arbitary use of royal power must have been welcomed by the common people, the gwerin, of Gwent. The gwerin, who worked on the farms, were the backbone of the kingdom. The Llandaff charters are important in describing farms and other units employed in exploiting the land in arable as well as pastoral production. Among secular settlements there are references to the tref and the villa, terms which seem to have been used almost interchangeably. Religious settlements could be ecclesia, a church, or podum, a religious settlement as in the monastic community of the clas church. All of these, including the ecclesiae, had attached land and a majority were three modii estates. A modius was approximately 40 acres so 120 acre farms can be seen as the norm in the kingdom of Gwent. Of particular interest is the fact that where these units can be identified today, they generally still include only one major modern settlement suggesting a correlation between modern Gwent and the kingdom before the Norman conquest. Also of interest is the fact that these units generally had a working population of between 30-40 people.[10] Since this is substantially larger than a single nuclear family, the best model is one of agricultural hamlets rather than family farms.

Many of those working on the farms of Gwent were not freemen. There are, for example, charter references to the heres and the hereditarius. The hereditarius was probably a man with hereditary rights to claim produce from an estate. The heres, on the other hand, seems to have been a tenant who was hereditarily tied to the land. Parallels to serfdom obviously spring to mind. Nevertheless, some caution should be exercised in forming a view of free and unfree men in Gwent. Clearly social stratification was an important feature of society and there were numerous people who were not free. This does not, however, confirm the widespread existence of slavery which has sometimes been suggested. Charter references to slavery are few and those which exist are interesting. In one case a wealthy man, Tudwg, gave himself into 'perpetua servitute' in atonement for evil done. A captured Saxon woman was given as a slave in another grant. The general picture which emerges is that slavery resulted from crime or conquest and may not have been a major feature of the social system.[11]

If caution is required on questions such as the extent of slavery in the kingdom of Gwent, equal circumspection is necessary in forming a view of the economic system of the kingdom. Agriculture was clearly the principal concern. Gwent has been referred to as non urban and non commercial and the paucity of evidence for markets could suggest a lack of economic sophistication. The principal means of exchange was certainly barter. Nevertheless, a cattle standard existed and goods were priced in cattle or silver. Application of the standard was consistent, suggesting the recognition of the concept of fixed values for a variety of commodities. In addition, provision for landing rights at Caldicot, Pwllmeurig, Mathern, Chepstow and Caerleon implied seaborne trade. Also, the use of the unusual description urbs for Caerwent suggests the possibility of an urban, or at least proto-urban, role for that site.[12]

Whatever the degree of sophistication of the economic system, it is clear that Gwent did not evolve in a vacuum. As has been seen, the consolidation of the kingdom grew from the threat of Saxon expansion. While the immediate threat seems to have been eliminated before the death of Meurig, renewed Saxon activity must always have been an unsettling possibility. Similarly, Saxons east of the Wye must also have felt at risk from Welsh raids. This tension between the two nations was in a sense institutionalised in about 784 when the Mercian king Offa began to build his dyke, a project unprecedented since Roman times, running from 'sea to sea' between Wales and England. The dyke appears to have been designed more as a means of delineating a frontier rather than creating an impregnable fortification. Of particular significance is the line of the dyke along the lower Wye. Where possible, the dyke incorporated natural features and above Redbrook the border follows the Wye. It easily could have done all the way to the Severn and the fact that it does not is very important for two reasons. Both banks of the Wye, for as far as the river was tidal, were left in Welsh hands demonstrating that navigation of the river was important to the kings of Gwent. Fishing, especially for salmon and eels, was also important. Perhaps most significant is the fact that the line of the dyke left Beachley in Welsh hands and it seems certain that the kings of Gwent had a special interest in this terminus of the ferry from Aust. Even more important than the obvious interest of Gwent in the lower Wye, however, is the fact that the kings of Gwent were able to extract this concession from Offa, the dominant king in England whose reputation extended even to continental courts. The ability to wrest both banks of the lower Wye from Offa says a great deal about the interests and the influence of the kings of Gwent. [13]

An ability to treat with Offa argues that Gwent was a powerful entity. On the other hand, fractionalization was at times a serious problem. In the tenth century, for example, Gower was lost and for approximately 50 years, Gwent Iscoed was ruled by the intrusive dynasty of Nowy ap Gwriad. The family of Nowy were involved in an episode which gives an especially interesting picture of Iscoed in the mid tenth century. In 955 a deacon, Eli, killed a farm labourer, rusticus, during an argument in St. Arvans. The peasant was reaping near the village when he was approached by the deacon. An argument broke out between the men and as the exchange became heated, the labourer struck out and cut one of Eli's fingers. Feigning serious injury, Eli asked the man to bind the wound. Obviously regretting his act, the peasant began to do so. As soon as he was off his guard, however, the deacon stabbed and killed him. It was now Eli's turn to regret his action and fearing retribution, he ran to St. Arvans church for sanctuary. On discovering the murder, however, six local men who were members of the familia or kindred of Nowy, rushed to the church. Ignoring the conventions of sanctuary, they broke in and murdered the deacon before the altar. The scandal caused a sensation, less because of the murder than the fact that kinsmen of the king had violated sanctuary. At this stage, the church stepped in and bishop Pater summoned Nowy to Caerwent where a settlement was agreed resulting in the imprisonment of the guilty men in the monastery of Teilo. The episode is instructive, giving a glimpse into a society where violence was not uncommon but where social conventions were maintained even against the kindred of the king. [14]

If fractionalization was at times a factor in Gwent, incorporation into a wider Welsh state was also a feature, especially in the tenth and eleventh centuries. While Hywel Dda did not rule Gwent directly, he exerted influence on the kingdom until his death in 950. Later, Gruffudd ap Llywelyn gained control over the whole of Wales including, after 1055, Gwent. A tendency to move in the direction of a Welsh national state was in part the result of a recognition of common interest among the Cymry. There was certainly commonality in resisting growing external threats. The Vikings swept up the Severn, Wye and Usk managing even to capture

Cyfeilliog the bishop of Ergyng and holding him for ransom. Despite the devastation of the Vikings, however, the greatest danger was renewed Saxon, or by the tenth century, English incursions. Particularly threatening to Gwent were Harold Godwinson and his brother Tostig who, in 1063, arranged the murder of Gruffudd ap Llywelyn. In the ensuing upheaval, Caradog ap Gruffudd re-established an independent kingdom in Gwent. Godwinson, however, attempted to claim Gwent Iscoed for his earldom of Hereford and invaded in 1065 to try to realize that ambition. His stay was a short one although before withdrawing he ordered construction of a building, probably to serve as a manorial court, at Portskewett. Almost immediately, however, Caradog attacked, razing the structure to the ground and killing Godwinson's retainers. [15]

It is impossible to know whether, having suffered this reverse in his attempt to snatch Iscoed, Godwinson still harboured ideas of moving into Wales. He was, of course, overtaken by events elsewhere. To most local observers at the time, the assertion of authority by Caradog ap Gruffudd probably implied stability and maintenance of the traditional lifestyle of Gwent. The appearance was deceptive. In the event, this was only the calm before the storm, since 1066 was drawing near.

NOTES

[1] Davies, Wendy, *An Early Welsh Microcosm* (London: 1978) pp. 93-100 and 132n. Gwynllyw is thought to have been buried at his monastery in Newport suggesting that the family gained influence in the east fairly rapidly. See also Howell, R., *The Kingdom of Gwent* (Newport: 1986). This is the teacher's introductory booklet for the first teaching pack in the 'History of Gwent' series.

[2] Ll., pp. 141-143; and Charters, p. 97. Wendy Davies suggests that the battle, sometimes dated as 597, was probably nearer 620.

[3] Davies, W. Microcosm, pp. 93-95. The line of the kings of Gwent appears in the appendices.

[4] Ibid., pp. 92-93.

[5] Charters, pp. 76-77; Ll., various references; and Ibid., pp. 93-95 and 102-103.

[6] Davies, Wendy, *Wales in the Early Middle Ages* (Leicester: 1982) pp. 29-30; and Davies, W., Microcosm, p. 108. Cemais has been corrupted to today's Kemeys.

[7] Davies, W., Middle Ages, pp. 41 and 129; and Davies, W., Microcosm, pp. 101-107.

[8] Details of the law codes are in Jenkins, Dafydd, *Cyfraith Hywel* (Llandysul: 1970) and *The Law of Hywel Dda* (Llandysul: 1986). See also Davies, W., Middle Ages, pp. 43, 60-84 and 131-132 and Microcosm, pp. 37-39. The nuclear family was central, despite the importance of the kindred. The head of a kin group was the pen cenedl.

[9] Brut Y Tywysogion (with notes and introduction by Thomas Jones, Cardiff: 1955) pp. 16-17; Ll, various references; Davies, W., Microcosm, p. 63 and 108-116; and Davies, W., Middle Ages, pp. 63, 82-83 and 132-133. Estates seem to have become smaller in the changes of the eighth century. Einion, frequently spelled Einon, was king in Dyfed. Brut y Tywysogion is cited below as Brut.

[10] Davies, W., Microcosm, pp. 33-40.

[11] Ll. p. 127; and Ibid. pp. 43-47.

[12] Davies, W., Microcosm, pp. 59-62.

[13] Stanford, pp. 191-198; and Stenton, F., *Anglo Saxon England* (Oxford: 1971), pp. 212-215. See also Fox, Cyril, *Offa's Dyke* (Oxford: 1955). See also Noble, F., *Offa's Dyke Reviewed*, (ed. Gelling) (B.A.R.: 1983). It is conceivable that a maritime tradition in Gwent is also suggested. Welsh sailors from Gwent were undoubtedly the scipwealen described in later English references.

[14] Ll., pp. 218-221; Charters, p. 120; and Howell, p. 16. St. Arvans church which today has a Celtic cross on display, is described in Guy, J. and Smith, E. *Ancient Gwent Churches* (Newport: 1979), p. 60. The incident with Nowy is also significant in demonstrating the continuing significance of Caerwent. The role of Blegywryd in the case demonstrates the influence of lawyers in the Gwent tradition.

[15] Charters, p. 77 and note 60, p. 88; and *Anglo Saxon Chronicle*, 1065. A readily available version is the translation by G. N. Garmonsway (London: 1972). Pressure from Viking raids sometimes forced an accommodation with English kings. Edgar posed a particular problem, having attacked Caerleon in 973. Five Saxon/Norman coins from Caerwent are interesting as confirmation of trade contacts. As is discussed in the text, landing rights existed at several points and a silver standard was widely accepted. The existence of trade links may also impact on the 'urbs' description used in the charters. The coins do not, of course, suggest any permanent Saxon presence; social/political discontinuity in Gwent Iscoed almost certainly resulted from the Norman conquest. For a description of the coins, see Dolley, M. and Knight, J. K., *Archaeologica Cambrensis*, 1970, pp. 75-82.

The Norman Invasion

On the 14th of October 1066, William of Normandy succeeded in dramatically changing the direction of British history. By the evening of that day, Harold Godwinson lay dead at Hastings and William had become the Conqueror. On Christmas day, William was crowned king of England and within a comparatively short period, his control over the English heartland was secure. News of these developments rapidly reached Gwent where Caradog ap Gruffudd undoubtedly welcomed the removal of Harold who had proved a considerable nuisance. It did not take long, however, to recognize that a new threat had emerged which was far more serious than the old one. Soon the Normans were making their presence felt west of the Wye. There had actually been Norman activity on the border from about 1050 when Edward the Confessor introduced Norman knights in an attempt to organize Herefordshire into a strong frontier province. The Confessor's nephew Ralf was given the earldom of Herefordshire in 1053 and he encouraged the construction of fortifications until his death in 1057.[1] Given first-hand Norman knowledge of the region, it is not surprising that William moved almost at once to secure the potentially dangerous Welsh border. With the powerful and ambitious William, however, it soon became clear that the intention was not simply defensive. He intended to extend his control into Wales.

As a part of his plan, three great marcher earldoms were created at Chester, Shrewsbury and Hereford, the latter having a major impact on the course of the history of Gwent. Hereford was particularly important, in part because of its potential as a base for a thrust into Wales. Another consideration for William was the instability within the region itself which led to the rebellion of Eadric the Wild, bolstered by Welsh support, in 1069. The significance of the region was reflected in William's choice as earl of Hereford, William Fitz Osbern. Not only was Fitz Osbern a trusted commander from Hastings, he was also the king's cousin. The bond was particularly strong since Fitz Osbern's father had been William's guardian who was killed resisting an attempt to murder the young duke. William and Fitz Osbern fled together and as they grew to maturity, Fitz Osbern became one of William's most trusted officials. A key figure in the planning and organization of the invasion of England, Fitz Osbern commanded the right wing of the Norman army at Hastings.

When, some six months after landing in England, William felt secure enough to visit Normandy, the co-regents left in charge of his new realm were his half-brother Odo and Fitz Osbern.[2]

Fitz Osbern soon began probing the Welsh borders, building castles at key points including Monmouth. Most important, however, was his construction programme at Chepstow. Recognizing the strategic significance of the river cliff protecting the crossing near the mouth of the Wye, he began erecting a massive stone castle. The fact that the castle was built of stone from the start is particularly noteworthy. In the early stages of the conquest, the Normans adopted the rough and ready expedient of the motte and bailey with wooden pallisades and keep. At Chepstow, however, an imposing rectangular hall-keep was stone-built, with bonding courses of Roman tiles robbed from Caerwent. This in itself would have made the castle unique, but its date of construction made it even more so. The first phase of building was certainly completed by Fitz Osbern's death in 1071 and the best estimate for start of work is 1067/68. This makes Chepstow castle the oldest dateable stone secular building still standing in Britain.[3] It should be stressed that the site of the castle was chosen for more than its defensive qualities. Located on the west bank of the Wye, Chepstow afforded a strong base for an advance into Wales. Chepstow was to become the 'thin end of the wedge' in establishing Norman control in Wales.

From the strong base at Chepstow, Norman influence was extended in the west. Gwent Iscoed was brought almost completely under Norman control fairly rapidly. This expansion, however, then began to slow partly due to the death of Fitz Osbern and the subsequent imprisonment of his son for his part in the rebellion of the earls in 1075. The advance into south Wales was so stalled that William himself mounted the last British military expedition of his reign into south Wales, visiting St. David's in 1081. By this time, however, Norman fortunes had been improved by internal disputes in Wales. For example, Caradog ap Gruffudd, king of Gwent-Morgannwg, was killed at the battle of Mynydd Carn in 1081 fighting, not to stop the Norman advance, but to extend his own authority in the west. For a time, Rhys ap Tewdwr, the victor at Mynydd Carn, appeared to offer the last hope for the independent Welsh kingdoms of the south. When he was killed in 1093, Norman control appeared to be assured.[4] A network of castles extended through

Gwent and into the Glamorgan lowlands suggesting permanency and secure control.[5] The appearance was, however, deceptive.

Welsh resistance in remote regions remained strong and there was a widespread determination to reassert independence. Moreover, serious difficulties arose for the Normans on the death of Henry I, the Conqueror's youngest son, in 1135. Henry's own son and heir had pre-deceased him and as a consequence the throne was claimed by a nephew, Stephen. This claim was disputed by Henry's daughter Matilda and chaos ensued. A nineteen-year civil war, the period known as the Anarchy, raged through England. The protracted dynastic struggle was particularly significant because well before the full extent of the conflict had become clear, Welsh leaders were already moving to re-establish their authority in many parts of south Wales. The confusion of the Anarchy made their task an easier one.[6]

Among the most powerful Norman families in Wales were the de Clares with Walter Fitz Richard holding Chepstow and his brother Gilbert, Cardigan. Within a week of Stephen's coronation, however, there was a major rising on the Gower with over 500 Anglo-Norman colonists killed. Some three months later, in April 1136, Richard Fitz Gilbert was returning to the lordship of Cardigan after visiting Stephen. In Coed Grwyne in the Vale of Usk, he was attacked and killed by a group of men from Gwent led by Iorwerth ap Owain, grandson of the last king of Gwent, Caradog ap Gruffudd. The news of the death of the powerful de Clare was electric and sparked more widespread revolt through other parts of Wales. Norman strongholds, including Aberystwyth, were taken and the chaotic situation in England made Stephen's response ineffectual. The re-establishment of Welsh authority in the west was mirrored in Gwent. Much of Gwent Uwchcoed was in Welsh hands, controlled from strongholds like Castell Arnallt. In 1137 Morgan ap Owain took Usk, allowing him to extend his control over Gwynllwg and claim the lordship of Caerleon.[7]

One important consequence of this re-emergence of the indigenous Welsh leadership was that the peculiar institutions of the March, created for military conquest, were maintained. The continuing scope for conflict meant that the development in Normanized Gwent, in common with the rest of Wales, would inevitably be significantly different from that of Norman England. A period of distinctive historical development, and of continuing conflict, had begun.

NOTES

[1] Stenton, pp. 569-570; and Stanford, pp. 204-205. In 1057, the earldom passed to Harold who used it as a platform for incursions into Gwent. Nevertheless, it was necessary for Fitz Osbern to make the claims to Gwent Iscoed a reality through military conquest.

[2] Stenton, p. 599; Stanford, pp. 204-205; and Douglas, D. C., 'The Ancestors of William Fitz Osbern', *The English Historical Review*, LIX (1944) pp. 62-79.

[3] Stanford, pp. 208-209; and Perks, J. *Chepstow Castle* (London: 1967), pp. 5, 20-21, 42. A new and visually exciting guide is Knight, J. *Chepstow Castle* (Cardiff: 1986).

[4] Brut, pp. 30-33; Stenton, p. 616; and Poole, A. L. *From Domesday Book to Magna Carta* (Oxford: 1954), pp. 287-288. Robert Fitz Hamon was in control of Cardiff and parts of Gwynllwg and Philip de Braose established himself at Radnor in 1095. Soon Walter Fitz Richard was granted Striguil and William Fitz Baderon held Monmouth. Abergavenny, dominating Gwent Uwchcoed was held first by Hamelin, then Brian, Fitz Count. It should also be noted that Caradog was quite happy to use Norman military assistance to further his ambitions.

[5] A pattern emerged with Striguil dominating most of Gwent Iscoed. Usk, Trelech and Caldicot including Shirenewton were eventually detached. Other important lordships were Gwynllwg and Caerleon, Monmouth often including the three castles, Abergavenny, and Ewias Harold. The lordships of Mathern and Goldcliff were in ecclesiastical hands. Large holdings were subdivided into smaller manors and castles like Penhow held by knight's fees.

[6] Poole, pp. 129-166, 290-292; and Brut, pp. 112-115.

[7] Brut, pp. 112-113; Poole, pp. 290-291; Evans, Gwynfor, *Land of My Fathers* (Swansea: 1974) pp. 175-178; and Giraldus Cambrensis, *The Journey Through Wales*, Book 1, Chapter 4. Giraldus reported that the over-confident Richard had dismissed the bodyguard provided by Brian de Wallingford. The family name, de Clare, was taken from the manor of Clare in Suffolk. In 1158 Morgan of Caerleon was killed and his brother Iorwerth succeeded him. The Brut identifies Morgan as the leader of the attack on de Clare, but Giraldus says it was Iorwerth. The Domesday Book offers useful insight into developments in parts of Gwent. See, for example, Moore, John, 'Gloucestershire' in Morris, John (ed), *Domesday Book* (Chichester: 1982). The general background is provided in Davies, R. R., *Conquest, Co-existence and Change, Wales 1063-1415* (Oxford: 1987). A useful overview of the historical geography of the region is Courtney, Paul, *The Rural Landscape of Eastern and Lower Gwent* (doctoral thesis, University of Wales: 1983).

The Marcher Lords

The continuation of a measure of Welsh authority assured the perpetuation of the March, a term borrowed from the French 'marche' meaning frontier. Powerful barons placed in control of virtually autonomous territories meant that the character of Norman control in Wales was inevitably far different from that which had succeeded in England. The marcher lords held their lands through right of conquest and Norman kings were willing to achieve that conquest at the cost of granting the right to exercise high and judicial power to the lords. The consequence was that regions were created in which, quite literally, the king's writ did not run.[1] A pattern of small, largely autonomous, states emerged. In Gwent the most powerful of the early marchers were the lords of Striguil (Chepstow) and at times they had a significant influence in shaping the course of history not only in south Wales, but in the whole of Britain as well. As has been seen, Fitz Osbern, the first to hold the lordship, was an excellent example of an immensely powerful border lord. So were several of those who followed him. Fitz Osbern was succeeded by his son, Roger of Breteuil, but after his imprisonment Striguil reverted to the king. In 1115, however, the lordship was granted to Walter Fitz Richard, becoming a part of the extensive de Clare holdings. When Walter died childless in 1138, his lands were regranted to his nephew, Gilbert, the first of two successive holders of Striguil known as Strongbow. The second of these, his son Richard who succeeded in 1148, was in many respects the archetypal marcher lord. Times were difficult, however, and de Clare fortunes were at a low ebb owing in part to increasing Welsh pressure on the earldom of Pembroke also held by Strongbow. Looking for ways to renew his fortunes, in 1166 he was presented with an opportunity to do so when Dermot McMurrough, king of Leinster, arrived in Bristol. Dermot had fallen foul of Rory O'Conor, the Irish high king, and had fled to England seeking support. Henry II, who harboured designs on Ireland, was not in a position to act immediately so instead he simply issued letters patent empowering his barons to assist Dermot. It was this which enabled Strongbow, sensing a golden opportunity, to enter into a bargain with the deposed king. In return for support, Strongbow would marry Dermot's daughter and succeed to his kingdom.

Emboldened by this agreement, Dermot gained the immediate support of the Anglo-Norman half brothers, Robert Fitz Stephen and Maurice Fitz Gerald, and returned to Ireland in May of 1169. Some initial success was achieved but the critical intervention came on 23rd August 1170 when Strongbow himself landed near Waterford with a force of about 200 knights and 1,000 light armed troops, some recruited in Gwent. Waterford was captured almost immediately and within a month Dublin had fallen. In May 1171, Dermot died leaving Strongbow, who had duly married his daughter Eva, as his successor. There was, however, considerable opposition to a Norman king in Leinster, not least from the Irish high king. As a consequence, a large Irish army tried to take Dublin but was beaten back. Then Strongbow with his comparatively small, but highly disciplined force, sallied out and routed the army of the high king on the banks of the Liffey. Strongbow appeared to be on the verge of total victory. Developments had, however, gone too far for Henry II who now saw his own Irish designs threatened by this marcher adventure. Aware of developments, Strongbow was pragmatic enough to do a deal with the king. He agreed to cede Dublin, Waterford and Wexford but was enfeoffed with the remainder of Leinster, an acceptably profitable result from his point of view. Henry landed with a large army in October 1171, professing to have come to control the Anglo-Norman adventurers who were threatening the peace of Ireland. Of course he had actually come to assert royal control and the whole protracted question of English rule in Ireland had begun.[2] The most significant aspect of the episode for this study is the clear demonstration of the power and influence of the marcher lord of Striguil who, if not having changed the course of Anglo-Irish relations, had at least accelerated the timing of Henry's intervention.

Strongbow was powerful; his successor as lord of Striguil was even more so. William Marshal was an outstanding soldier who was a key figure in four reigns. He served Henry II, acting as guardian to the young prince Henry until the boy died in 1183. After the death of the prince, Marshal remained in royal service until the death of the king in 1189. The summer of that year found the sons of Henry II in revolt against their father and in a skirmish Marshal unhorsed none other than Richard 'the Lionheart' himself. Later in that year, Richard became king and, respecting Marshal's considerable abilities, granted him the hand of Isabel de Clare, Strongbow's daughter and only heir. As earl of Pembroke and lord of Striguil, Marshal emerged as a champion of royal legitimacy, supporting Richard and trying to prevent usurpation of power by John. In 1199 when Richard was killed, however, he became one of John's only reliable advisors. His influence was so great that he was appointed regent for Henry III and played a key role in stabilizing the realm before his own death in 1219. Marshal was obviously influential nationally and much of his life was spent away from the March. Nevertheless, Striguil was an important power base for him and he stamped his personality on south Wales. The defences at Chepstow castle were modernized through addition of a curtain wall with two half round towers which are probably the earliest examples in Britain of the new technique of building round towers projecting from a curtain. A new gate was also constructed. Perhaps most significantly for Gwent, it was also Marshal who succeeded in capturing the Welsh stronghold of Caerleon in 1217.[3]

The Marshal era at Striguil was a long one as on the death of the powerful elder William, the lordship passed to his son, also William Marshal. It was then held by each of his four other sons in turn until the death of the youngest Marshal in 1245. By 1270, however, the lordship had come into the hands of Roger Bigod III who demonstrated the continuing influence of the marcher lords at Chepstow. A well known story survives describing Bigod's confrontation with Edward I, one of England's strongest medieval kings. Edward demanded that Bigod, in his role as earl marshal, should lead a campaign into Gascony. The earl's response was that his obligation was to accompany the king and not to lead an unaccompanied campaign. Edward was furious and thundered 'Sir Earl, by God, you shall go or hang'. The equally furious retort of Bigod, confronting the powerful king, was 'Sir King, by God, I shall neither go nor hang'. The earl marshal retired to his stronghold at Chepstow and neither went nor hanged.[4] The point to be drawn from all of these examples is that the marcher lords were powerful men who could, and did, confront kings with impunity.

Given the power of the lords of the March, it is not surprising that unusual alignments developed along the Welsh borders. A case in point is the change in attitude by Henry II when faced with the growing strength of Strongbow and other marcher lords. Henry had led a disastrously unsuccessful campaign into north Wales against Owain Gwynedd in 1165. In the aftermath, the king continued to face a significant challenge in south Wales from Rhys ap Gruffudd, the grandson of Rhys ap Tewdwr and a supporter of Owain Gwynedd. When Owain died in 1170, Rhys emerged as the principal leader of the Welsh resistance. By this time, however, other problems were distracting Henry. One was the murder of Beckett in December 1170. Even more important in a Welsh context was Strongbow's Irish adventure. Facing what he perceived as a threat from the over powerful marchers, Henry turned to Rhys. The king met Rhys at Laugharne and appointed him justiciar of south Wales. In accepting the appointment, the previously rebel prince of south Wales became the king's chief deputy in the region—the Lord Rhys as he was henceforth known. Rhys continued to dominate south Wales until his death in 1197. Notable among his achievements was the first documented eisteddfod, held under his patronage at Cardigan castle in 1176.[5] What is particularly instructive about the role of the Lord Rhys is that the English king was happy to rely on the native Welsh prince to reduce the power of the marcher lords.

Similarly, the marcher lords were willing to align themselves with the Welsh in controversies with the king. For example, in 1233 when Richard Marshal found himself in conflict with Henry III who had seized his castle at Usk, he turned to Llywelyn ap Iorwerth, Llywelyn Fawr, for an alliance. Regaining Usk, Marshal then joined forces with Owain ap Gruffudd, grandson of the Lord Rhys, and attacked and burned Monmouth before capturing Cardiff, Abergavenny and several other castles.[6] Probably the best known example of co-operation between lord and Welsh prince was the alliance between Simon de Montfort and Llywelyn ap Gruffudd. Combining forces in 1265, they stormed Monmouth castle. Llywelyn then attacked the de Clare holdings in Gwent as de Montfort moved down the Usk, attacking Abergavenny, Usk and Newport. In July, however, de Montfort was forced to withdraw, losing several ships in the Usk, beginning the retreat which eventually led to Evesham.[7] The critical conclusion to be drawn from all of these examples is that there was a tri-partite power structure in the March with the king, the marcher lords, and the Welsh princes all contesting for control. Any possible combination of alliances within this structure could and did occur. Far from simply being agents of extending the authority of the English king into Wales, the marcher lords were frequently laws unto themselves whose principal concern was their own self interest and the history of Gwent can only be fully understood in this context.

NOTES

[1] A good explanation of the system can be found in Rees, W., *South Wales and the March* (Oxford: 1924), especially pp. 43-49. This source is a very useful one which was issued as an Academic Reprint in 1967. See also Davies, R., *Lordship and Society in the March of Wales 1282-1400* (Oxford: 1978) and Reeves, A. C. *The Marcher Lords* (Llandybie: 1983).

[2] Poole, pp. 302-312; and Perks, pp. 5-6. An almost contemporary account is found in *The Conquest of Ireland* by Giraldus Cambrensis.

[3] Brut, pp. 216-217; Perks, pp. 6-7; Poole, various references, especially p. 347; and Knight, J. 'The Medieval Castle in Monmouthshire' in *Gwent Local History*, No. 42, 1977, especially pp. 43-44. It is likely that Marshal was responsible for the destruction of the great Roman baths at Caerleon, using building material for his re-constructed castle. The Marshal inheritance was partitioned after the death of Anselm, the youngest of the sons of William Marshal, in 1245. One significant development was the acquisition of the lordship of Usk by Richard de Clare. His son, Gilbert, later acquired the lordship of Caerleon. There is a long chanson or poem which chronicles the life of William Marshal, the elder. It has formed the basis for two biographies, Painter, Sidney, *William Marshal* (Baltimore: 1933) and Duby, Georges, *William Marshal, The Flower of Chivalry* (London: 1986).

[4] For a good general account of the period, see Powicke, M., *The Thirteenth Century* (Oxford: 1962).

[5] Brut, pp. 158-159; Poole, pp. 293-295; and, for a concise summary, Williams, A. H., *An Introduction to the History of Wales*, Vol. II, Part 1, pp. 37-44. The office justiciar or justice would be better understood today as Viceroy. For a discussion, see Griffiths, Ralph, *The Principality of Wales in the Later Middle Ages: The Structure and Personnel of Government*, I (South Wales) (Cardiff: 1972) especially pp. 19-34.

[6] Brut, pp. 230-233; Powicke, pp. 53-55; and Kissack, K. E., *Mediaeval Monmouth* (Monmouth: 1974) pp. 11-14.

[7] Brut, pp. 254-257; Powicke, pp. 200-202; and Williams, A. H., pp. 90-92.

A Tripartite Structure

The conflicting interests and shifting alliances within the tri-partite structure of marcher Gwent meant that warfare was endemic. A particularly instructive example of the frequently violent life of the March began to unfold during unrest in 1173. Fighting swept Gwent as Hywel ap Iorwerth ranged from Caerleon as far east as Chepstow, subduing the whole of Iscoed apart from the castle strongholds. Further north, Seisyll ap Dyfnwal, leader of the Welsh in Gwent Uwchcoed, managed to capture Abergavenny castle. Two years later, however, in an effort to gain a general peace settlement, the Lord Rhys persuaded Seisyll, his brother-in-law, to return the castle to Norman control. As a consequence, in 1175 the castle passed to William de Braose who also held Brecknock, Builth, Radnor, and the three castles.[1] The gesture appeared to be reciprocated at Christmas in that year when de Braose invited Seisyll, his eldest son Gruffudd, and other Welsh leaders of Uwchcoed to a banquet at the castle. It was not, however, to prove the seasonal feast of peace and reconciliation expected by the Welsh. Instead it was a calculated attempt to wipe out the native leadership. When the Welshmen arrived and were seated in the hall, the trap was sprung. De Braose's men pounced and murdered all of the unsuspecting guests. Even that carnage did not satisfy de Braose who then sent his men to attack Seisyll's home at Castell Arnallt near Llangattock nigh Usk. They destroyed it and when they found Seisyll's seven-year-old younger son Cadwaladr, shielded in his mother's arms, they cut him down too.

The marcher de Braose had hoped to eliminate the Welsh dimension from Gwent Uwchcoed at a stroke. He failed. Almost immediately surviving Welsh leaders began to plan retaliation and in 1182, Iorwerth of Caerleon and other kinsmen of the murdered Seisyll attacked and captured Abergavenny castle again. Scaling ladders were dragged to the wall and the Welshmen poured into the castle, seizing the constable and his wife. They then, in the words of Giraldus Cambrensis, 'burned the whole place down'. Giraldus also described the devastating effect of the longbow, the speciality weapon of the men of Gwent. In the attack, arrows penetrated oak doors as thick as a man's palm. Shortly afterwards, the Welsh struck Dingestow where Ranulf Poer, sheriff of Herefordshire, was building a new castle at the behest of de Braose. The

Herefordshire men were expecting the attack and were drawn up fully armed. Nevertheless they were forced back into the defences they had erected and there Ranulf, nine of his captains, and many of his men were killed. [2] These bloody exchanges typified the violence which persisted in the region.

One dimension of marcher society did, however, tend to reduce violence to a degree, although it complicated it from other points of view. The Welsh-marcher distinction became progressively less clear with time. From the outset, marcher lords found marriage a convenient way to enhance their authority in newly-acquired territories. There are numerous examples of Norman lords taking Welsh wives but undoubtedly the best known was Nest, the daughter of Rhys ap Tewdwr. Nest was married to Gerald of Windsor, one of the leading Normans in Dyfed. Sometimes described as the Helen of Wales, her beauty prompted her celebrated abduction by Owain ap Cadwgan in 1109. It also led to her having children by three leading Normans other than Gerald, including a son by Henry I. She also had five legitimate children. Her sons, including a Fitz Stephen and two Fitz Geralds, were in the vanguard preceding Strongbow to Ireland. One of Nest's daughters, Angharad, married William de Barry, lord of Manorbier. Giraldus Cambrensis was their son. Giraldus, Gerald of Wales, is a classical example of the cultural fusion of the March. He was closely linked to both leading marcher and Welsh families; he was a cousin of, among others, the Lord Rhys. Contemptuous of the English, Giraldus was proud both of the Normans and of the Welsh and wrestled with conflicting loyalties throughout his life. [3] As the March evolved, among leading families, Welsh, English or French became less a question of birth and more one of linguistic and cultural preference.

This ability to exercise choice did not extend to the common people. Nevertheless, there were anachronisms in this respect too. In many parts of the March, including Gwent, Welsh law, customs and language flourished in regions closely linked to the strongest of the marcher lordships. One of the most significant consequences of the Norman conquest in England was the imposition of a rigid feudal system with its associated pattern of manorial organization. Practical difficulties, however, prevented this from happening to the same extent in the March. In Wales and the border country, there was a clear distinction between the Englishry and the Welshry. The former was comprised of introduced populations which were concentrated in lowland regions and particularly in the towns. These towns were new developments, generally growing up around the castles and frequently enclosed by walls. In the early stages of the March, the towns were exclusively English with Welshmen prohibited from settling within the town walls. Chepstow today offers the classical example, often repeated throughout south Wales, of a Welsh Street just outside the medieval town gate—a lingering legacy of this period. One of Gwent's most interesting examples of an attempt to establish an intrusive English town in an area which was strongly Welsh is Trelech. Today a small agricultural village near Monmouth, Trelech was once one of the largest towns in Wales. It was a speculative venture by the de Clares. The motte and bailey had been erected before 1231 and by 1288 the town was flourishing with a population larger than Chepstow. At the beginning of the fourteenth century, Trelech was one of the eight largest towns in Wales. There was a slow decline after 1300 but the town remained an important centre at mid-century as sheep rearing had become an increasingly important element in bolstering the economy. It was only after 1369 that events, including plague and warfare, sent Trelech into irreversible decline making it one of the best examples of a decayed settlement in Wales.[4] The Englishry did sometimes extend into rural regions although it was usually confined to easily controlled lowland areas. The Caldicot levels are the most obvious examples in Gwent. In these Anglicised regions, manorialism could develop. The situation was, however, substantially different in the Welshry.

In highland Welsh regions, the strength of the kindred and the traditional application of the laws of Hywel made imposition of the English system impracticable. As a consequence, marcher lords were generally willing to settle for political control without attempting to encourage direct economic exploitation on the English model. The traditional obligations owed to the Welsh leader, in this case the king of Gwent, were simply transferred to the marcher lord. In much of the Welshry, the community held lands from the lord as a body and continued to render their accustomed dues in a slightly modified form.[5] In these Welsh areas the fact of manorial organization frequently did not imply manorial cultivation. In many cases the term manor was used simply to describe a 'manorial district' created solely for the purpose of collecting dues. Throughout these highland districts the staple crops tended to be oats, or oats and wheat in the more fertile regions. The traditional medieval three-field pattern frequently did not apply; crops were sometimes repeated for two years in succession, then the field would lie fallow for a year. Much land was given over to grazing with pasture particularly important throughout the Welshry. There were customary or bond tenants in both the Englishry and the Welshry although their obligations were different. The main task of the English serf was to provide labour supporting cultivation on the home farm of the manor. He was obliged to work on the lord's demesne on two or three days per week, week-work, in addition to boon-work, providing special services at harvest time. This pattern of villeinage was difficult to apply to pastoral economies especially in Wales. In the Welshry customary obligations tended to emphasize haulage and 'building work' and the week-work of the English manors frequently did not apply. In Striguil, for example, Welsh tenants owning two or more oxen were expected to haul timber from Wentwood to Chepstow castle. Welshmen were also expected to build mills and haul mill stones. Interestingly many mills were owned collectively by the Welsh tenants. Administrative rents, such as the cylch, were extracted from both the Englishry and the Welshry[6]

An important related feature in Gwent was that the marcher lords, like the Norman kings, attached great importance to hunting and tracts of the Welshry were set aside as forest preserves. Here forest law, administered in forest courts, applied although it was still necessary to accommodate Welsh usages. There were large forest tracts, like that in Striguil extending from the Wye towards Trelech. In these forests, in part to support the foresters, a cylch was extracted from the tenants of the Welsh hamlets. These residents did, however, retain certain common rights. For example, local communities had recognised rights to pasture except in clearly delineated enclosures or hays; such rights are indicated by surviving records of pannage payments from places including Tintern and Llangwm. Other rights included that of collecting firewood, haybote (the right of tenants to take timber for fences) and housebote (the right of tenants to take timber for making and repairing buildings).[7]

Among the most interesting features of the Welshry was how closely it impinged upon the most powerful of the marcher lordships. In Striguil, for example, villages like Porthcaseg and St. Arvans, little more than two miles away from Chepstow castle, remained Welsh in language, custom and law. Remarkably, in 1309 the manor of St. Arvans was actually held by a Welshman, Ieuan ap Morgan, for a quarter of a knight's fee. These hamlets, almost within sight of Chepstow castle continued to be Welsh throughout the medieval period. [8] This Welsh continuity in east Gwent was mirrored throughout the county. The assize roll of the Great Sessions at Newport, for example, shows a strong Welsh dimension even in low lying regions like Wentlwg right into the fifteenth century. [9]

There is a final point which must be made about the unique nature of the Welshry and that is that among the obligations owed by men from the Welshry was military service. The military obligations which had once been owed to the kings of Gwent were transferred to the marcher lords. The demand for military service could be applied so rigidly that Welshmen living in hamlets in the Englishry might retain military obligations which did not apply to the English villeins among whom they lived. It is known that provisions within Striguil obliged Welsh tenants to follow the lords to war. If the fighting were confined to the bounds of Striguil, they went at their own expense. It was only when they had to cross Chepstow bridge or Newport Bridge, for example, that the lord would undertake the cost. [10] This military service was of immense value to the marcher lord since it allowed him to tap a large pool of trained soldiers. As Giraldus Cambrensis observed, among the Welsh it was not only the leaders who were trained for warfare. With the call to battle, 'the peasant will rush from his plough and pick up his weapons as quickly as the courtier from the court'. Moreover, the men of Gwent offered special expertise in the weapon which was revolutionising medieval warfare—the longbow. According to Giraldus, 'the men of Gwent, for that is what they are called, have much more experience of warfare, are more famous for their martial exploits and, in particular, are more skilled with the bow and arrow than those who come from other parts of Wales'. To prove the point he described an attack in which a mounted knight was hit by an arrow fired by a Gwent archer. The arrow went through his thigh, his leather tunic, and the iron cuishes protecting his leg inside and out. Having pierced man and armour, the arrow penetrated the saddle, driving in so deeply that the horse was killed. The bows were carved from the dwarf elm of the forests. 'Nothing much to look at' but very effective. [11] This military expertise was significant not only in the incessant conflicts in Gwent, but also in wars further afield. Even at the time of the Hundred Years War, Welshmen made up the large majority of the archers who dominated the set piece battles. The archers at Crecy, Poitiers and Agincourt included large numbers of men from Gwent.

NOTES

[1] The three castles—Grosmont, Skenfrith and White Castle—controlled the important gateway to Gwent between the Black Mountains and the Wye above Monmouth.

[2] Giraldus Cambrensis, *Journey Through Wales*, I, 4; and Brut, pp. 162-167.

[3] Summaries can be found in Evans, G., p. 172; and Williams, A. H., pp. 52-56. Giraldus Cambrensis is the traditional form with Gerald of Wales more widely used today. Alternatives are Geraldus and the Welsh Gerallt.

[4] Soulsby, Ian, *The Towns of Medieval Wales* (Chichester: 1983), especially pp. 256-259; Soulsby, I., 'Medieval Trellech', a lecture for the Gwent History Council Summer School, 1982; and Rees, p. 196. Today's village of Trelech offers a good example of the difficulties arising from English spelling of Welsh names. The three main approaches to the village are all signposted, and each offers a different spelling of the village name—Trelech, Trellech and Trelleck. The author's continuing excavation at Trelech, conducted in association with Stephen Clarke and the Monmouth Archaeological Society, will shed light on development of the medieval town.

[5] Rees, pp. 25-30.

[6] Ibid pp. 25-30, 76, 131, 167, 237-238; and Williams, A. H., pp. 21-26. Payment in food or money was usually associated with boon work. For example, in Striguil customary tenants received between them a sheep, the med sheep, or the equivalent of one shilling as payment for mowing the meadow. There was also growing diversification. By the fourteenth century, for example, dairy farming was becoming more significant in areas like Caerleon and Usk.

[7] Rees, pp. 109-128; and Rent Rolls of the lordship of Chepstow. Much of the Court Roll material was used by Bradney, see especially I, IV, pp. 9-12.

[8] Howell, pp. 22-23.

[9] See Pugh, T. B. (ed.) *The Marcher Lordships of South Wales* (Cardiff: 1963) especially, pp. 21-25.

[10] Rees, pp. 64. The terms of service which survive pertain specifically to Pentirch hamlet, but they probably applied widely in the lordship.

[11] Giraldus Cambrensis, *The Description of Wales*, I, 6 and 8; and *The Journey Through Wales*, I, 4.

Life in Medieval Gwent

A major problem confronting historians examining early periods is the difficulty in forming any clear picture of the common people. Surviving accounts and chronicles deal almost exclusively with the high and mighty of the land and as a consequence it is far easier to picture life in the castle than it is to visualize conditions in the hinterland. Historians of Gwent, however, are particularly fortunate in having access to a unique description of the common people in the late twelfth century. Giraldus Cambrensis accompanied the archbishop Baldwin through Wales, preaching a crusade, in 1188. The journey was described in Giraldus' third book, *The Journey Through Wales*. At about the same time he wrote a companion volume called *The Description of Wales* and in it provided a most useful view of life in the Welshry.

In dealing with the description of what he saw as his own country, Giraldus dealt with the whole of Wales from 'Anglesey to Portskewett in Gwent'. Much of his material, however, was drawn from the southern marches which he knew intimately. The first feature of the Welsh stressed by Giraldus was their ferocity and pre occupation with training for war. Ostensibly quoting from a letter written by Henry II, he described the Welsh who were 'so brave and untamed that, though unarmed themselves, they do not hesitate to do battle with fully armed opponents'. There is an appealing sequel to this passage which observes, with a certain degree of incomprehension, 'this is all the more surprising because the wild animals in the island are not particularly fierce, whereas the Welsh show no sign of losing their ferocity'.

The people were described as generally lithe and agile, wearing only a thin cloak and a tunic to keep out the cold. Frequently going barefooted, they sometimes wore roughly sewn, untanned leather boots. Their staple diet was based on oats and the produce of the herds. Most land was used for pasture but when fields were ploughed oxen were used, sometimes in pairs but usually in teams of four. 'They eat plenty of meat, but little bread', the reader is told. There was, however, a tradition of serving the main dish on a sort of bread, baked daily and rolled thin. The description sounds very much like an early Welsh version of the pizza or of paratha bread.

A detailed description is provided of the appearance of the people and elements of their personal hygiene. We are told that both men and women cut their hair short and 'shape it around their ears and eyes'. Women covered their heads with a 'flowing white veil, stuck up in folds like a crown'. Both men and women went to great lengths to care for their teeth. Giraldus says that they took more pains with their teeth than people in any other country he had seen, constantly cleaning them with green hazel shoots and then polishing them with woollen cloths 'until they shine like ivory'. Particularly noticeable was that the men shaved their beards, leaving only their moustaches.

An obvious observation is that descriptions of agile and particularly ferocious men sporting distinctive moustaches sounds surprisingly like much earlier descriptions of Silurian warriors in the Gwent highlands. The fact was not lost on Giraldus who suggested that moustaches were a habit which went back 'to time immemorial'. Similarly, other descriptions do not sound totally foreign to today's observers of Gwent. Giraldus reported that when Welshmen came together to sing their traditional songs, they did not sing in unison as in most places, but instead in parts. He wrote, 'when a choir gathers to sing, which happens often in this country, you will hear as many different parts and voices as there are performers, all joining together in the end to produce a single organic harmony and melody in the soft sweetness of B-flat'. Three main musical instruments were played including the harp, pipe and crwth (an early stringed instrument). Particularly important was the harp, which was an important feature in provision of hospitality which was so significant in Welsh society. Generosity and hospitality were cited as the greatest of Welsh virtues with all homes open to anyone. 'When you travel there is no question of your asking for accommodation or of their offering it: you just march into a house and hand over your weapons to the person in charge', Giraldus observed. Tradition then dictated that the new arrival would be offered water to wash his feet as a symbolic invitation to stay. Refusal of the water to wash meant that the traveller had only dropped in for refreshment and did not intend to spend the night. Guests who arrived early in the day would be entertained until nightfall by girls playing the harp. 'In every house there are young women just waiting to play for you, and there is certainly no lack of harps.'

When mealtime came, the fare was simple. There was little variety and, to Giraldus' palate, a lack of seasoning to the food. There were no tables or napkins and 'everyone behaves quite naturally, with no attempt whatsoever at etiquette'. Guests tended to sit in threes rather than in twos, a habit which Giraldus put down to the celebration of the Trinity. Food was presented in a large trencher resting on rushes, in ample quantity for the three eating from it. Much about the lifestyle was rough and ready. The communal bed stuffed with rushes and covered by a single 'harsh' sheet, for example, was pictured as being particularly uncomfortable:

A fire is kept burning all night at their feet,
just as it has done all day, and they get some
warmth from the people sleeping next to them.
When their underneath side begins to ache through
the hardness of the bed and their uppermost side
is frozen stiff with cold, they get up and sit by
the fire, which soon warms them up and soothes away
their aches and pains. Then they go back to bed
again, turning over on their side if they
feel like it, so that a different part is frozen and
another side bruised by the hard bed.

The complicated, alliterative works of the bards impressed Giraldus. The fascination with words found among the bards, however, extended to all levels as did a boldness and confidence in speech. 'This is true of all of them, from the highest to the lowest,' claimed Giraldus. Among other points considered noteworthy was the long Christian tradition and the devotion to Christian practice in Wales. There was also, according to Giraldus, an obsession with genealogy and noble descent. 'Even the common people know their family tree by heart and can readily recite from memory the list of their grandfathers, great-grandfathers, great-great-grandfathers, back to the sixth or seventh generation.' The general picture presented of the Welsh was favourable in many respects. 'They are quicker-witted and more shrewd than any other Western people,' Giraldus asserted.

The Description of Wales did not, however, simply dwell on virtues. The second section of the book is devoted to the negative features of the Welsh. Among the descriptions which appear in this section are inconstancy and instability. It is clear that Giraldus disapproved of the guerilla tactics which had been adopted on the march. Spirited resistance would cause them to 'turn their backs, making no attempt at a counter-attack'. Nor did reverses seem to make any impression. 'They do not lose heart when things go wrong, and after one defeat they are ready to fight again,' he claimed. Of course, Giraldus did recognize factors making guerilla tactics necessary. Losses to armies of English mercenaries were of little consequence, he explained. 'There is enough money to ensure that the ranks of battle will be filled again and more than filled tomorrow. On the other hand, for the Welsh 'who have no mercenaries and no foreign allies, those who fall in battle are irreplaceable'.

Other aspects of the Welsh criticized by Giraldus included greediness. 'If they come to a house where there is any sign of affluence . . . there is no limit to their demands. They lose all control of themselves and insist on being served with vast quantities of food and more especially intoxicating drink'. A related theme was land hunger. 'The Welsh people are more keen to own land and to extend their holdings than any other I know,' he reported. 'They are prepared to dig up boundary ditches, to move stones showing the edges of fields and to overrun clearly-marked limits'. Quarrels over land, of course, became particularly significant when the conflicting parties were princes and Giraldus emphasized the damaging effects of the internal dissension which repeatedly surfaced.

Internal conflict led naturally to the final section in which Giraldus considered invasion of Wales from two points of view. He offered advice as to how the Welsh should be conquered. A determined invader would have to be prepared for a protracted struggle since it was impossible to defeat a people who never drew up forces for a single decisive battle in the field and who never allowed themselves to be besieged in any stronghold. The only answer was 'patient and unremitting pressure' while fomenting internal dissension and fueling the hatreds and jealousies existing within Welsh society. Finally, however, Giraldus offered advice to the Welsh for resisting invasion. What was most needed was strong leadership and a sense of national unity. 'If they were united, no one could ever beat them,' he argued. It would also help, he believed, if they would learn to fight in disciplined ranks, 'instead of leaping about all over the place.'[1]

The descriptive passages of Giraldus are particularly significant in giving us a glimpse of Welsh life style. The fashions and foibles, the strengths and weaknesses, allow us to form a mental image which applies to life in the Welshry of Gwent. The lifestyle described was under constant, and increasing, threat but continuity was a persistent feature. Welsh historians will be perpetually indebted to Giraldus for, in his own words, 'writing about such humdrum matters.'

NOTES

[1] The descriptions are drawn from *The Journey Through Wales* and *The Description of Wales* by Giraldus. The most readily obtainable version of the two, is the volume in the Penguin Classics series translated and introduced by Lewis Thorpe. It is this version which is quoted throughout. References to matters such as physical endurance and hospitality in Welsh society are also found in Walter Map. See Walter Map, *De Nugis Curialium, Courtiers' Trifles*, edited and translated by M. R. James and revised by C. N. L. Brooke and R. A. B. Mynors (Oxford: 1983).

The Monastic Tradition

Continuity in the lifestyle of the Welshry demonstrates that the upheavals associated with the incursion of the Normans and the creation of
marcher society did not change traditional usages as dramatically as
might have been expected. In fact, a case can be made for arguing that, in
some respects, the greatest threat to established practice came less from
the marcher lords, than from the institution which was only in part their
client—the church. Despite its ancient roots and traditions, the Welsh
Church found itself under siege after the Norman conquest. The
Normans saw ecclesiastical control as an element in political domination
and set about to destroy the existing church structure. The old influence
of the claswyr, for example, was undermined with the introduction of
Latin monasticism. Foundation and endowment of a monastery had
become a conventional act of piety among the Normans, but intrusive
religious houses could also be integrated into the feudal fabric as a tool of
political control. Once again, Striguil offers an excellent example.
William Fitz Osbern had founded a monastery at Cormeilles in 1060
and, after gaining Chepstow, he founded a monastery there as a daughter
house in about 1070. Establishment of dependent Benedictine priories
like Chepstow became the norm in south Wales. No fewer than nineteen
were established although most of these always remained mere cells.
Seven, however, were significant enough to acquire the status of conventional priories and four of these—Chepstow, Monmouth, Abergavenny
and Goldcliff—were in Gwent. The founding of a conventional dependent priory generally led the mother house to require payment of an
annual sum as a token of subjection. This was the case with each of the
Gwent houses. Chepstow paid £3 13s. 4d. to Cormeilles, Monmouth £6
13s. 4d. to St. Florent, Abergavenny £5 7s. 0d to St. Vincent, and Goldcliff £1 to Bec.[1] The influence of these early Benedictine foundations
was inevitably limited. Confined to the Englishry, they usually sheltered under the protection of the Norman castle and had little impact on
the Welshry. Size was a factor. It was assumed that conventional priories
should have at least 12 monks in order to perform liturgical prayers and
other required functions. It seems unlikely that many did so through
much of the medieval period. It is known, for example, that in 1319
Abergavenny had only five monks. The position was even worse in

Chepstow in 1370 when there were only four. In view of such difficulties, the spiritual influence of these foundations was limited. The financial impact, however, was rather greater. Chepstow priory, for example, was endowed with property in the surrounding area and the tithes, or part tithes, of Chepstow, Newchurch, Trelech, Howick, Mounton, Llanfair Discoed, Tidenham and Usk. Similarly Abergavenny was in possession of the rectories of Abergavenny, Grosmont, Llangadog Lingoed, Llanelen, Llanfihangel Crucorney, Llanddewi Rhydderch and Mitchel Troy in addition to part of the tithes of Llanddewi Skirrid, Llanfoist, Llanwenarth, Bryngwyn, Goytre, Llanfair Cilgedin, Llantilio Pertholey, and Llangadog juxta Usk. In addition to property in the Wye Valley and the Forest of Dean, Monmouth also had the spiritual income from St. Cadog in Monmouth, Rockfield, Wonastow, Llangadog vibion Avel and Welsh Bicknor. Assessed values for the houses in 1291 were: Abergavenny £51 17s. 10½d.; Chepstow £35 19s. 11d.; Goldcliff £171 14s. 1d.; and Monmouth £85 18s. 8d.[2]

It is obvious from the assessed values that Goldcliff was wealthier than the other early foundations. Robert de Chandos had granted the church of St. Mary Magdalen at Goldcliff to the abbey of Bec, along with lands and tithes, for the establishment of a monastery. The grant was confirmed in 1113. The difference with this foundation, apart from a location more isolated than that of its contemporaries, was the extent of its arable holdings. For all the grants of property to the other Benedictine houses, their arable holdings were always small. None exceeded 500 acres with Monmouth holding 480, Abergavenny 240, and Chepstow 201 acres of arable along with 28½ of meadow and 82 of waste and pasture. The later Benedictine foundation of Llangua had 480. Goldcliff, on the other hand, had an exceptional estate of 1,221 acres of arable and 125 acres of meadow in Gwent. In addition, it also held manors in Somerset which were valued at some £50 per annum in the early fourteenth century. Goldcliff was also unusual in having 25 monks in 1295. The priory became the largest and richest Benedictine house in south Wales.[3] Unique for another reason was Monmouth which was founded by a Breton noble, Wihenoc. Monks in the Benedictine houses were usually supplied from Normandy, but Wihenoc's foundation drew monks from Britanny who were familiar with the ecclesiastical traditions of the Celtic peoples among whom they had settled.[4] This affinity with the Welsh was unique. In addition to the Benedictine tradition, there was an

Augustinian influence in Gwent which began with the foundation of Llanthony Prima in about 1118. Unlike the Benedictine houses, the Augustinian foundations were autonomous and were, therefore, forced to recruit locally. Llanthony did not, however, recruit from the Welshry and indications are that monks were drawn almost exclusively from among the Anglo-Normans of the march.[5]

Despite the introduction of a limited Augustinian presence, the main thrust of early Latin monasticism in Gwent was Benedictine. Even allowing for the large land holdings of Goldcliff and a certain rapport between the monks of Monmouth and the Welsh, the inescapable conclusion is that the influence of these early foundations was limited, particularly in the Welshry. That was less true, however, of the next wave of monks to reach Gwent. As the early dependent priories were reaching maturity in south Wales, dissatisfaction with monastic usages was growing on the continent. Desirous of a more rigorous life style and greater austerity, a group of monks founded a new monastery at Cîteaux near Dijon in 1098. By 1119 a constitution and set of rules had been drawn up for the new order by the abbot Stephen Harding, an Englishman. The Cistercians, as they were called, continued to follow the rule of St. Benedict but with a new emphasis on austerity. Remote abbeys were to be established and manual labour, centering on the outlying farms or granges, was emphasized. The abbeys were to become working communities relying in part on the work of the conversi, lay-brothers. The real key to the success of the new order, however, was its administrative framework. New abbeys could only be established if clear conditions had been met and then only as colonies of established houses with close supervision through annual visitations. Annual General Chapter meetings held at Cîteaux issued decrees binding on the whole order. The first of these Cistercian foundations in England was in 1128, and in 1131 Tintern became the first abbey in Wales, established on land granted by Walter Fitz Richard, the de Clare lord of Striguil.[6] The association between the abbey and the lords of Striguil was a close and continuing one which placed Tintern in a very strong position in eastern Gwent. The financial situation was secure enough for the abbey to be almost completely rebuilt during the thirteenth century. Work on a new refectory began in about 1220 but the major construction project was the rebuilding of the church itself. Under the patronage of Roger Bigod, work began in 1270 with the consecration of the new High Altar in 1288.

The final phase of building, the west front of the church, was not completed until 1301, making a total of 32 years in building the new structure.[7]

The emergence of the Cistercians gave a new impetus to monasticism in Wales where eventually thirteen monasteries were established with three in Gwent. Following Tintern were Caerleon, later and more commonly known as Llantarnam, in 1179 and Grace Dieu in 1226. These Cistercian foundations were unlike their Benedictine predecessors in several respects. The basis of their economies was different and the new arrivals inevitably sought out more remote locations. Moreover, the emergence of strong Welsh leadership in the person of the Lord Rhys allowed a new relationship to develop between the Cistercians and the Welsh. Rhys became a patron of the order and many of the houses took on a distinctive Welsh outlook. This was especially true of colonies from Whitland. It was certainly the case with the second Cistercian foundation in Gwent. In 1179 a colony from Strata Florida established a daughter house at Nant-teyrnon near Caerleon under the patronage of Hywel ap Iorwerth, lord of Caerleon. The abbey of Caerleon, or Llantarnam, was a Welsh house from the outset and this continued to be true even after the Welsh lords of Caerleon had been displaced. Some Welsh recruits to these new Cistercian houses came from among the younger sons of leading families. Interestingly, others seem to have been the sons of clergy, confirming that clerical celibacy continued to be spurned by the Welsh. The Welsh orientation of Llantarnam was not reflected in the last of the Cistercian abbeys, Grace Dieu. The house was founded by John of Monmouth in 1226 as a daughter house of Dore. Far from attracting Welsh postulants, the new abbey was attacked and burned by the men of Gwent who claimed that it had been built on land seized from them. The hostility was so great that a new site had to be found for the monastery in 1236.[8] It is perhaps not surprising that Grace Dieu, like Tintern, retained a strong Anglo-Norman orientation and never achieved the degree of rapport with the Welsh which other Cistercian houses enjoyed.

In assessing the general influence of this monastic tradition in Gwent, spiritual questions must be considered first. Undoubtedly the early Cistercians were devoted to their creed although the nature of their organization invariably gave the abbeys an introspective outlook. In the early Benedictine foundations, discipline seems to have been good. Later, however, this was not necessarily the case. In 1319, for example, complaints led to a formal investigation of Abergavenny priory conducted by Adam de Orleton, bishop of Hereford. He found that there were only five monks and they had so misappropriated monastic goods that the priory was in ruins. Worse was that the monks had abandoned observance of the rule and were living shockingly dissolute lives. They were discovered to be consorting with prostitutes, gambling when they should have been reciting the divine office, and conducting parodies of the passion of Christ. As Cowley puts it, 'the monastic life at Abergavenny had reached the nadir of decadence and corruption even by secular standards'.[9] In fairness, it should be stressed that effective remedial action was taken quickly at Abergavenny. Nevertheless, it is difficult to avoid the conclusion that the spiritual influence of these early houses, which was never significant in the Welshry, was also limited and, at times, negative in the Englishry. Even with the Cistercians there were lapses. In 1217 there were complaints that the abbot of Tintern drank with the bishop and his monks and that women lived near, and worked on, at least one of Tintern's granges.[10]

A legacy of the monasteries which is particularly significant in a historical context is the literature copied or produced by the monks. While much was lost at the dissolution, crucially important works have survived. The monasteries were a pool of literacy and the traditions of the scriptoria of the Welsh churches was, to an extent, continued, especially in the Welsh houses. Among the four 'Ancient Books of Wales' the Black Book of Carmarthen was almost certainly transcribed at the scriptorium of the Augustinian priory of St. John's, Carmarthen, perhaps as early as 1170. The Book of Aneirin was probably a product of Basingwerk Abbey and the Book of Taliesen that of Margam. It is likely that the Red Book of Hergest which was the source of the Brut y Tywysogion was transcribed at Strata Florida. Strata Florida may also have been responsible for preserving the tracts now a part of the Peniarth collection which include copies of the tales of the Mabinogi. Also significant is that in the later midddle ages, a close relationship developed between some Welsh monasteries and the bards. Among the surviving contributions to this literary heritage are two examples from houses in Gwent. The Homilies of St. Gregory, with annotations, belonged to Llantarnam and Tintern preserved the Flores Historiarum, the last section of which describes events at Tintern between 1305 and 1323. Of course, no discussion of the literary inheritance of Gwent would be complete without mention of

Geoffrey of Monmouth whose imaginatively fictional but hugely influential Historia Regum Britanniae can be credited with having launched
the Arthurian legend onto the European stage.[11]

This literary legacy is clearly important retrospectively but to contemporary observers the most significant influence of monasticism may well
have been economic. This was especially true of the Cistercian foundations
with their grange economies. The grange was the main unit of exploitation and generally included a range of farm buildings and living quarters
for the lay brethren and hired labourers. In some cases there was also a
grange chapel. At the end of the thirteenth century, Caerleon had
thirteen granges while Tintern and Grace Dieu each had eight. The size
of the Tintern holdings, however, was immense. In 1291 Tintern held
over 3,200 acres including the large Trelech Grange and Rogerstone
Grange near the abbey and smaller holdings as distant as Undy and
Magor. In the early stages, the emphasis on the granges was arable
farming but livestock soon began to predominate. By the beginning of
the thirteenth century, sheep had become the mainstay of the Cistercian
economy with most of the livestock income coming from the sale of
graded wool. By 1200 surpluses were being exported. It is true that
Grace Dieu had few sheep and Caerleon only slightly over 500 in 1291.
Tintern on the other hand had over 3,000 generating export revenue in
excess of £150 per year. Profitable and less labour intensive, sheep
clearly emerged as a principal interest of many Cistercian houses. An unfortunate aspect of medieval life, however, was that when sheep came
into an area, people were frequently forced out. There are numerous
examples of wholesale eviction of local inhabitants to make way for
creation of granges and introduction of flocks. The Cistercian reputation as land-grabbers, attributed to them by Giraldus Cambrensis
among others, was, in many cases, earned.[12]

An interesting demonstration of the fact can be found in one of the last
monastic foundations in Gwent. St. Kynmark near Chepstow was a late
foundation, established sometime between 1254 and 1271 in an area
with a surfeit of monasteries. Always poor, it seems an anachronistic
foundation. Its reason for being, however, may be suggested by the
churches impropriated to it. The three churches tied to the new abbey
were St. Kynmark itself, St. Arvans and Porthcaseg. Porthcaseg was on
the edge of one of Tintern's earliest granges which had become the
central court for all the abbey tenants west of the Wye. St. Arvans was

located nearby on the edge of Rogerstone Grange. The three small, but old churches, had long associations with the bishopric of Llandaff and it seems highly likely that the establishment of St. Kynmark was a move by the bishop to forestall further expansion by Tintern and to protect the threatened villages from being swallowed up in the abbey's land hunger.[13]

It is possible that the English orientation of Tintern may have been a factor increasing tension with neighbouring populations. Whatever the case, there can be little doubt of the importance of the large Cistercian foundations like Tintern. Even with Tintern, however, the impact on lifestyle was limited apart from those physically removed from the granges themselves. While customary obligations of residents of hamlets nearby were sometimes employed on the granges and wage labour was important, the traditions and usages of the Welshry remained largely unchanged on the very doorstep of the abbey and its granges.

NOTES

[1] Cowley, F. G., *The Monastic Order in South Wales 1066-1349* (Cardiff: 1977) especially pp. 9-17, and Williams, Glanmor, *The Welsh Church from Conquest to Reformation* (Cardiff: 1976) pp. 16-19.

[2] Davies, E. T., *An Ecclesiastical History of Monmouthshire* (Risca: 1953), pp. 64-65; and Cowley, pp. 40-43, 110-111, 274-275.

[3] Cowley, pp. 15, 42, 57-58. The total of 25 monks plummeted sharply. In 1296, five were removed for 'lack of sustenance' and five more were removed in the following year, leaving a total of 15 at the end of 1297. Smaller foundations like the priory cell at Bassaleg, founded in 1116, relied almost exclusively on spiritual income. The same applied to the Cluniac cell at Malpas founded in about 1122. Eventually, an Austin Friary was established at Newport.

[4] Ibid, pp. 14-15. Wihenoc became a monk later in life. A variation in the spelling of the name is Gwethenoc. See Kissack, pp. 11-14. Provisions for religious houses for women were limited in Wales. Gwent had one of the few, the Benedictine foundation at Usk which was established before 1236.

[5] Ibid. pp. 43-44.

[6] Knowles, David, *The Monastic Order in England* (Cambridge: 1950) pp. 208-226; Craster, O. E., *Tintern Abbey* (London: 1956) pp. 5-6; and Lewis, J. M. and Williams, D. *The White Monks in Wales* (Cardiff: 1976). This booklet offers a concise summary of Welsh Cistercian activity. The best local survey is Williams, David H., *White Monks in Gwent and the Border* (Pontypool: 1976). See also Mahoney, T., *Llantarnam Abbey*—a substantial commemoration of the 800th anniversary of the foundation of the abbey in 1979. Tintern's primacy as the first Welsh foundation is based on a technicality. Neath, established in 1130, would have the better claim except that it was founded as a colony of Savigny and was not formally Cistercian until 1147. The new guide to Tintern is Robinson, David, *Tintern Abbey* (Cardiff: 1986).

[7] Craster, pp. 6-7.

⁸Cowley, pp. 25-28, 47-52, 212-213 and Williams, David H., pp. 59-60. The lay brethren in Welsh houses had a reputation for unruly behaviour and a liking for their beer. The situation was such that Welsh abbots were ordered to prevent beer from being drunk on their granges. This was easier said than done. When the abbot of Cwm-hir tried to ban beer, the lay brethren reacted by stealing all of his horses. The lay brothers actually revolted and seized Margam in 1206. The influence of Dore abbey in Herefordshire was significant in northern Gwent.

⁹Ibid. pp. 109-112.

¹⁰Ibid. p. 118; and Williams, David H., p. 104.

¹¹Lewis and Williams, pp. 14-22; and Cowley, pp. 139-164. Geoffrey and his influence is discussed in more detail in the appendices. Adam of Usk must also be noted among the literati of medieval Gwent.

¹²Cowley, pp. 69-92, 238-239, 272; Williams, David H., pp. 119-120 and Howell, pp. 24-26. See also Muir R., *The Lost Villages of Britain* (London: 1982) pp. 86-91, 137-140. Tintern was also responsible for a limited development of local industry and enjoyed fishing rights on the Wye. The possessiveness of the monks could run to extremes. Walter Map related that the monks of Tintern hanged a man at Woolaston for stealing their apples. The Cistercians pointed to increasing demands for provision of hospitality as justification for expansion of their holdings.

¹³Cowley, pp. 34-35. Much about the foundation of St. Kynmark, originally Cynmarch, is uncertain. Its affiliation, for example, is not clear. E. T. Davies identifies the foundation as Premonstratensian and others have accepted this supposition. L. A. S. Butler, however, in the *Journal of the Historical Society of the Church in Wales* (XV) 1965, pp. 9-19, argues that it should be identified as Augustinian and Cowley accepts this interpretation. The evidence is a reference to an Augustinian canon at the monastery in a letter from Pope Innocent VI in 1355. It is unlikely that the matter will ever be settled beyond doubt. Some authorities prefer the use of appropriation to impropriation to describe tied churches.

Alignments and Power Struggles

The power struggles of the March dictated a stormy course for Gwent's history. Moreover, the strength and independence of the marcher lords meant that developments in the March frequently had a profound impact on developments in England and at times Gwent provided the stage for events which changed the general direction of British history. As has already been noted, the tripartite power structure sometimes produced strange alignments. One such emerged through the growing power of Llywelyn ap Iorwerth, Llywelyn Fawr. A grandson of Owain Gwynedd, Llywelyn had gained control of north Wales after a power struggle. He was influential enough to marry Joan, the daughter of King John. The fact that the Welsh prince was his son-in-law did not, however, prevent John from manoeuvering in Wales, attempting to play one Welsh leader off against another. The king's interests in south Wales were considerable because as a result of his marriage to Isabella of Gloucester he had become Lord of Glamorgan and a marcher in his own right. Furthermore, conflict between the sons of the Lord Rhys presented opportunities to undermine the Welsh position. In the event, however, the king managed only to unite the opposition which soon included both Llywelyn and leading marcher lords. An important figure in the opposition was Giles de Braose, bishop of Hereford, who was instrumental in bringing the Welsh and discontented barons together, hoping to revive his own family fortunes in the March.[1] The bishop sent his brother Reginald to join Welsh leaders in attacks on castles previously held by the de Braose family including Abergavenny, Skenfrith and White Castle in addition to Pencelli, Brecon, Hay, Radnor, Builth and Blaen Llyfni. The unlikely alliance between the de Braose family and the Welsh was cemented by the marriage between Reginald and Gwladus, Llywelyn's daughter. Eventually, baronial opposition forced John to agree to Magna Carta in 1215 and among the provisions of that document was restoration of all lands illegally deprived from the Welsh. When, in December 1215, Llywelyn arrived in south Wales he was the focal point of unprecedented national unity.[2] John died in October of 1216 and in 1217 insurgent barons reached an agreement with the new king, Henry III, in the Treaty of Lambeth. Initially Llywelyn resisted a similar agreement and during the year his ally, Morgan of Caerleon, was attacked and displaced by the elder William Marshal. In the following year, however, Llywelyn decided that prudence dictated an accommodation and agreed the Peace of Worcester which confirmed him in his possessions. It appeared that stability had been achieved and peace did last for about five years. Then conflict broke out again, this time between Llywelyn and the second William Marshal who had succeeded his father in 1219. The source of trouble was not Striguil, but Pembroke where Llywelyn accused the tenants of the new earl of harrying their Welsh neighbours. In response, Llywelyn invaded Dyfed in 1220. Marshal's retaliation was delayed but in 1223 he landed in Dyfed with a force from Ireland and secured several strongholds including Carmarthen and Cardigan before returning to Chepstow. At this stage, Hubert de Burgh, the influential and ambitious justiciar who was rapidly becoming a dominant power in south Wales, entered the fray in support of Marshal, relieving the seige of Builth and then beginning construction of the new castle at Montgomery. It was at this point that Llywelyn again decided to reach an accommodation. This time peace lasted until 1228 when de Burgh began to use Montgomery as a base for further conquests in the Welsh regions nearby. In order to put a stop to these activities, Llywelyn attacked and scattered a marcher force, capturing William de Braose, the son of his former ally Reginald. In the aftermath, it appeared possible that a new alliance might be forged between Llywelyn and de Braose with the latter offering Builth as a dowry for his daughter who would marry Dafydd, the son and heir of Llywelyn. The situation changed, however, when the foolishly amorous de Braose was found in the bedchamber of Llywelyn's wife Joan. Llywelyn did not hesitate in having de Braose hanged in public.[3]

Shortly afterwards, developments in Gwent became critical. Llywelyn had watched the increasing influence of de Burgh in the southern march with growing alarm. He had held the three castles since the accession of Henry III and had more recently presented a serious threat from his base at Montgomery. On the sudden death of Marshal in 1231, custody of the former de Braose holdings including the lordship of Abergavenny as well as Brecon and Radnor also passed to de Burgh. Already having effective control of Glamorgan, de Burgh then held a stretch of territory running from Cardigan Bay to the Wye. This provided ample reason for intervention but the final straw was the beheading of Welsh prisoners held at Montgomery. Llywelyn gathered a large force and attacked south into Gwent. He overran and burned Montgomery, Radnor, Hay, Brecon and finally Caerleon in 1231. Meanwhile other opponents of de Burgh were at work in England engineering his fall from power. In 1232 he was supplanted as justiciar by Peter de Rivaux.⁴ By this time, the Marshal holdings had passed to Richard who was suspicious of de Rivaux and of the king. His fears were well founded as by 1233 the king had decided that the new earl marshal was untrustworthy. Henry sent a royal army into Gwent, laying seige to Marshal's castle at Usk. Trying to avoid open warfare with the king, Marshal agreed to a token surrender of the castle on the understanding that it would be returned to him after fifteen days. Failure to regain custody as agreed, convinced Marshal of treachery and he recovered Usk by force. At this stage, Marshal inevitably emerged as the main opponent of the king and even took the recently deposed de Burgh under his protection in Chepstow castle. More importantly, however, Marshal took the obvious step of entering into an alliance with Llywelyn.⁵

The Welsh prince and powerful marcher soon had full control of Gwent and much of the southern march. Marshal joined forces with Llywelyn's supporter Owain ap Gruffudd, a grandson of the Lord Rhys, and they ranged through the Usk and Wye valleys. First castles at Pencelli, Blaenllyfni and Bwlchydinas were taken; then they attacked and captured Abergavenny before moving on to take Newport and Cardiff. A royal army attempting to re-establish some measure of control encamped at Grosmont. In November of 1233, however, Marshal and his Welsh allies staged a surprise night attack and overran the unprepared forces of the king. The royal army fled leaving behind many of their horses and most of their baggage. Marshal went on to attack Monmouth while the king, his army scattered, retired to Gloucester. From that time, Henry III, in the words of Roger of Wendover 'did not dare to meet his enemies'. In January of 1234, Llywelyn and Marshal took Shrewsbury while the king impotently remained in Gloucester.⁶

The king's discomfort was such that he yielded to pressure for reform and also expressed willingness to settle with Llywelyn. In June of 1234 a truce was agreed which confirmed Llywelyn's dominant position in Wales and left strongholds like Cardigan and Builth in his hands. The pact was renewed every year until Llywelyn's death in 1240, assuring his position in Welsh history as Llywelyn Fawr—Llywelyn the Great. The king would also have found it necessary to heal the rift with Marshal. He, however, had gone to secure his lands in Ireland and in April had fallen victim to treachery, being mortally wounded in Kildare. He was succeeded by his brother Gilbert. The combination of Marshal and Llywelyn, however, had been formidable enough to intimidate a king and to place Gwent on the centre stage of British history. [7]

Following the turbulence of this period of Welsh-marcher cooperation against the king, relative calm prevailed for a time. Llywelyn Fawr attempted to avoid the fratricidal struggle for succession, which all too often accompanied the death of a Welsh leader, by assuring the succession of his son. In the event, Dafydd ap Llywelyn did follow his father in 1240. His reign, however, was a short one as he died suddenly in 1246. In the aftermath, a grandson of Llywelyn Fawr, Llywelyn ap Gruffudd, emerged as the new dominant figure in north Wales. Slowly he consolidated his grip and extended his authority. As Llywelyn's power grew, the concern of Henry III increased and in 1257 the king set out on a disastrous military campaign into north Wales. Having achieved nothing, he agreed a truce and by the spring of 1258 baronial discontent was so strong that Henry could not contemplate further action against Llywelyn. In 1258, Llywelyn adopted the title Prince of Wales and began attempting to extend his authority into parts of south Wales. Henry was unable to respond in view of the growing baronial revolt. [8]

In 1258, barons including Simon de Montfort forced the Provisions of Oxford on the king. The provisions were an attempt to restrict arbitrary abuses of royal authority but in the aftermath the barons fell out with one another and de Montfort was forced abroad. In April 1263, however, he returned and civil war broke out in England. In May of 1264, de Montfort defeated the king at Lewes, capturing Henry and his son and heir, Edward. In the short term, de Montfort appeared all-powerful but as he monopolized power he alienated important marchers including Gilbert de Clare, earl of Gloucester and Roger Mortimer. The powerful marchers arranged Edward's escape from Hereford and then challenged de Montfort. As the new confrontation developed, de Montfort's best hope was the military support of Llywelyn who had already helped in the capture of several castles including Hereford. Even firmer support was achieved by a formal alliance agreed at Pipton near Glasbury-on-Wye in June of 1265. Llywelyn was recognized as Prince of Wales and de Montfort's daughter Eleanor was betrothed to the Welsh leader. Having agreed the alliance, the two men moved on to Monmouth and Gwent once again became the focus of conflict. Llywelyn and de Montfort struck at the Clare estates. Llywelyn ranged through the Clare holdings in Gwent, as de Montfort captured the castles at Abergavenny, Usk and Newport. Then, however, things began to go badly wrong for de Montfort as Edward managed to block his way to Bristol, sinking several ships containing de Montfort's baggage in the Usk. This reverse put Simon in a difficult position and forced him to retrace his route up the valley of the Usk towards Hereford. From there he attempted to reach Kenilworth and an army commanded by his son, unaware that it had already been defeated by Edward. On the 4th of August, de Montfort's small force was trapped at Evesham. The Welsh infantry were scattered and cut down. Then Simon and many of his knights who had formed into a tight defensive circle were also slain. [9]

Not surprisingly, the defeat of de Montfort, while decisive in England, did not spell the end of conflict in the marches and in May 1266, Llywelyn achieved a notable victory over Roger Mortimer in Brecknock. Partially as a consequence, the king agreed to the Treaty of Montgomery on 25th September 1267. Some eleven years of conflict were brought to an end by the settlement which left Llywelyn at his most powerful. That power, however, led to continuing confrontation with Gilbert de Clare who recognized that Llywelyn was a threat to his holdings in south Wales. De Clare attacked and imprisoned Gruffudd ap Rhys, lord of Senghenydd, and in 1268 began construction of a new castle at Caerphilly. Llywelyn's response was to attack and in 1270 he destroyed the castle. De Clare in turn decided to build again, this time trying to create a truly impregnable fortress. The result was the 30-acre, concentric design, with its water defences, which dominated the region. Throughout his life, Llywelyn dreamed of uniting the whole of Wales. In his later years, however, his activities were necessarily concentrated in the north and were typified by increasing pressure from the English king, especially after the accession of Edward I in 1272. In general, Gwent was only peripherally involved in the conflict between the two although there were obvious implications for the region when, in December 1282, Llywelyn was killed at Cilmeri. [10] The death of 'ein Llew olaf' obviously had profound implications for Welsh leaders in the March as well as in the Principality.

It should not be thought, however, that the demise of Llywelyn brought an end to marcher practice. Nor did Edward's victory fundamentally undermine the tripartite power structure in regions like Gwent, although the relative strengths within that system certainly did change. It is important to note that Edward did not attempt to administer his new Welsh holdings as a simple extension of England. Instead Welsh practices were acknowledged and English statutes did not automatically apply. In practice a royal march had been created and the king had become the leading marcher. [11]

Moreover, in south Wales there continued to be Welsh leaders able to raise substantial military forces. One example was Llywelyn ap Rhys, the son of the deposed lord of Senghenydd, more commonly known as Llywelyn Bren of Gelligaer. Incensed by erosion of traditional privileges, he led a major revolt which spread into Gwent. He attacked Caerleon among other strongholds. In the end, the rising failed largely due to Llywelyn's inability to capture the by then virtually impregnable Caerphilly although he laid seige to it for nine weeks. A large army commanded by Humphrey de Bohun the powerful marcher who held, among other lordships, Caldicot, was dispatched from Gloucestershire to put down the revolt. Enroute, the army camped at Trelech. The force was sufficiently overwhelming to convince Llywelyn that further resistance would only lead to devastation of the Welshry. He surrendered at Ystradfellte saying that 'It is better for one man to die than for a whole population to be killed'. De Bohun used his influence to try to assure that Llywelyn's life was spared. Later in 1318, however, custody of the Welsh leader was given to Hugh Despenser the younger who staged a mockery of a trial and then had his prisoner hanged, drawn and quartered. Despenser staged the butchery to provide an example which he hoped would strengthen his attempts to build up a strong power base in south Wales. These machinations of the Despensers once again pushed Gwent into the national spotlight. By any standard, Edward II was an unsuccessful king. A bad choice of associates, including the flirtation with Piers Gaveston, undermined his credibility. After the death of Gaveston, the king fell under the influence of the Despensers, elder and younger. The younger Despenser married Gilbert de Clare's sister bringing him the extensive de Clare holdings in the southern march. His growing influence with the king allowed him to expand these holdings even further. From 1308, for example, he was constable of Chepstow castle which had reverted to the crown after the death of Bigod. The growing power and obvious ambition of the Despensers produced opposition, especially from among marcher lords who felt particularly threatened by developments. Unrest exploded into open revolt in 1321 with yet another example of an alliance between marcher lords and Welsh leaders directed against the king. Leading marchers including Roger Mortimer and de Bohun joined forces with the family of Llywelyn Bren and captured Newport, Cardiff and Caerphilly. Opposition was great enough to force Edward to banish the Despensers, but only until he felt sufficiently strong to counter attack. He strengthened royal forces until he was confident enough to attack Mortimer who he imprisoned. The king then recalled the Despensers who immediately began to re-establish their position in south Wales. This power base was strengthened by the acquisition of new holdings from the 'treasonable earls' including Monmouth, Trelech, Caldicot, Usk and Caerleon. In the meantime, however, Mortimer escaped and fled to France where he joined with the queen, Isabella. In September 1326, Mortimer and the queen returned to England with an army. Their force was only about 700 strong but they had substantial popular support and the threat they posed was great enough to cause the king and the Despensers to flee into Gwent. The party arrived in Tintern on 13th October and on the following day proceeded to the stronghold of Chepstow castle. The castle had been provisioned for a seige and the plan seems to have been to hold Chepstow. After arriving, however, the panicked trio had second thoughts and decided to flee further. The elder Despenser went to Bristol where he was captured and executed. The king and the younger Despenser set sail for France but were forced back into port at Cardiff. They then moved to Caerphilly but once again decided to abandon a strongly fortified position and fled towards Neath. They were pursued by Mortimer's forces and were eventually hunted down by the sons of Llywelyn Bren and captured near Llantrisant. The younger Despenser was taken to Hereford where he was hanged. Edward II was murdered in Berkeley castle in the following year. [12]

NOTES

[1] The elder William de Braose, responsible for the massacre at Abergavenny castle, had fallen foul of king John. He fled to France where he died in penury. His wife and son were imprisoned by John who starved them to death.

[2] Brut, pp. 200-207. There are good secondary accounts of this period including Williams, A. H. and Evans, G. The English background is in Poole.

[3] Brut, pp. 208-229; Williams, A. H., pp. 71-75; and Powicke, Maurice, *The Thirteenth Century* (Oxford: 1962), pp. 392-396. The marriage between Dafydd and de Braose's daughter went ahead and Llywelyn retained Builth.

[4] The complicated manoeuvres surrounding the English court during this period are explained in Powicke, pp. 55-60. De Burgh was responsible for the stone re-construction of the Three Castles.

[5] Ibid, pp. 54-55, and Williams, A. H., p. 77.

[6] Brut, pp. 230-233; Williams, A. H., p. 77; Powicke, p. 55; and Knight, J. K., *Grosmont Castle* (Cardiff: 1980) pp. 7-8.

[7] Brut, pp. 232-233; Powicke, pp. 57-58. Gilbert Marshal was killed in a tournament in the summer of 1241, to be followed as lord of Striguil in rapid succession by his two brothers, Walter and Anselm.

[8] Brut, pp. 236-251; and Williams, A. H., pp. 81-89.

[9] Brut, pp. 254-257; Powicke, pp. 201-202; and Williams, A. H., p. 91.

[10] Brut, pp. 256-271; Williams, A. H., pp. 93-130; and Evans, G., pp. 226-236.

[11] Rees, pp. 32-33.

[12] McKisak, M., *The Fourteenth Century* (Oxford: 1959) pp. 82-83, 94-95; and Perks, p. 10. See also Saul, N., 'The Despensers and the downfall of Edward II' in *The English History Review*, XCIX (1984) pp. 1-33. Lleucu, the widow of Llywelyn Bren, was given a pension and protection by Bohun.

Llys Ifor Hael

It is important to note that Llywelyn Bren maintained a Welsh court in south Wales in the early fourteenth century. Cultured and literate, he represented the continuation of a tradition which was also well entrenched in Gwent. Undoubtedly the best known example is Ifor ap Llywelyn whose court, Gwern y Clepa, was flourishing near Bassaleg in the mid-fourteenth century. Ifor is better known as Ifor Hael, Ifor the Generous, the description used by Dafydd ap Gwilym who benefitted from his patronage. Dafydd ap Gwilym, the giant of medieval Welsh literature, was one of the great poets in any language. His poems of love and nature were a departure from the more common praise poetry of his contemporaries and the themes give his work a particular appeal today. He did, however, address some laudatory pieces to his friends including four cywyddau to his patron Ifor.[1] The encouragement of the leading Welsh poet by a Welsh lord of Gwent was notable and was made more so by the fact that Ifor could trace his descent back to the lords of Caerleon and, through them, to the kings of Gwent. Ifor represents a remarkable demonstration of the durability of the Welsh aristocracy in Gwent and of their commitment to their cultural heritage.[2] Moreover, Ifor's influence brought Dafydd ap Gwilym, a west Walian, to Gwent for a time.

Dafydd left no doubt that he was familiar with Gwent and that he had enjoyed residing in the court of Ifor. He was also fulsome in his praise of his patron. In the Cywydd i Ifor Hael, Dafydd wrote:

Hyd y gŵyl golwg digust,	as far as the unclouded eye may see
Hydr yw, a hyd y clyw clust,	—strong he is—and far as ear may hear,
Hyd y mae iaith Gymraeg,	as far as the Welsh tongue is known,
A hyd y tyf hadau teg,	and as far as fair crops grow,
Hardd Ifor hoywryw ddefod,	splendid Ifor, of sprightly ways
Hir dy gledd, heir dy glod.	—long your sword—your praise will be sown.[3]

Perhaps even more important is the poem Bassaleg in which Dafydd gave a glimpse of life in the Gwent court at Gwern y Clepa. He described it by saying:

Mawr anrhydedd a'm deddyw:	Great is the honour which I have received:
Mi a gaf, o byddaf byw,	For while I live, I am allowed
Hely â Chŵn, nid haelach iôr,	to hunt with hounds—there is no more
	generous lord—
Ac yfed gydag Ifor,	And drink with Ifor,
A saethu rhygeirw sythynt,	and shoot a straight course at the stags,
A bwrw gweilch i wybr a gwynt,	and cast hawks to the wind and sky,
A cherddau tafodau teg,	and (enjoy) sweet songs by word of mouth
A solas ym Masaleg.	and entertainment (here) at Basaleg.[4]

Dafydd's association with Gwent is interesting in its own right, but it is particularly significant in proving that the Welsh elements in the tripartite structure of marcher Gwent, while weakened through the fourteenth century, continued not just to survive, but also to thrive.

NOTES

[1] Bromwich, Rachel, *Dafydd ap Gwilym, a selection of poems* (Llandysul: 1982), especially p. 178. See also Parry, Thomas, *Gwaith Dafydd ap Gwilym* (Cardiff: 1982).

[2] The descendants of Caradog ap Gruffudd can be traced to the late thirteenth century through the Brut y Tywysogion.

[3] Bromwich, pp. 166-167.

[4] Ibid. pp. 168, 169.

The Black Death

Ifor Hael was a good example of continuity. There were, however, notable changes in fourteenth century Gwent. Among the most important of these were economic developments with farming techniques improving and agricultural productivity increasing rapidly. Returns for wheat and oats more than doubled in many areas and since there was not a corresponding increase in acreage ploughed, improved farming techniques must have accounted for the growth in production. It is true that the revolt of Llywelyn Bren caused crop shortages which, when combined with bad weather and high prices, produced famine in parts of Gwent. Nevertheless, recovery was fairly rapid and prices were stabilized in the years following the revolt. Furthermore, there was an increasing emphasis on mixed farming. Dairy herds, for example, were introduced into several areas including Caerleon and Usk. In 1327, sale of milk from the thirty-eight cows in the Caerleon herd generated almost £8 for the year. Sheep, too, were becoming more important in the economy as the Cistercian monopoly began to disappear. Secular interest in sheep developed rapidly in places like Usk and Trelech with flocks being increased at a rapid rate. In 1317, for example, the flock at Usk consisted of 300 sheep. Within only seven years, however, that number had almost trebled to some 800. The expansion in agriculture was reflected in other areas as well. Fishing, for example, was an important local industry for places like Chepstow, Caerleon and Usk. Fishermen paid a fixed rent or a proportion of their catch to maintain rights to fish from boats or coracles. Profits could be substantial; in 1330 at Usk, fishing receipts reached the substantial figure of £43.[1]

The towns were also reaching a peak in the fourteenth century reflecting the general economic growth. It has been estimated that in 1300 the growing urban population of Wales may have represented something between 15 and 23 per cent of the total. Gwent centres like Usk and Trelech were benefitting from economic developments and, significantly, the number of Welshmen living in the towns was increasing. Previous restrictions were relaxed and while still a relatively small proportion of the urban population, Welshmen were playing an increasing role in the towns.[2]

At mid-century there was a general air of optimism bred by expansion. Conditions, however, changed dramatically as society was plunged into an abrupt and dramatic decline by a calamitous series of outbreaks of plague. During the second half of the fourteenth century, Europe was devastated by the pandemic known as the Black Death. The disease swept through Gwent with three major outbreaks between 1348 and 1369. In the first of these, during the winter of 1348-1349, parts of Gwent Uwchcoed were badly affected. The degree of devastation in hamlets near Abergavenny is reflected in rents collected within the lordship. Rents from Llanover, for example, fell from £12 to £4 while 'the mortality' caused rents in Tregare to decline from £4 6s. 8d. to £1 10s. 6d. The plague also struck in surrounding lordships including the region of the Three Castles and Raglan. The next outbreak of plague, in 1361, hit Gwent Iscoed particularly hard with serious economic effects on Striguil. The most serious outbreak in the whole of south Wales, however, seems to have been at Caldicot. Rents plummeted 'because very many of the tenants are dead'. Of 62 bond tenants before the outbreak, only 11 were left in 1366.[3]

The outbreak of 1369 ravaged all of Gwent with the possible exception of Gwynllwg. It was particularly severe in Uwchcoed. As has already been noted, Trelech was particularly hard hit and the plague was a major factor in its decline as an urban centre. Again, the hamlets around the Three Castles suffered badly as did Monmouth, Llangwm, Usk, Raglan, Tregrug, Caerleon, Llantrisant near Usk, and Llanfair Discoed in Striguil. The problems associated with these outbreaks were immense and were exacerbated by continuing re-visitations of the plague. Parts of Gwent were hit again in 1381 and chroniclers refer to local outbreaks in 1375, 1379, 1390-91, 1393, 1407 and 1413. When the disease was rampant, agriculture was neglected and harvests were left ungathered. Markets disappeared with trade stagnating and prices falling.[4] Among the obvious consequences was an acute labour shortage which undermined all aspects of the traditional economic structure. Agricultural wages rose dramatically. Reapers and harvesters, who had been paid at a daily rate of 1d. or 2d. could be receiving 4d. and in some places even 6d. at the end of the century. The monasteries, were not immune from this changing pattern. Quite apart from the immediate losses from the plague, Cistercian houses like Tintern found it almost impossible to recruit lay brothers and had to adjust their grange organization accordingly.[5]

One of the most striking aspects of the upheavals of this period was the decline of manorialism. Ravaged customary tenancies gave way to rental of land with increasing emphasis on wage labour. The implications were probably even greater in the Welshry since vacant holdings were redistributed among the kindred who held the land in common and who were still responsible for the entire amount of dues. Collective obligations like the cylch continued to be extracted at the same rate, placing a heavy burden on the remaining Welsh tenants.[6] Difficulties arising in 'native' tenancies were one of several factors underlying the revolt of Owain Glyndŵr.

It is obvious that the horrors of the plague produced significant social and economic disruption. Recovery was very slow in coming, in part due to the immensity of the disaster. Perhaps even more significant, however, was the political unrest which followed in its wake.

NOTES

[1] Rees, pp. 191-198.

[2] Soulsby, pp. 19-24.

[3] Rees, pp. 246-256. The disease did not strike uniformly through the lordship. For example, losses were not as high in Shirenewton. The manor of Caldicot ceased to cultivate altogether in 1366.

[4] Ibid.

[5] Craster, pp. 8-9. An additional, and by comparison highly paid, source of employment was provided by the recruiting of soldiers, especially archers, for campaigns on the continent. An archer could earn some three times as much as a tradesman or agricultural labourer. The leader of a company of bowmen could treble that amount, earning 2s. a day.

[6] Rees, pp. 258-269.

Owain Glyndŵr

In some respects Owain Glyndŵr can be viewed as a marcher lord. He held his estates of Glyndyfrdwy and Sycharth from the king in the same way as the marchers of Gwent. Moreover, he spent some seven years in London studying law at Westminster. In keeping with the traditions of marcher society, however, he made his reputation as a soldier, campaigning in the armies of the English king. A squire to the future Henry IV, he distinguished himself in the English campaign into Scotland in 1385 and was probably also involved in fighting against the French and the Irish. There was, however, a notable difference between Owain and his contemporaries arising from his impressive family background. A descendant of rulers of north Wales, he also claimed descent from Rhys ap Tewdwr and the Lord Rhys. Not only did he thus combine the royal lines of north and south, uniquely among the major Welsh landowners of the time, he also held lands from the crown which his ancestors had ruled as princes. It was this impressive Welsh genealogy which became particularly significant when Glyndŵr came into conflict with Reginald Grey, the lord of Ruthin, who attempted to seize land belonging to him. As has already been seen, conditions had created widespread distress in Wales. Furthermore, national sentiment had remained strong since the death of Llywelyn, fueled by the bards who sang of the 'mab darogan', the son of prophecy who would restore Wales. All these factors combined to such an extent that when Owain took up arms against Grey, an otherwise limited marcher quarrel was transformed into a major nationalist revolt. In September 1400, a band of nobles met and proclaimed Owain prince of Wales; the results were electric. The town of Ruthin was burned; attacks then followed on other English towns in the northern march including Denbigh, Rhuddlan, Flint, Hawarden, Holt, Oswestry and Welshpool. By January of 1401 when Parliament met, disquieting reports were arriving of a remarkable exodus. Welsh students at Oxford and Cambridge, whose numbers were substantial, had abandoned their books and left the university. Welsh labourers from throughout England had left their employment and returned home to prepare for war. As a consequence, stringent anti-Welsh legislation was passed and preparations were made to combat what was rapidly becoming a full-blown nationalist revolt. [1]

The campaigns in the rising ebbed and flowed, but major success came to Glyndŵr in 1402. In April of that year, he managed to draw his foe Reginald Grey into a trap and capture him. Grey was bundled off to the mountains for safe keeping and Glyndŵr turned his attention south. In June he struck into Radnorshire and territory controlled by the powerful Mortimer family. The ten-year-old Mortimer heir Edmund, later fifth earl of March, was held by the king in close custody, reflecting the fact that the boy, by the generally accepted rules of descent, was heir to the crown. The family fortunes in the March were, therefore, in the hands of the younger brother of the late earl, also Edmund Mortimer, and it was he who confronted Glyndŵr. The two armies met on June 22nd at Bryn Glas, a hill near the village of Pilleth. Mortimer relied heavily, as the family had done for years, on Welsh archers, many recruited from Gwent and Glamorgan. The assumption was that well-established marcher loyalties would override any lingering Welsh sentiments among the bowmen. That assumption proved false. As battle was joined, the archers defected en masse to Glyndŵr who won a sweeping victory. Many of Mortimer's men were killed and he himself was taken prisoner. The implications were far reaching. Eventually, Glyndŵr ransomed Grey for a substantial sum and tried to do the same with Mortimer. The king, however, was less than anxious to see the potentially dangerous Mortimer released and his reluctance was not lost on the marcher lord. Eventually, Mortimer threw in his lot with Glyndŵr, marrying his daughter Catrin, and becoming one of his staunchest supporters.[2]

In 1403, Glyndŵr's new relationship with Mortimer led to a wider alliance with the marcher's brother-in-law, Henry Percy — Hotspur. The alignment could have been decisive but it was brought to an abrupt end by the defeat of Hotspur, who was killed in the battle of Shrewsbury in July. The reverse, however, did not affect Owain's position in Wales which became progressively more secure. One factor strengthening Glyndŵr's hand was that he managed to negotiate an alliance with France. On the royalist side, attempts were made to coordinate actions by placing the 16-year-old 'English' prince Henry in control. Edward, duke of York, served as his lieutenant for south Wales and Thomas, earl of Arundel, in the north. The Monmouth born Henry, whose mother was a Bohun, had already seen action against Glyndŵr and it was in the revolt that he gained the experience which served him well at Agincourt. In the short term, however, he could do nothing to check the revolt in

Wales. During 1404, the castles of Aberystwyth and Harlech fell to Owain and he succeeded in making the transition from rebel leader to ruling prince. Styling himself 'Owynus dei gratia princeps Wallie' Owain established his court and a government under his chancellor Gruffudd Young. Even more significant is that during the year Owain called the first of his Parliaments. Based on the model of Hywel's assembly at Whitland in the tenth century, the first Parliament met at Machynlleth, with a second following at Harlech. Among the notable provisions to come from these meetings was the decision, taken in the midst of a fight for survival, to establish two national universities, one in south Wales and one in the north. [4]

In the summer of 1404, Glyndŵr campaigned into Gwent, striking into Archenfield, the old Ergyng. In response, the forces of four English counties were mobilized and, moving past Grosmont, they defeated the Welsh at Campstone above Abergavenny. Shortly afterwards, however, Owain counter attacked at Craig y Dorth on the Troddi near Trelech. The English army was heavily defeated and broke toward Monmouth. They were pursued all the way to the Monnow gate, suffering heavy casualties in their flight. By the beginning of 1405, such successes had helped smooth the way for a new grand design. Glyndŵr reached agreement with Mortimer and the earl of Northumberland, Hotspur's father. Mortimer was to become king but his England was to consist only of the Thames valley and the south. Northumberland's realm was to extend from the north into the midlands. Glyndŵr was to have Wales but this Cambria Irredenta was to have a boundary running along the Severn to the north gate of the city of Worcester then along the high road from Bridgenorth to Kinver and then by the 'old road' to the source of the Trent, then on to the source of the Mersey following that river to the sea. Of course, agreeing the partition was not the same thing as implementing it and Glyndŵr soon met substantial reverses — in Gwent. In March, Owain's son Gruffudd collected a force with many men of Gwent and attacked Grosmont. Henry, however, sent a large army from Hereford which relieved the castle and scattered the attackers. Worse followed in May, when Gruffudd attacked Usk only to be heavily defeated at Pwll Melyn, a hill near the town. The retreating Welsh army was pursued to Monkswood, between Usk and Little Mill where Gruffudd was taken prisoner. Gruffudd was moved to the Tower where, after some six years of imprisonment, he died of plague. Other prisoners captured in Monkswood were taken to Usk where they were slaughtered. The defeat at Pwll Melyn was a major blow to Glyndŵr. Not only was Gruffudd taken, among those killed in the battle was Owain's brother Tudor. Another casualty of the battle was the notable churchman John ap Hywel, prior of Llantarnam abbey. John, who had been abbot since 1400, enjoyed a reputation for piety and for a fervant commitment to the national cause. A preacher of note, his eloquence on the eve of the battle was directed at rallying the troops who he charged to defend their homes, wives and children. Unlike some of his church contemporaries, John ap Hywel went on to lead by example, dying in the fighting at Pwll Melyn.[5]

These developments in Gwent brought Glyndŵr's fortunes to a low ebb. Pressure was relieved almost immediately, however, by the revolt of Northumberland. The northern rising was put down quickly but it did lift the immediate pressure in south Wales. Soon the initiative was back with Glyndŵr as, in the summer of 1405, a French force of 800 men-at-arms, 600 crossbow men and 1200 light armed troops, arrived at Milford Haven. They were met by Owain with a Welsh force which has been estimated at up to 10,000 men. Immediate successes were achieved in west Wales with Cardigan and Carmarthen among the strongholds captured. There then followed the critical phase of the revolt, as Glyndŵr and his French allies moved to re-establish control in Glamorgan and Gwent and then strike into England. Many details of the advance are unclear although it is known that the army passed through Caerleon before marching through Herefordshire and camping about eight miles from Worcester to await the king. On August 22nd, the king arrived from Leicester and the two armies faced one another in what was to prove the crucial confrontation of the war. Skirmishers probed the valley between the two armies but in the event a decisive battle did not take place. The king refused to come out and engage Glyndŵr. That in itself proved critical as Glyndŵr was not strong enough to attack the city and had gone too far into hostile territory to supply his army for any period of time. In the end, Glyndŵr was forced to retire back into Wales. The withdrawal was orderly and Glyndŵr's hold on Wales remained firm. He would not, however, find himself so close to victory again, especially since the French returned home shortly thereafter. There were assurances that they would return in future campaigning seasons, but they did not. In the main, the final stages of the revolt unfolded away from Gwent.

English control was slowly re-established in many regions and concentration inevitably focused on the castle strongholds held by Glyndŵr. Aberystwyth finally fell in September of 1408 and Harlech was taken early in 1409, but not before Mortimer had starved to death holding it for Owain. Even then, however, the revolt was not over as Glyndŵr withdrew to the mountains to resume a guerilla campaign. He was strong enough to attack the outskirts of Shrewsbury in 1410. In that year, Glyndŵr retained active adherents from Gwent including Philip Scudamore of Troy near Monmouth. Philip, however, was captured in the campaigns of 1410 and was beheaded at Shrewsbury. As late as the summer of 1412, Glyndŵr held Dafydd Gam to ransom.[6] In 1415, Gruffudd Young was still working in France on Glyndŵr's behalf. Henry V, who succeeded to the throne in March of 1413, desired a general settlement and offered a pardon to Glyndŵr but there was no response. Glyndŵr simply disappeared and it seems likely that he ended his life near the borders of Gwent, in the home of his daughter, at Monnington Straddel in the Golden Valley of Herefordshire above Ewyas Harold.[7]

The implications of the revolt were profound. Much land lay idle and there was economic destruction on a scale even larger than that seen in the wake of the Black Death. It is clear that the Welsh appreciated the possibilities of economic warfare and as a consequence attacked not only English towns but also systematically devastated the manors. Manors were pillaged, buildings burned, and stock driven away. Most mills were destroyed and many customary tenements were lost altogether. There was, of course, no hope of collecting rents in most parts of the Welshry. For example, in 1404 no manorial courts were held in White Castle, Grosmont, Monmouth or Dingestow 'because the tenants are rebels'.[8] Similarly in 1403 no revenue at all could be drawn from the lordship of Gwynllwg and Machen. There were substantial losses in and around Usk with manors like Llantrisant reported as virtually worthless. The same was true of Caerleon. The demesne of St. Maughans near Monmouth had still not recovered from the effects of the revolt in 1420. Attempts to recover lost revenue were made through the imposition of fines and a difficult position was made worse by legislation imposing a series of restrictions on Welshmen. The Welsh found themselves unable to acquire land in or near the towns, to hold certain offices, or to become citizens of the towns. Not surprisingly, many of Glyndŵr's supporters feared to return to their homes and violence and robbery became wide-spread. Economic and social stagnation were inevitable and a situation was created in which, as Rees describes it, 'the years following the Black Death seem by comparison almost progressive'.[9]

There is another important aspect to the end of the revolt. The fact that Glyndŵr spurned a pardon and vanished enhanced the mystical reputation which he already enjoyed. For example, the Annals of Owain Glyn Dŵr written in the mid-sixteenth century by the poet Gruffudd Hiraethog are notable in this respect. The poet concluded his account by suggesting that, 'very many say that he died, the diviners say that he did not'.[10] The almost Arthurian vision of an Owain who would return suited many well. With widespread Welsh dissatisfaction and impover-ishment, prophetic poetry again took up the quest for the mab darogan who would save Wales. Interestingly, this quest soon focused on Gwent.

NOTES

[1] There are a number of works on the Glyndŵr revolt. Among the better ones are Lloyd, J. E., *Owen Glendower* (Oxford: 1931) and Williams, Glanmor, *Owen Glendower* (Oxford: 1966). The spelling in these titles is the Anglicised version used by Shakespeare who portrayed Owain as possessing supernatural powers, able to 'call spirits from the vasty deep'.

[2] Lloyd, pp. 42-52. Roger Mortimer, fourth earl of March, had been declared heir apparent by Richard II. It is hardly surprising that the usurping Henry IV should keep his son in captivity and regard the whole family with suspicion.

[3] Ibid. pp. 54-55.

[4] Lloyd and Williams, G., various references. See also Evans, G., pp. 263-267. Mary de Bohun gave birth to her son in Monmouth, which had been one of the 'favourite castles' of her father-in-law, John of Gaunt. See Kissack, Medieval Monmouth, pp. 44, 48.

[5] Ibid; Knight, Grosmont, pp. 3-4; and Kissack, pp. 49-50.

[6] Dafydd Gam of Brecknock supported Henry who purchased his release. He later went on to fight with Henry at Agincourt where he was killed. Credited with saving Henry in the battle, Dafydd was knighted as he died on the field. He is generally regarded as the model for Shakespeare's Fluellen. Large numbers of Welshmen were in Henry's service, including Maredudd ap Owain, Glyndŵr's last surviving son who had accepted a pardon.

[7] Lloyd, pp. 126-146.

[8] Ministers' Accounts, Public Record Office 729/12003 (5H.IV) quoted in Rees, p. 276.

[9] Rees, pp. 273-280

[10] Lloyd, p. 154. Those who claimed that Glyndŵr lived on were the brudwyr which Lloyd chose to translate as seers.

Herbert, Tudor and the Mab Darogan

Dramatic changes in the economic and social structure followed in the wake of the Glyndŵr revolt. Many economic factors represented an acceleration of developments which preceded the rebellion and which were among its causes. An extension of the application of English land law, for example, brought wider use of escheat, surrender of land to the lord in the absence of an heir, to areas where Welsh law would previously have caused it to be distributed among members of the kindred. Moreover, the development of a cash economy provided the additional opportunity to purchase holdings which might become available through partible inheritance in regions still practising gavelkind in accordance with Welsh law. While this was occurring, Welsh traditional services were also being commuted for cash. These changes came at the same time that manorialism was declining, providing an increase in the number of leased 'free' farms. As has been seen, the collapse of the manors was accelerated by the Glyndŵr revolt. These changes produced a new pattern of land holding although the basic elements of marcher society continued to exist within the modified structure. [1]

Many Welshmen were anxious to capitalize on the new situation. Application for denizenship from Parliament allowed them to sidestep restrictive anti-Welsh legislation and numbers availed themselves of the opportunity. The process was encouraged from London because the king and his advisors recognized the necessity of Welsh support if there were to be any hope of sustaining stability in Wales. Moreover, many Welshmen had distinguished themselves in the service of Henry V, notably at Agincourt. There were many reasons for Welshmen, some of them supporters of Glyndŵr, to take service with the king. His Monmouth birth may have made the decision more palatable. As Shakespeare had his Henry avow, 'I am Welsh, you know, good countryman'. [2] Probably more important, however, was that service in France offered a means of recovering lost fortunes through the use of military skills well-honed in the recent rebellion. Whatever the reasons, the result was a new class of Welsh leader returning from the wars enriched and with increased self confidence, ready to exploit the changed situation at home. It was not long before opportunities for self enhancement became even greater with dynastic conflict in England. There was

Chepstow castle with (centre) the rectangular hall keep of William FitzOsbern built 1067/68

(Cadw: Welsh Historic Monuments. Crown Copyright)

(Cadw: Welsh Historic Monuments. Crown Copyright)

Above, the Marshal gate and round tower at Chepstow. Left, the main gate of the castle today

(Wales Tourist Board Photo Library)

The tomb effigy of William Marshal

(RCHM)

The great seal of Gilbert deClare

(National Museum of Wales)

Abergavenny castle, scene of the massacre of Seisyllt ap Dyfnwal and the men of upper Gwent

(Wales Tourist Board Photo Library)

Caldicot castle
(Wales Tourist Board Photo Library)

Raglan Castle
(Cadw: Welsh Historic Monuments. Crown Copyright)

Giraldus Cambrensis
(National Library of Wales)

Dafydd ap Gwilym
(National Library of Wales)

The tomb effigies of William ap Thomas and Gwladys ddu in Abergavenny church
(National Monuments Record for Wales)

Tŵr Melyn Gwent, the great tower of William ap Thomas at Raglan
(Cadw: Welsh Historic Monuments. Crown Copyright)

Richard Herbert
(National Monuments Record for Wales)

certainly significant fragmentation of political power in the March and the violence which had been endemic may well have intensified; old scores from the Glyndŵr revolt were settled and various brigands capitalized on the ability to flee easily from one lordship to another.[3]

An archetypal example of this new breed of Welsh leader was a man of Gwent, Sir William ap Thomas. A soldier of fortune, he earned himself the picturesque description—Y Marchog Glas, the blue knight, from the armour which he wore. He married Elizabeth Berkeley, widow of the lord of Raglan, and lived with her at Raglan until her death in 1420. He officially gained possession of the lordship in his own right in 1432 by which time he had re-married. His second wife was Gwladys—Seren Y Feni, the star of Abergavenny—daughter of Dafydd Gam and widow of another hero of Agincourt, Roger Vaughan. Sometime about 1435, ap Thomas began rebuilding Raglan to reflect his growing status. The most notable surviving relic of his building programme is the massive Great Tower—Tŵr Melyn Gwent, the yellow tower of Gwent—which dominated the countryside. Interestingly, its construction reflected significant new developments in warfare since not only was it built to withstand gunpowder, its arrow slits were made on top of gun ports to allow the castle defenders to return cannon fire. Knighted in 1426, ap Thomas became steward of the lordship of Usk and Caerleon under the duke of York shortly thereafter. These holdings gave him a strong power base in central Gwent which he used to good effect. A band of armed retainers allowed ap Thomas to dominate Gwent, and also much of Glamorgan. He was eventually made sheriff of Glamorgan. Conditions in Gwent during the mid-fifteenth century, and ap Thomas' approach to local government, are characterized by an incident in 1441. There was a dispute over appointment of a new prior at Goldcliff with ap Thomas supporting one of the candidates. In order to assure success, he provided his chosen churchman with a band of eighty armed men who broke into the priory and seized the rival prior. They took him to Usk castle where he was imprisoned in chains. William then ordered the prior to resign in favour of his candidate, warning that 'if not, he would make him, with violence, even if he were on the high altar of the priory'.[4]

William ap Thomas died in 1445 and his holdings passed to his son William Herbert.[5] Herbert was able to amass substantial wealth in part from his commercial connections. He did not, however, forget the techniques of his father and he, too, maintained an armed band of retainers. In 1457 he was outlawed for the 'mischief and grievance he has brought upon the king's liege subjects in divers parts, robbing some of them, beating and maiming some, and causing the death of many'. He was restored quickly and his fortunes improved dramatically after the Yorkist victory at Mortimer's Cross in 1461 when Edward, earl of March, seized the throne as Edward IV. Herbert, who had raised and maintained an important Yorkist force which he led in the battle, became one of the king's most trusted advisors. Already holding his father's lands and offices, he was soon appointed Chief Justice and Chamberlain of south Wales and was raised to the peerage, eventually being granted the earldom of Pembroke. Herbert continued to make Raglan his home and principal court and began a substantial rebuilding programme which gave the castle its present form. In 1468 he gained the lordship of Chepstow which left him in complete control of southern Gwent.[6] As will be seen, Herbert's meteoric rise and abrupt fall were critical features in the Wars of the Roses. There is, however, an important additional aspect to the fortunes of this Gwentian dynasty. As has been seen, the disappearance of Owain Glyndŵr, led many in Wales to seek a new mab darogan—a successor to the son of prophecy who would restore the fortunes of Wales. During this period the bards began to focus on ap Thomas and Herbert as the most likely candidates. There is no doubt that both men kept a Welsh court at Raglan. As one bard proclaimed, 'Gwinllan fu Raglan i'r iaith—Raglan was a vineyard for our language'. When Herbert was created Chief Justice of Wales, the bard Guto'r Glyn called on the 'king of our language' to serve Welsh interests and was confident that he would do. He wrote:

> Na âd arglwydd swydd i Sais
> Na'i bardwn i un bwrdais;
> Barna'n iawn, brenin ein iaith
> Bwrw yn tân eu braint unwaith . . .
> Dwg Forgannwg a Gwynedd,
> Gwna'n un a Gonwy i Nedd;
> O digia Lloegr a'i dugiaid,
> Cymru a dry yn dy raid.

> My lord, don't give the English office
> Nor pardon to a burgess;

king of our language, be aware
their rights were once thrown in the fire . . .
Bring Glamorgan and Gwynedd,
make one from Conwy to Neath
if England and her dukes with anger burn,
all Wales to your need will turn.

Nor was Welsh poetry alone in expressing the view that the sentiments
of the Glyndŵr revolt lived on. In 1436, The Libell of English Policye
warned:

Beware of Wales, Christ Jesu must us keep
That it make not our child's child to weep.

Prophetic poetry continued to be a major facet of fifteenth century
Wales, and as long as he lived, a central figure in that poetry was William
Herbert of Raglan.[7] The vision of a restored Wales, and powerful
magnates able to draw on the expectations of the Welsh, meant that men
like Herbert were able to exercise immense influence on the dynastic
struggle which gripped England. Significantly, the prophecy became
critical in the final stages of the Wars of the Roses.

The train of events leading to a thirty-year dynastic struggle in
England began with the early death of Henry V in 1422. Poised on the
brink of total victory in France, Henry contracted dysentery at the siege
of Meaux on the Marne and died, leaving as his heir a son who was less
than one-year-old. Plagued by bouts of insanity, Henry VI proved a
singularly ineffective king; dynastic manoeuvres plagued his reign, with
the Lancastrian and Yorkist descendants of Edward III struggling for
control. The background to the situation was, briefly, that Henry VI was
the great-grandson of John of Gaunt, third son of Edward III and duke of
Lancaster. The heir apparent in the early years of the reign was Richard,
duke of York who claimed descent from two lines—Lionel duke of
Clarence, Edward's second son, and more directly Edmund duke of
York, the fourth son. In 1454, when the king lapsed into insanity,
Richard was made protector. In 1455, however, Henry recovered his
wits and in the meantime a son and heir had been born to him. Richard,
dispossessed of power and the succession took up arms and in May of
that year the first open military clash took place. Fortunes ebbed and

flowed and the death of Richard in the battle of Wakefield in December 1460 was not the end of the Yorkist challenge. The following February, Richard's son Edward, earl of March, won a victory over Lancastrian forces at Mortimer's Cross then marched on London and claimed the throne. In the next quarter century, the throne was to change hands six times and three of five kings died violently. Not only that, by the end of the conflict both the families of Lancaster and York had been eliminated in the direct male line. [8]

As fortunes ebbed and flowed in the conflict, control of Wales and the marches was important to both sides. Many participants had direct interest in the region. The earl of Warwick, for example, whose machinations earned him the title 'kingmaker' was a member of the Neville clan who held, among other things, the lordship of Abergavenny. Also significant were the Tudors who had strong Lancastrian connections. The Tudors of Anglesey had been important supporters of Owain Glyndŵr and the family fortunes had suffered as a consequence. One of their number, however, Owain ap Maredudd ap Tudur—Owen Tudor —joined the numbers of Welshmen in the court of Henry V. He made more impact than most, as he married the king's widow, Katherine of Valois. They had two sons, Edmund and Jasper, who were made earls of Richmond and Pembroke respectively, by their half brother, Henry VI. Edmund married Margaret Beaufort who was a great-granddaughter of John of Gaunt and through her their son Henry gained a Lancastrian claim to the throne. Not surprisingly Edmund and Jasper were seen as the key to controlling Wales against the threat of the powerful Yorkist interests in Gwent and Glamorgan represented by Warwick and supporters including William ap Thomas and William Herbert of Raglan. Early in 1456, Edmund was sent to west Wales to try to consolidate the Lancastrian position and rally local support. In August, Herbert led a force of about 2,000, including men from the lordship of Raglan, to challenge him. Edmund was captured and died at Carmarthen in November of 1456. Three months later, Margaret Beaufort gave birth to his son, Henry Tudor. They were taken under the protection of Jasper who had become the main hope of Lancastrian Wales. Jasper recruited a Welsh force which fought at Mortimer's Cross. After the defeat, he managed to escape although Owen Tudor was captured and beheaded. Following the Yorkist victory and the accession of Edward IV, establishing effective control in Wales became a matter of priority. The task was entrusted to Herbert who had fought beside Edward in the battle and who was emerging as one of the most powerful figures in the court. It was at this stage that Herbert was elevated to the peerage as Baron Herbert and led another force into west Wales. In September 1461, Pembroke castle was surrendered to Herbert and while Jasper escaped, the four-year-old Henry Tudor was captured. For almost ten years, Henry was a member of Herbert's household where he was well-treated. Herbert provided tutors for the boy and appears to have planned to marry him to his own daughter, Maud. While some of Henry's time was spent at Pembroke, a portion was in the Herbert stronghold of Raglan.[9]

An interesting aspect of the situation is that the bards were anxiously looking for an advantage during this chaotic period. As has been seen, Guto'r Glyn was in the vanguard of those looking to Herbert as a saviour for Wales and the Welsh language. At times, poets like Lewis Glyn Cothi presented Jasper Tudor as the great national leader although Lewis hedged his bets by praising Herbert as well. The point to be drawn is that the bards, undoubtedly reflecting widespread Welsh attitudes, had little interest in the vagaries of the English dynastic struggle and were interested only in finding a strong Welsh leader who could be persuaded to put Welsh interests first.[10]

A key supporter of Edward IV was Warwick who undoubtedly expected to control the young king. To Warwick's discomfort, however, the king refused to be dominated and began to rely more and more heavily on other advisors, notably Herbert. One demonstration of Edward's independence was his marriage, against the wishes of Warwick, to a commoner, Elizabeth Woodville. The marriage of Herbert's son, William, to Elizabeth's sister Mary, was a confirmation of the standing of the Herberts at court. During this period, Herbert became the effective Yorkist ruler of Wales. In 1461, for example, he was named Chief Justice and Chamberlain of south Wales for life. By 1466, these offices had become hereditary, passing automatically to Herbert's male heirs. In 1467, he also became Chief Justice of north Wales—an unprecedented concentration of power. In June of 1468, Jasper Tudor returned from Normandy and landed near Barmouth in support of Henry VI who was by this time a prisoner in the Tower. Herbert and his brother Richard, a man of considerable military prowess, pushed north to stop Jasper and in August, Harlech surrendered to them. In that year, Jasper's earldom of Pembroke was granted to Herbert who was at the pinnacle of his power—the lord of Raglan effectively ruled Wales. Achieving such heights, however, helped lead to his undoing as Warwick, fearing his loss of influence, took up arms against Edward. The king's leading military commanders, including Herbert, were summoned by the king only to be defeated near Banbury in July 1469. On the following day, Warwick had William and Richard Herbert executed at Northampton. Many bards regarded the deaths as a Welsh national disaster. In the short term it was certainly disastrous for Edward who, in October of 1470, was forced to flee. Warwick, in a remarkable turnabout, brought back Henry VI as a figure head for his own government.[11]

Edward fled to France where with help from his brother-in-law, the duke of Burgundy, he collected an army and returned to England in March of 1471. In the meantime, however, Jasper seeing the improvement in Lancastrian fortunes had returned to Pembroke and from there marched to Chepstow which he intended to use as a base for a force which would join with Queen Margaret, wife of Henry VI. That plan came to nothing as on 14th April, Edward defeated Warwick who was killed in the battle at Barnet. On the same day, Margaret landed at Weymouth. On May 4th, Edward defeated her force; in the battle the Lancastrian heir, prince Edward, was killed. News of these calamities reached Jasper at Chepstow but he had the consolation of having been reunited with his nephew Henry who had become, as a result of these recent developments, the Lancastrian claimant to the throne. Edward, who had Henry VI put to death in the Tower, sent Sir Roger Vaughan of Tretower to take Jasper. In the event, it was Jasper who captured Vaughan and executed him at Chepstow. He and Henry then retreated to Pembroke and from there to Britanny where they began fourteen years in exile. Edward IV, having disposed of virtually all the opposition, enjoyed relative security for the remainder of his life. In 1483, however, he died at the age of 40 leaving two young sons, Edward and Richard. The twelve-year-old Edward V and his brother had the misfortune of being entrusted to the protectorship of their uncle Richard who installed them in the Tower. Acting quickly and ruthlessly, Richard eliminated all who had opposed his assumption of the role of protector. The young princes were then murdered in the Tower and Richard usurped the throne, being crowned on July 6th as Richard III.[12]

It was at this stage that the prophetic quest for the mab darogan became pivotal in the final act of the Wars of the Roses. Richard was widely unpopular and Henry Tudor embodied the Lancastrian claim to the throne. To succeed, however, he had to have military support in Britain. The obvious place for a Welsh-speaking, Welsh prince to turn for that support was Wales. The bards were already making that task easier as many had turned to Henry as the son of prophecy. Among the more influential of the prophetic poets was Dafydd Llwyd. Dafydd had expressed fulsome praise for Dafydd ap Ieuan who had held Harlech for the Lancastrians and for William Herbert who had taken it for the Yorkists. Clearly, Lancaster or York were of no consequence to Dafydd who was concerned only with finding a leader who would restore Welsh fortunes. Applying that criterion, he decided that the true son of prophecy must be Henry Tudor. For his part, Henry encouraged the growing support. For example, writing from exile to John ap Meredith of Eifionydd, Henry promised to deliver Wales and the Welsh people from 'such miserable servitudes as they have long piteously stood in'. Henry was able to convince adherents that Welsh interests would be advanced under his leadership and Wales rallied to his cause. On the 7th of August 1485, Henry landed at Milford Haven and began the march to Bosworth. It was of considerable significance that he proceeded through Wales under the banner of the red dragon of Cadwaladr. The bards had prepared the way for Henry and Wales answered his call, most notably with the contingents from south Wales under Rhys ap Thomas whose force was swelled as he marched to Brecon. There he collected marcher forces from Gwent and other parts of the southeast including members of the Vaughan and Gam families. Rhys then moved along the upper Wye on his way to his rendezvous with Henry. In the meantime, forces from north Wales led by men like William Griffith of Penrhyn and Richard ap Howell of Mostyn also joined them. This combined army, still fighting under the red dragon banner, was decisive when on 22nd August Henry triumphed at Bosworth. Richard III was killed in the battle and his crown was placed on Henry's head, symbolizing an end to the chaotic Wars of the Roses and the beginning of a new era in British history. This result could not have been achieved without the military support Henry gained from Wales and that support was stimulated by the notion of the mab darogan. Henry used the bardic tradition to his advantage and the Welsh dimension was crucial in his success. It should be noted, however, that while Henry exploited the longing for the mab darogan, there was a part of his own psyche which accepted the prophecy. There was more to the Welsh dimension in the reign of Henry VII than simply keeping a Welsh harpist at court and celebrating St. David's Day. There was a sense of prophecy in Henry's decisions to name his eldest son Arthur; there was a sense of purpose in sending this Welsh Prince of Wales to Ludlow in 1501 to govern Wales and the marches. To some observers, Bosworth appeared to be the point at which Wales had finally conquered England. The Viennese ambassador, for example, reported that the Welsh 'have won back their old independence'. While Henry VII was on the throne, that notion did not seem too far fetched. [13]

The role of Gwent in these developments was a major one. Forces recruited in the region were active throughout the period of conflict. Furthermore, men like ap Thomas and Herbert not only stamped their authority on Gwent, but also influenced developments in and around the court. Moreover, they also fuelled the prophetic vision which Henry was able to harness so effectively. Significantly, of course, Henry himself had his Gwent connections, having been tutored in the Herbert court not only at Pembroke, but also at Raglan. Of particular interest to the history of Gwent was the brief dominance over Wales achieved by William Herbert. The king's Viceroy for the whole of Wales, Herbert continued to hold court at Raglan. Consequently, there is a case for arguing that during this period, Raglan can be seen as a de facto capital of Wales.

NOTES

[1] Rees, pp. 258-269, 273-280; and Williams, Glanmor, Welsh Church, pp. 249-270. See also Pugh, T. B. *The Marcher Lordships of South Wales 1415-1536* (Cardiff: 1963).

[2] King Henry V, Act IV, Scene 7.

[3] For a concise overview of the period see Rees, David, *The Son of Prophecy* (London: 1985) pp. 24-32.

[4] Taylor, A. J., *Raglan Castle* (Cardiff: 1950) pp. 5-9, 42-46, 53; and Thomas, D. H., *The Herberts of Raglan as Supporters of the House of York in the Second Half of the Fifteenth Century* (M.A. thesis, University College Cardiff: 1967). Ap Thomas obtained the castle in an outright conveyance on 31st July 1432. The Tower was obviously imposing to contemporaries. The poet Guto'r Glyn wrote:

| Uchel yw'r llys uchlaw'r llaill | The court is high, high above the others |
| A'ch twr uwch y tai ereill | and your tower higher than the other houses |

See, Williams, John Ll. and Williams, Ifor, *Gwaith Guto'r Glyn* (Cardiff: 1939) pp. 126-128.

⁵ The reluctance to continue with the use of the Welsh ap reflects lingering suspicions from the rising of Owain Glyndŵr; the ap smacked of treachery in many English minds. The choice of Herbert was probably an attempt to claim a connection with the Fitz Herberts. An important family record is the *Herbertorum Prosapia*, Cardiff Ms.5.7.

⁶ Taylor, pp. 9-13. Trade was becoming progressively more important. There were many Welsh sailors engaged in a thriving trade with Bristol which was emerging as the principal western metropolis. Wool, hides and cloth were shipped from Newport, Usk, Caerleon, Chepstow and Tintern. Welsh family names like Gough, Lloyd, Vaughan, Howell and ap Meurig began to dominate in Bristol's commercial sector. See Williams, Glanmor, Welsh Church, pp. 249-250.

⁷ For these and other examples, see Evans. G., pp. 273-281. See also Rees, David, p. 24 and Humphrey, Emyr, *The Taliesin Tradition* (London: 1983) pp. 36-39. In his Moliant Syr Wiliam o Raglan, Guto'r Glyn wrote of William—Cymro o Went (Welshman from Gwent). A copy is in Evans, M. B., *Y Canol Oesoedd* (Rhan 2) in Cyfres Llygad y Ffynnon (Cardiff: 1978) pp. 43-44. See also 'Prophecy, Poetry and Politics in Medieval and Tudor Wales' in Williams, Glanmor, *Religion, Language and Nationality in Wales* (Cardiff: 1979) pp. 71-86, Williams, J. E. Caerwyn 'Guto'r Glyn' in Jarmon, A. O. H. and Hughes, G. R., *A Guide to Welsh Literature* (Swansea: 1979) pp. 218-242, Williams, John Ll. and Williams, Ifor, and Thomas, D. An especially useful synthesis of bardic material is Lewis, William, *Astudiaeth o Ganu'r Beirdd i'r Herbertiaid hyd Ddechrau'r Unfed Ganrif ar Bymtheg* (Ph.D. thesis, Bangor: 1982).

⁸ For details of the intricacies of the period see Jacob, E. F., *The Fifteenth Century* (Oxford: 1961).

⁹ Rees, David, pp. 40-72. There is a study of the war from a Welsh perspective—Evans, Howell, *Wales and the Wars of the Roses* (Cambridge: 1915). Traditionally, Henry was taught Welsh by his nurse, the wife of Philip ap Howell of Carmarthen. The *Herbertorum Prosapia* is definite as regards Henry's residence at Raglan—'the said Lord Henry . . . . remained with the said Countess (Lady Herbert) at Raglan'.

¹⁰ Ibid, pp. 102-107; and Evans, G., pp. 275-281. For background concerning Lewis, see Jones, E. D., 'Lewis Glyn Cothi' in Jarmon and Hughes, pp. 243-261.

¹¹ Jacob, pp. 510-511, 527; and Rees, David, pp. 70-75.

¹² Jacob, pp. 607-645; and Rees, David, pp. 75-78.

¹³ Rees, David, pp. 107-148; and Evans, G., pp. 284-285. The ill-fated rising of the duke of Buckingham in 1483 also had a Gwent dimension with Caldicot used as a marshalling point. The Herbert reaction to Henry Tudor is of particular interest. The largely ineffectual younger William Herbert, by this time Lord Huntingdon, at the least did not resist the accession of his childhood companion. The much more energetic younger son, Watkin to his father, probably actively assisted Henry. He certainly maintained the family control at Raglan which he occupied although, as the Calendar of Close Rolls suggests, 'by what right and title was not known.'

Creation of the Shires

Henry VII was 28 years old when he took the throne. Half of his life had been spent in continental exile while the other half had been spent in Wales. Familiar with Wales and the intricacies of Welsh society, his knowledge of England was slight. In view of this background and the crucial Welsh dimension in his success, it is hardly surprising that Welshmen played an important role in the new regime. Many followed him to court where they were rewarded with a variety of offices. Lewis of Caerleon, for example, became the king's doctor. The Welsh influence in London was so pervasive that it produced an envious reaction. Welsh accents and an apparently obsessive interest in ancient pedigrees, prompted the English poetical response:

> Py Got they be all shentlemen
> Was descended from Shoves own line,
> Part human and part divine . . .[1]

Among the 'Welsh jokes' current in London was the suggestion that St. Peter had become so tired of the growing number of Welshmen in heaven that he devised a plan. He arranged for someone to shout caws pôb—toasted cheese—outside the heavenly gates; he then slammed them shut as the Welsh rushed out for their national treat.[2]

Clearly, the Welsh influence at court was strong enough to elicit considerable reaction. Far more important to the historical development of Gwent, however, was the fact that Henry rewarded his Welsh supporters with lands and offices in Wales itself. The king's uncle Jasper, the architect of his success and his closest advisor, was made duke of Bedford. In addition, his earldom of Pembroke was restored and he was granted other lordships including Glamorgan, Newport and Abergavenny. Second only to Jasper in Wales was Rhys ap Thomas, whose military support had been crucial to Henry. Among the offices granted to him was chamberlain of west Wales. Ten years later, when Jasper died, Rhys succeeded him as chief justice and effectively became the king's viceroy in south Wales, controlling the region as firmly as William Herbert had done. Significantly, Henry also broke a sequence of alien bishops by naming Welshmen to the Welsh sees. The most influential of these was

John Morgan of Tredegar. This member of an increasingly important Gwent family, had been a strong supporter of Henry during his years in exile. Following the king's succession, Morgan became his first clerk of Parliament and then bishop of St. David's.[3]

An important administrative development was Henry's decision to revive the Council in the Principality and Marches of Wales as an extension of the judicial dimension of the king's council into Wales. The council had been established by Edward IV to deal with the minority of his heir. With Edward's death in 1483 and the subsequent murder of the prince, however, the council was suspended. Henry re-established it and in 1501 sent the 15-year-old prince Arthur, recently wed to Catherine of Aragon, to preside over the council. Sadly for Henry's plans, the young prince was dead within five months. The council, however, was retained and the lord president, as the presiding officer was soon to be styled, gained increased authority. No longer regarded as a personal body of advisors to the prince, the council soon exercised considerable influence as the Council in the Marches of Wales.[4] The council was a useful tool in extending royal control into Wales. Even more important, however, was the growing proportion of Wales held directly by the king. He directly ruled the shires of Anglesey, Caernarfon and Merioneth in the north as he did Cardigan and Carmarthen in the south. Henry also brought Flint into his personal domain. Moreover, he had inherited the holdings of the Duchy of Lancaster and claimed the vast marcher holdings of the Mortimers after the victory of Bosworth. Among these personal holdings was Monmouth. When Jasper Tudor died, his estates also reverted to Henry. As Henry lay on his death-bed in 1509, he is reported to have charged his son to 'have special care for the benefit of his own nation and countrymen, the Welshmen.' In the main, Henry VIII ignored the injunction but he did follow at least one of his father's Welsh policies —the acquisition of territory for the crown. The extent of royal holdings became such that one of the few major remaining lordships not in the king's hands was that of the Herbert heirs including the lordships of Chepstow, Raglan and Gower. The balance between king and marcher was tipped decisively in favour of the king who retained Welsh support on the strength of his father's memory. Nevertheless, in some respects, the early years of the reign of Henry VIII saw a continuation of Welsh policy since Henry left government in the hands of 'Father' Rhys ap Thomas. When Rhys died in 1525, however, his offices were not passed on to his grandson and heir, Rhys ap Griffith. Instead Walter Devereaux, lord Ferrers, was made chamberlain of south Wales. The young Rhys might have been inclined to accept the loss of status, but other members of the family, notably James ap Howell, pushed him to action. Finally in 1529, the conflict with Ferrers became so intense that it led to serious rioting in Carmarthen. In the aftermath, Rhys was arrested. After being released, he was re-arrested and was finally executed in 1531.[5]

The execution of Rhys ap Griffith sent shock waves through the powerful families of Wales. It seemed a clear indication that the cosy relationship with the court which existed in the time of Henry VII had ended and that the new king was becoming ominously more assertive. It certainly did nothing to reduce the inclination of leading families to maintain substantial bodies of men-at-arms in the tradition of William ap Thomas. In fact, the lawlessness which had bedevilled the March may have increased through the widespread practice of arthel, the maintenance of retainers, by leading magnates. Many of these members of the household were kinsmen and most enjoyed reputations for disreputable behaviour. In 1534, for example, the president of the council reported on the lordship of Magor where retainers were said to include five men who were known to have committed wilful murder, eighteen who had committed murder and twenty-five others who were guilty of lesser crimes. An ability to steal cattle was regarded as a particularly useful asset. The situation gave the king an excuse to extend his authority and in 1534, he appointed Rowland Lee as president of the council, instructing him to restore order in the marches. Lee's approach to establishing order became a judicial reign of terror; repression was the only solution on offer. Interestingly, one aspect of administrative tidying during this period had a lasting impact on Gwent and other regions. Lee objected to the use of the Welsh ap and began to impose surnames. The process was an arbitrary one. Morgan ap Maredudd would become Morgan Meredith; Maredudd ap Morgan, Meredith Morgan. There were inevitably corruptions with, for example, descriptions like fychan, meaning short, rendered as Vaughan. Similarly there was no consistency concerning retention of the ap in the surname. Sion ap Hywel might become John Howell, John Howel, or John Howells. On the other hand, the ap might be incorporated making the name John Powell. Similar examples include Price from ap Rhys, Prichard from ap Richard, and Probert from ap Robert. The latter examples clearly stem from a growing tendency to adopt English Christian names which in turn became Welsh surnames like Davies, Hughes, Thomas and Williams. Perhaps the most striking example, however, grew from an expedient adopted to deal with the numbers of Welsh names which were considered impossible to spell and too difficult to Anglicise. This legacy can be seen today by examining a modern Gwent telephone directory and looking at the listings for people who owe their surname to the process of recording all such names as Jones. [6]

Within two years of the appointment of Lee, the decision was taken to embark on much more far-reaching changes in the government of Wales. Acts of Parliament passed in 1536 and 1543 formed the Act of Union of England and Wales which fundamentally altered the course of history in Gwent. In a sense, the legislation of 1536 provided a framework for union while the 1543 act implemented the changes in detail. The union was justified in part by the need to reduce the lawlessness of the marches. More important, however, was concern over the reformation settlement which was being implemented at the same time and which increased the dangers of invasion. Henry undoubtedly wished to assure firm control of Wales in an attempt to secure the western approaches to his realm. There is also a possibility that he saw the union as a first step for a broader unified state which would eventually include Scotland and Ireland. Whatever the justifications, there were voices of opposition raised. One of the loudest of these was Lee who argued that introducing justices of the peace in Wales would be giving responsibility for law and order to those most likely to threaten it — the local gentry. On the other hand, there may have been some calls from Wales itself for union and the legal protections which it would presumably offer. [7]

Among the most significant provisions of the act was the official ending of the March. Marcher power had been so eroded by the extension of royal authority, that there was little opposition to provision that the lordships of the March would become shire-ground. Some lordships were simply attached to the existing border shires of Shropshire, Herefordshire and Gloucestershire. The most arbitrary example of the process was the transfer of Ewias Lacy to Herefordshire. As a consequence, the old Welsh region of Ergyng was incorporated into the English county despite the fact that it was Welsh in speech and would continue to be for some 300 years. In addition, entirely new shires were created including Brecon, Denbigh, Montgomery, Radnor, and, most significantly, Monmouth. For the first time there was to be Welsh representation in Parliament. Each Welsh shire was to have one knight of the shire except for Monmouthshire which had two. Each shire town, with the exception of Merioneth, was to be represented by one burgess. Among the provisions of the act most criticised by later observers concerned language. Welsh was deprived of all legal standing. All courts and oaths were to be 'in the English Tongue' and no one would be appointed to any office 'unless he or they use and exercise the English speech or language'. The long-term implications of these provisions were highly significant although in the short term it was virtually impossible to enforce them. With the passage of time, the premium placed on English tended to create a gulf between the upper classes and the vast majority of the population in Wales. The Council of Wales was continued as an administrative body with authority over not only the thirteen Welsh counties but also over Gloucestershire, Herefordshire, Shropshire and Worcestershire.

A final aspect of the act requires consideration. Administrative convenience dictated arrangements for judicial organization. Circuits were established to cover units consisting of three shires. The justice of north Wales held courts twice annually for six days in the three shire towns of Anglesey, Caernarfon and Merioneth. The justice of Chester did the same for Flint, Denbigh and Montgomery. Similarly, circuits in the south included Cardiganshire, Carmarthenshire and Pembrokeshire as well as Glamorgan, Breconshire and Radnorshire. Because it did not fit easily into the three-shire system and because it was 'the nearest part of Wales to London', Monmouthshire was placed under the courts of Westminster. Ecclesiastically, as well as culturally and linguistically, there was no question that the new county was a Welsh one. The apparent anomaly of its judicial arrangements was no more than an administrative convenience; there was certainly no sense in which Monmouthshire had been singled out for quasi-English status. Clearly no one believed that Chester had been annexed to Wales nor was there any question of Monmouth being separated from Wales or more fully incorporated into England than other Welsh shires. The framers of the act would have been horrified at the suggestion since the whole point of the Act of Union was to incorporate all of Wales into England. There were to be no degrees of submersion.[8]

NOTES

[1] 'The Gentry of Wales' and 'The Welsh in Tudor England' in Williams, Glanmor, *Religion, Language and Nationality in Wales* (Cardiff: 1979) pp. 148-199.

[2] This story is one of the most often cited as an indication of English reaction to Welsh influence. Its survival is attributed to the poet Skelton. See Williams, David, *A History of Modern Wales* (London: 1950) p. 23. This book provides a firm basis for the study of modern Welsh history.

[3] Ibid. pp. 22-23; and Williams, Glanmor, Welsh Church, pp. 308 and 544. Jasper took an interest in these holdings, building the great tower of Llandaff cathedral and leaving bequests to friaries including the one in Newport.

[4] Williams, David, pp. 24-26. A good general background is provided in Mackie, J. D., *The Early Tudors* (Oxford: 1952). A biography of Henry VII is Chrimes, S. B., *Henry VII* (London: 1972).

[5] Ibid. pp. 26-29 and Williams, Glanmor, Welsh Church, pp. 546-547. Lee delighted in hanging offenders of all ranks. He once boasted of having hanged 'four of the best blood in Shropshire'.

[6] The process is discussed in Williams, Gwyn, *When Was Wales?* (London: 1985) pp. 118-119. Perhaps the best example was the cheerful eighteenth century bankrupt who signed himself, 'Sion ap William ap Sion ap William ap Sion ap Dafydd ap Ithel Fychan ap Cynrig ap Robert ap Iorwerth ap Rhyrid ap Iorwerth ap Madoc ap Ednawain Bendew, called after the English fashion John Jones'. See also Mackie, pp. 366-369.

[7] Williams, David, pp. 33-35. The example most often quoted to demonstrate Welsh support for union is a petition which may have originated with Sir Richard Herbert. Its authenticity is not universally accepted. See Williams, W. Ogwen, 'The Union of England and Wales' in Roderick, A. J. (ed.) *Wales Through the Ages*, Vol. II (Llandybie: 1960) pp. 16-23. The architect of the act was undoubtedly Thomas Cromwell. See also Rees, J. *Tudor Policy in Wales* (Cardiff: 1936) and Rees. W. *The Union of England and Wales* (Cardiff: 1948).

[8] Ibid. pp. 33-45; see also Evans, G. pp. 294-300. Further implications of the status of Monmouthshire are discussed below. For the choice of Monmouth as the county town, see Kissack, K. *Monmouth, The Making of a County Town* (London: 1975) pp. 9-11. See also, Michael, D. P. M., *The Mapping of Monmouthshire* (Bristol: 1985).

The Reformation

The marital manoeuvres of Henry VIII led directly to the English reformation and the Act of Union assured that the break with Rome would also apply to Wales. The change was achieved by a series of acts in 1534. In March, the Act of Succession required that subjects accept the king's marriage to Anne Boleyn as valid. Additional legislation followed which severed financial links with the papacy. Finally, in November the religious revolution was completed by the Act of Supremacy which proclaimed Henry the 'Supreme Head of the Church of England'. With some notable exceptions, these changes were generally accepted with little opposition. This was certainly true of Wales although there is little evidence of doctrinal dissatisfaction or protestant sympathies during this period. A possible exception was Gwent where there may have been considerable Lollard activity. This 'proto-protestant' forerunner of the reformation began with John Wyclif who taught at Oxford in the late fourteenth century. Wyclif challenged the sacramental system and argued that neither absolution nor indulgences could remit sin. He also challenged the doctrine of transubstantiation, teaching that the substance of the bread in the eucharist was unchanged although there was a spiritual presence of Christ. Scripture was paramount and neither tradition nor Church councils could contradict its authority. Consequently, he argued that no priestly or papal hierarchy could stand between man and God. Wyclif's followers, the Lollards, gained considerable influence in parts of England and seem to have been particularly strong in Herefordshire and eastern Gwent. Notable among the Herefordshire Lollards was Walter Brut who loyally served Owain Glyndŵr. A leading Lollard figure in England was Sir John Oldcastle, who also originated in the southern march. Condemned as a heretic, he fled to Wales in 1415 where he sought assistance from the sons of Glyndŵr. Oldcastle was finally captured and executed in 1417. Interestingly, the bard Sion Cent, patronized by the Scudamores who probably sheltered Glyndŵr at the end of his life, has been described as an early poet of puritanism. Some of his themes were certainly in keeping with Lollard tradition. Whatever the extent of Lollard sentiment in eastern Gwent, however, the doctrine was not an important factor in the acceptance of the Act of Supremacy. Instead, that acceptance was passive and generally resulted from a superficial approach to religious teaching which was well entrenched and the fact that doctrinal differences resulting from the Act seemed slight to most laymen. Glanmor Williams, in reviewing the state of Welsh religion at the time, suggests:

> At its best religious life was pietistic and unmilitant. At its worst it was credulous and ignorant. At all levels it was not the stuff of which martyrs were made.[1]

Having broken with Rome, Henry inevitably turned his attention to the wealth held by the monasteries. These institutions were already in decline, never having fully recovered from the Black Death. Important changes came about during the fourteenth century conflict with France when alien priories became objects of suspicion. As has been seen, many houses were linked to French mother priories and in 1415 an act of Parliament transferred all of these alien priories to the crown. Small Welsh houses were attached to English foundations; larger monasteries were allowed to become independent and choose their own priors. As a consequence, Abergavenny and Monmouth became independent priories in 1415 and Chepstow followed, possibly in 1442. Goldcliff was initially transferred to Tewkesbury abbey but in 1467 was granted to Eton college.[2] These changes did nothing to enhance the fortunes of the local houses and by the time of the dissolution all were mere shadows of their former size and influence. Most of the Gwent houses seem to have had between three and six monks with only one having a dozen or more. The largest Gwent house was still Tintern, but even there only 13 monks remained. This general decline and an increasing secularization, which was widespread through Britain, offered an excuse to suppress the monasteries. The real reason, however, was the substantial land holdings belonging to the monks. The process of dissolution began in 1536 when all houses with an income of less than £200 per year were suppressed on the grounds that they were too small to function efficiently. All the Gwent houses fell into this category, with Tintern valued at £192 per annum. By 1539, the process was complete with all the religious houses dissolved and their estates incorporated into the crown lands.[3]

The priors of Gwent houses accepted the inevitable and agreed to receive pensions. William Marley of Abergavenny, Richard Talybush of Monmouth and Eleanor Williams, the last prioress of Usk, were all granted pensions of £9 per annum. Roger Shrewsbury of Chepstow received £6 per year and John Griffith of Grace Dieu, £4. John Clerke of Malpas received £6 13s 4d. Doing best from the dissolution were Richard Wyche, the last prior of Tintern, who was granted an annual pension of £23 and Jasper ap Roger of Llantarnam, a Welsh house to the end, who received £15. It is more difficult to be sure of the fate of the monks themselves. Judging from English practice, it is likely that most applied to be licensed as parish priests in the local area.[4]

The most significant question arising from the dissolution concerned the disposition of the land which had been held by the monks. Many abbots, perhaps anticipating developments, had already leased large tracts in return for cash payments. In many cases, too, management of abbey affairs was placed in the hands of a lay steward who was frequently a member of a leading local family. At Tintern, for example, the steward was Charles Herbert who was well placed to capitalize on the suppression of the monastery. The Herberts continued to be a major force in Gwent. After the death of William Herbert, his son, also William, succeeded as earl of Pembroke and lord of Raglan. In 1469, he exchanged his title for that of earl of Huntingdon. As there was no male heir, the holdings passed to William's daughter Elizabeth who married Sir Charles Somerset, a son of Henry Beaufort, duke of Somerset. He adopted the title Baron Herbert of Raglan, Chepstow and Gower and served as lord chamberlain to both Henry VII and Henry VIII. In 1514, he was made earl of Worcester. It was his son and heir, Henry, who acquired the extensive Tintern estates.[5] The site and lands of Grace Dieu passed to Dr. John Vaughan who had been a crown visitor there in late 1535 or early 1536. Commissioners had been sent to visit all the monasteries in order to enquire into the morals of the houses and thereby provide justification for dissolution. They were also to itemize monastic revenues and Vaughan obviously used his position to good advantage. In 1545, he leased the property to William Herbert. Herbert also obtained land from Abergavenny although some priory land there was used for the endowment of a new King Henry VIII Grammar School in the town.[6]

Monastic buildings themselves were sold for the salvage value of the lead, glass and iron which they contained. Profits accrued to the crown and there is a record of payment of £8 to the king's plumbers for melting down the bells of Tintern in 1541. In 1546, the earl of Worcester paid £166 outstanding for lead from Tintern suggesting that the abbey became roofless within a few years of the dissolution.[7] Not all monastic churches, however, fell into ruin. Portions of the Benedictine foundations in the towns sometimes survived as parish churches. This was the case in several towns including Abergavenny, Chepstow, Monmouth and Usk.

As Protestantism became established, access to scripture became more important and an English Bible was soon produced. In 1545, the 'King's Primer' appeared containing the Creed, the Ten Commandments and the Lord's Prayer. In the following year, a translation by John Price became the first Welsh book to be printed. Because it had no title, the book was known by its first four words—Yn y lhyvyr hwn (Yn y llyfr hwn—in this book). The necessity of vernacular texts became even more pressing when Henry died in 1547. During the six year reign of the young Edward VI, the king's advisors moved quickly to establish a purer form of protestantism. The protestant Book of Common Prayer in English replaced the Catholic rite in Latin. As beneficial as the vernacular prayer book may have been in England, however, it was of little use in regions where the common people spoke only Welsh. This problem was partially remedied by William Salesbury's translation of the epistles and gospels, Kynniver Llith a Ban which was published in 1551.[8] The protestant movement was halted between 1553 and 1558 in the reign of Queen Mary. There was little reaction as Welsh parishioners who had been content with previous changes, generally had no objections to a return to the old order. There was, however, one important qualification —the gentry were not willing to sacrifice the gains made from church property.[9]

By the time of the accession of Elizabeth and the securing of the protestant settlement, there was a fair measure of theological pliability in regions like Gwent. Property obtained from the church, however, was firmly consolidated in the hands of the local gentry. Most significantly, by the reign of Elizabeth, the structure of life in Gwent had changed fundamentally. The two institutions which had been so important in shaping medieval Gwent—the March and the monasteries—had both disappeared.

NOTES

[1] Williams, Glanmor, 'Wales and the Reformation' in Roderick, A. J. (ed.) II, pp. 24-30. See also Lloyd, pp. 109-110; Williams, D. pp. 46-50; Evans, G., pp. 287-288; and Ruddock, G. E., 'Sion Cent' in Jarmon & Hughes, pp. 169-188.

[2] Davies, E. T., p. 83.

[3] Ibid. pp. 126-135; Williams, D., pp. 51-56; Craster, pp. 8-10; and Williams, G., 'Reformation' p. 25. See also Mackie, pp. 366-379; Lewis and Williams, pp. 30-33. Woodward, G. W. O., *Dissolution of the Monasteries* (London: 1966); and Williams, David H., various references.

[4] Davies, E. T., p. 136; and Williams, D., p. 56.

[5] Taylor, pp. 13-14. Descendants of the earl eventually became dukes of Beaufort.

[6] Davies, E. T., p. 138-139; and Williams, D., pp. 54-57.

[7] Craster, p. 10; and Davies, E. T., p. 137.

[8] Williams, G., 'Reformation' pp. 26-27; and Williams, D., pp. 59-60. The most important Welsh publication was Bishop William Morgan's translation of the Bible in 1588.

[9] Williams, G., 'Reformation' pp. 28-29.

The Elizabethan Settlement

The ending of the March marked a significant change in the historical development of Gwent. It did not, however, represent as dramatic a transformation as might have been anticipated. Certainly leading gentry families, the successors of the great marcher houses, continued to dominate local affairs. In many respects, too, their approach to local administration followed old patterns. Shire organization, for example, did nothing to loosen the grip of the Herbert clan. As has been seen, Baron Herbert became earl of Worcester in 1514 and, from his seat at Raglan, dominated Gwent. The first earl died in 1526, but his son exercised similar control after the Act of Union and extended the family holdings by the acquisition of substantial holdings from the monasteries. Other important family groupings were also emerging, including the Morgans of Tredegar. Llywelyn ap Morgan forfeited his home at Tredegar near Newport after taking up arms for Owain Glyndŵr. The family recovered the estate, however, and one of their number, Sir John ap Morgan, supported Henry Tudor in taking the throne. He was rewarded by appointment as sheriff of Wentlwg and constable of Newport castle.[1]

As has been seen, the Act of Union was drafted to establish English law and custom in regions like Gwent. Among the early objectives of legislation was to end the practice of maintaining armed retainers by local gentry. In the short term this attempt failed. The Gwentian gentry continued to keep large armed bands and used them to maintain their influence. As late as 1581, for example, local squires expressed their opposition to the notion of an elected mayor for Newport by sending armed followers to attack the election assembly. A table holding the town records was overturned and the recorder was forced to flee.[2] One way to support substantial numbers of armed retainers was the retention of cymorthau which remained an important source of income for the gentry. Originally a traditional tribute prescribed in the laws of Hywel, cymorth had become a widely applied 'free benevolence'. In the later years of the March, however, lords had extracted it for their own support, especially in maintaining their retainers. The practice was specifically banned by the Act of Union. In the event, however, not even the influence of Worcester could stop it.[3] One hundred years after the act, families like the Vaughans were still collecting cymorthau.[4] There were other similar holdovers. Application of English law implied inheritance by primogeniture. This suited the gentry in building up large estates. Partible inheritance by gavelkind, however, survived in some areas long after the Act of Union. One place where it did, for example, was Trelech, much to the annoyance of Sir Walter Herbert. A tenement there desired by Herbert had been divided between the son and a nephew of a deceased tenant in keeping with Welsh law. The nephew was willing to sell his portion but Herbert wanted the whole. As a consequence, he sent his retainers to assault and evict the son and then assured that a pliable jury supported his claim. Nevertheless, gavelkind continued in the region. Interestingly, in Monmouth town land was inherited by primogeniture but in the manor of Monmouth, which included holdings within the town, inheritance continued to be by gavelkind.[5]

Cymorth and gavelkind obviously represented a retention of traditional usages. There were other examples of continuity. As has been demonstrated, in medieval Gwent, a tripartite power structure existed. The Act of Union symbolized the ultimate royal domination of that structure. The Welsh dimension, however, proved remarkably persistent as leading gentry families like the Herberts and the Morgans confirm. At first, many of these families continued to view patronage of Welsh culture as an obligation of the uchelwyr. As a consequence household harpists and family bards continued to thrive. William Herbert, who rose rapidly at court through the influence of the earl of Worcester, was made earl of Pembroke in 1551. He had holdings in Gwent and exercised considerable influence at court. For example, he was made a privy councillor in 1547, master of the king's horse in 1548, and knight of the garter in the same year. In 1556 he became governor of Calais and he led the English military expedition into France in the following year. He became lord steward of Elizabeth's household in 1568. Despite this role at court and the many years spent away from Wales, throughout his long life Herbert remained more fluent in Welsh and was never fully comfortable in the English language.[6] With the passage of time, however, social pressures put an increasing value on English. A burgess holder in Newport, for example, desired that his children should be 'browghte up accordyng to the maneres and condicionez of the norture of Inglonde'. That could not, however, be done in Newport so he made arrangements for them to live in Bristol. Interestingly, towns like Newport became progressively more Welsh in the aftermath of the Act of Union. Two important factors were at work in the towns. A degree of demilitarization of Wales brought reduction of castle garrisons and many towns declined as a consequence. Most of Chepstow within the town walls, for example, was converted to meadows and gardens. Flax and hemp gardens in Usk sometimes reached an acre or more. At the same time, the lifting of all restrictions on Welshmen in the towns led to a rapid process of Cymricisation. Formerly English towns like Abergavenny became predominantly Welsh in speech as declining populations were partially offset by Welshmen from the surrounding countryside. As with Newport, Abergavenny residents wishing their children to perfect their English found it necessary to send them to England to do so. [7]

While numbers in the towns declined, circumstances for many 'yeoman' farmers in the surrounding countryside improved. Housing became more substantial and better off farmers began to furnish their houses with a range of cupboards, coffers, tables and chairs. Pewter utensils also became popular. Meat continued to be a staple but variety increased from the offerings described by Giraldus. Mutton, veal, beef and bacon appeared regularly. Most country tables also offered the traditional oatcake or rye bread. Some change was seen in the cawls, thick soups, which began to feature a range of vegetables including onions, parsnips and beans. Meals would usually by accompanied by beer. Not only were living standards improving, there was sufficient free time to allow sports to compete with more traditional pursuits like archery. In many parts, a precursor to rugby, related to the cnapan of Pembrokeshire, was popular. Entire parishes, with players sometimes keeping weapons readily at hand, contested across open fields. There was at least one fatality in the 1579 local derby between Crickhowell and Llangatwg. [8]

Improving living standards were a reflection of nationwide trends. The Elizabethan era saw developments in many areas and it should be noted that descendants of Gwent families were playing key roles. Particularly notable was the grandson of a member of the yeomen of the guard maintained by Henry VII. Many guardsmen were Welshmen who served Henry in his exile. One of these was David Seisyllt who was born in Ergyng at Alltyrynys. Seisyllt became sergeant of the guard and acquired land in Northamptonshire; his son was a page at court. Seisyllt's grandson, using the Anglicised version of the family name— William Cecil, became, as Lord Burghley, the leading statesman of Elizabeth's court.[9] For such Elizabethan administrators a continuing problem was applying English law to Wales. Welsh juries still showed a reluctance to convict and there was a general tendency to maintain old usages. For example, there was the fairly widely accepted custom which allowed a thief, when identified, to offer compensation in money or in livestock. The practice was common enough to become institutionalized with money offered to the injured party on a plate so that it wasn't necessary for him to take it from a thief's hand.[10] When disputes were brought to trial, there were particular problems. One of the most significant of these was the language and it was clear that the Act of Union prohibition on the Welsh language was impossible to apply. It was inconceivable that an almost totally monoglot people could deal with the complexities of a foreign legal system through the medium of an incomprehensible language. As a consequence, while courts were conducted in English, oral evidence as well as statements and interrogations were accepted in Welsh. Significantly, remembering the legal position of Monmouthshire, the same recognition of the necessity of using Welsh prevailed in the supreme courts in London where there was a plentiful supply of interpreters from among the numerous Welsh courtiers and merchants resident there. One of the pieces of legislation being enforced was the Poor Law which was a revolutionary Elizabethan experiment. The hope was to legislate a sense of communal responsibility for those disabled by ill health, age or circumstance. Parish overseers of the poor were appointed by the justices of the peace. In the new approach the poor were divided into two categories. The first group was made up of the old and the otherwise incapable who were allocated sums for their maintenance. Funds for this relief were provided by a compulsory Poor Rate and from Poor Boxes placed in parish churches for voluntary contributions. The able bodied unemployed were regarded as a separate category. Some were placed in the care of wealthier inhabitants who agreed to employ them as servants or apprentices. Another approach was for parish authorities to purchase flax, hemp, wool, or iron for distribution to the 'honest poor' who would then receive fixed payments for finished products. Houses of Correction were established where work could be provided for able bodied 'rogues'. A refusal to accept work or travelling as a vagabond would be a matter for the justices of the peace and could be punished by imprisonment or whipping 'until his or her body be bloody'. The application of provisions varied from region to region and there were notable individual interventions to alleviate poverty. A number of Welshmen who made their fortune in England attempted to relieve the distress of those less fortunate at home. Philip Gunter, a skinner by trade, was one of those who amassed considerable wealth. He was influential enough to be on friendly terms with Cecil. Gunter set aside money to provide 25 poor men in Monmouthshire with cloth coats worth 13/4d. each. He also provided an additional sum for twelve impoverished inhabitants of his native parish, St. Michael Dyffryn Usk. Another provider of endowment was Elizabeth Morgan who founded a charity for poor matrons of Caerleon in 1593.[11]

One of the most important aspects of Elizabeth's reign was the religious settlement. Insisting on outward conformity, the queen and her advisors recognized the necessity of a measure of freedom of conscience. Relative toleration was important in preserving order in regions where the gentry clung to catholicism and Gwent was certainly one of those. Not only did branches of the Morgan family support the old religion, the earl of Worcester did as well. The Act of Uniformity required that everyone attend the Church of England and Roman Catholics who refused, recusants, were subject to a fine of one shilling. It was estimated that about two per cent of the adult population of the county of Monmouthshire were convicted of recusancy between 1584 and 1603. A few became active in their opposition to the settlement. Particularly notable was Thomas Morgan, a member of the Gwent family, who may have been born at Llantarnam. He became an agent of Mary, Queen of Scots. It was Morgan who introduced Anthony Babington to Mary and two intercepted letters from Morgan led to Mary's trial and execution in 1587. Such activity, however, was unusual. In the main, most people in Gwent were happy to accept the new religious settlement. As long as they were not challenged directly, the leading gentry families were among them.[12]

By the beginning of the seventeenth century, there were numerous subtle but significant innovations in Gwentian society. Particularly important was what can be seen as increasing economic sophistication. The fledgling iron industry rapidly took root since Gwent offered the perfect combination of iron ore and extensive forests to provide charcoal for smelting. The most successful of the early iron masters was Richard Hanbury, a London goldsmith. In 1565 he started operations which included new forges and hammer mills at Pontypool and Monkswood and incorporated already established small works at Pontymoel and

Abercarn. Hanbury found that the best ore was at Blaenafon and he exploited it for his forges. Within a comparatively short time, he employed between 160 and 200 men including miners, woodcutters and charcoal makers who were called colliers. The destruction of the forests was startling. It has been suggested that within three years some six thousand beech trees had been cut down for charcoal; prices for wood increased by 100 per cent. The situation became so unbearable that tenants of the lordship of Usk attacked the charcoal makers at Glascoed. Meanwhile, however, additional industrial development was beginning in other parts of Gwent. A prohibition on the importation of wire led to an ambitious project to begin a wire works at Tintern. As will be seen, a major industrial complex eventually spread from Tintern up the Angidy valley. There is striking symbolism in the fact that, within thirty years of the dissolution, monastic tranquility at Tintern had given way to the pounding of hammers driven by the water wheels of the new wire works. [13]

Innovation was not confined to industry. In many parts of Wales men took up the profession of drover. Cattle were driven over well-established routes, some passing through Gwent, to be fattened in English pastures and sold in eastern markets. Movement of stock, expanded agricultural markets and industrial development all placed new demands on roads and bridges. Interestingly, these bridges provide a demonstration of a growing political sophistication as well. From about 1570, Welsh members of Parliament became more active, especially on matters of Welsh concern. Bills were given over to committees and an all-Welsh committee in 1597 dealt with the bill for bridges in Newport and Caerleon. The ports also became more important with traffic through Newport and Chepstow increasing. Chepstow had been an important medieval port, with a good traffic in wine and the wire works at Tintern expanded trade further. An associated development was that a growing number of Welshmen developed a taste for seafaring. For example, when Sir Humphrey Gilbert set sail to seek the Northwest passage in 1578 one of the ships in his fleet was commanded by Miles Morgan of the Tredegar family who was supported by Gwent sailors and 'gentlemen'. In Elizabethan England, there was a fine line between gentleman privateer and pirate. Whatever the distinction, there were seamen from Gwent who clearly crossed the line and qualified as pirates. Undoubtedly the best known of these was John Challice who was born in Tintern.

Leaving home at the age of 11, he was placed with a London alderman. Recognizing Challice's natural aptitude as a seaman, his guardian sent him on various trading voyages. In 1573, however, Challice did not return to London after a voyage. Instead, he arrived at Penarth on a Portuguese ship he had captured off the Azores. He then began a lucratively successful career of piracy in the Bristol channel. Challice was certainly interprising. While concentrating his activities near Cardiff, he would pursue merchant ships from Dover to the Azores. On one such foray, he was blown so far off course that he found himself in Newfoundland. Undaunted, he used the opportunity to raid the French fishing fleet there. Between 1575 and 1577, Challice began cooperating with a notorious English pirate, Robert Hicks. The activities of the two have been called a national scandal; Challice enhanced his reputation by attacking and capturing a Danish ship carrying a cargo bound for the Danish king himself. Not surprisingly, efforts to capture Challice were re-doubled and he was finally taken on the Isle of Wight. The by now infamous pirate was taken to the Tower and his fate seemed sealed. Incredibly, however, he was pardoned by the queen and walked from the Tower a free man. It is likely that influence at court, exercised by the Gwentian gentry, saved Challice. There is certainly evidence to suggest that the Herberts in Glamorgan had been happy to turn a blind eye to his activities. He also seems to have been helped by Edward Kemeys, a member of another Gwent family whose importance was growing. Kemeys was sheriff of Glamorgan four times and in his first term which lasted from 1575-76, he was charged by the judge of Admiralty with assisting Challice and other pirates. Kemeys decided it best not to answer the charge but this did not prevent him from additional terms as sheriff.[14]

Apart from economic expansion, legal and piratical, there is another aspect of Elizabethan society which is particularly noteworthy. There was a tendency throughout the country for the gentry to demonstrate their wealth and influence by the aggrandizement of their homes. Comfort and style became progressively more important than defence which had previously been the main consideration. As the architectural restraints imposed by fortification were lifted, ostentation could begin to thrive. This was the case in Gwent. As has been seen, there was new building at Tredegar house. Perhaps the best example, however, is the transformation of Raglan where Worcester began a modernization programme in the late sixteenth century. The centre wing of the castle was extended, the pitched stone court was enlarged, and the inevitable Elizabethan long gallery was built against the southwest side of the hall with extensive fenestration. The windows looked out on the fountain court. The hall itself was raised in height and its northeastern side was rebuilt with a huge, and still imposing, oriel window.[15] Such changes were symbolically significant as a reflection of a new outlook. Clearly, the economy, lifestyle, and the attitude of the gentry were changing rapidly as the Tudor era drew to a close.

NOTES

[1] The oldest surviving portion of Tredegar house appears to date from this period. Eventually, Herberts held the lord lieutenancies of Monmouthshire, Glamorgan and Montgomeryshire.

[2] Owen, G. Dyfnallt, *Elizabethan Wales* (Cardiff: 1964) p. 110. The threat of the retainers, combined with loyalties to the lord, were factors in giving Welsh juries a reputation for being unwilling to convict local men.

[3] Ibid. pp. 26-28.

[4] Dodd, A. H., *Studies in Stuart Wales* (Cardiff: 1952), p. 20.

[5] Owen, p. 76.

[6] Jones, Gareth, *The Gentry and the Elizabethan State* (Swansea: 1977) pp. 44-45. Henry Herbert, the second earl, became lord president of the Council in the Marches in 1586.

[7] Owen, pp. 42-43, 93 and 96.

[8] Ibid. pp. 40-43, 56. The social scene is described in Jones, Gareth Elwyn, *Modern Wales* (Cambridge: 1984).

[9] Williams, David, pp. 23-24. Cecil was a forebearer of the earls of Salisbury and Exeter. See also Black, J. B., *The Reign of Elizabeth* (Oxford: 1959) pp. 7-8. Williams, Penry, *The Council of the Marches of Wales under Elizabeth I* (Cardiff: 1958) is also useful.

[10] Owen, p. 171.

[11] Ibid. pp. 175, 188-190; and Black, pp. 264-267.

[12] Williams, Glanmor, 'The Welsh in Tudor England' in Religion, Language and Nationality, pp. 171-199; and 'The Elizabethan Settlement of Religion in Wales and the Marches 1559-60' in *Welsh Reformation Studies* (Cardiff: 1967) pp. 141-153; Black, pp. 14-17 and 372-385; Jones, Gentry, pp. 84-89; and Jones, E. Gwynne, 'The Religious Settlement' in Roderick (ed.) pp. 38-44. It has been argued that Morgan was an agent of the English government, acting as an agent provocateur.

[13] Owen, pp. 159-163. An interesting local industry was production of woolen 'Monmouth caps'. The caps, described in traditional ballads as well as Shakespeare, may have begun as a protective lining for archers' helmets. Monmouth was the traditional centre for producing the caps and their economic importance led to an act of Parliament protecting them when sales declined. The 1571 'Act for the Continuance of the Making of Caps' required common citizens over the age of six to wear a cap on Sundays and Holidays. Failure to comply brought a fine of 3s. 4d. For the most part the act was ignored. The law was repealed in 1597 but cap production continued. See Buckland, K., *The Monmouth Cap* (Monmouth: 1979) and Kissack, *County Town*, pp. 15-18. For a general economic overview, see Jones, G. E., pp. 3-28.

[14] Owen, pp. 125 and 144-147; Jones, Gentry, pp. 64-65; and Waters, Ivor, *The Port of Chepstow* (Chepstow: 1977). A later, and even more famous Gwent pirate was Sir Henry Morgan who eventually, in 1674, became deputy governor of Jamaica. Apprentice books place his birth in Abergavenny.

[15] Taylor, pp. 14-17; and Owen, p. 18.

The Civil War

The Stuart succession brought few changes to Gwent. A prosperous gentry continued to thrive and most observers must have believed that the conflict which typified so much of the medieval history of the region had gone forever. It was not long, however, before national conditions deteriorated and civil war began to loom. Gwent, in keeping with other parts of Wales, was generally royalist in its sympathies. The main reason was that most of the gentry supported the king and their tenants in turn supported them. Moreover, the lesser gentry, tradesmen, and freeholders who provided the corner-stone of parliamentary support in England were much less numerous in areas like Gwent. Furthermore, in so far as the common people had any views on the matter at all, they tended to look on Parliament with suspicion, seeing it as a foreign body which threatened their language and customs. This does not mean that the king's policies were universally welcomed. For example, the demand for ship money, at a rate of £2000 for the county of Monmouthshire, was certainly not well received. Monmouthshire, like other counties, was quickly in arrears in payment. Nevertheless, when the Long Parliament met in 1640, Welsh members were less aggressively anti royal than most. There were certainly strong measures taken by the Parliament and among them was one which sent tremors of apprehension into Gwent. A list of recusants was drawn up with a view to identifying and disarming them. A particular target was the earl of Worcester who, with the king's blessing, maintained some 700 armed retainers. It has been suggested that Worcester and his son, Lord Herbert of Raglan, were gaining such influence with the king that Raglan can again be seen as a de facto capital of Wales during this period. Parliamentary moves against recusants confirmed Worcester in the view that his fortunes lay with the king and assured that Gwent would be a strong royalist centre and a fertile recruiting ground for the king's army. [1]

Worcester's support was vital to Charles I for whom money was a continuing problem. The earl provided a startling sum for the king's coffers. A low estimate of his contribution is £600,000; some authorities put the total nearer to £1,000,000. Moreover, there was a substantial supply of manpower which helped to earn for Wales the description 'nursery of the king's infantry'. It should be noted that while most of the local gentry were royalist, some were not. The extensive Herbert clan, for example, was split with the earl of Pembroke supporting Parliament. The Morgans were similarly divided. These conflicting loyalties contributed to the opening skirmishes in Gwent as the war began. Pembroke, who was named lord lieutenant of Monmouthshire by Parliament, had holdings which included Newport, Caerleon, Usk and Cardiff. As a consequence, Parliament ordered the county magazine to be removed from Monmouth to Caerleon where it would be in Pembroke's safe keeping. The mayor refused the demand and was arrested. When the arms were moved toward Caerleon, however, they were captured by Worcester's men and taken to Raglan.[2]

Despite such skirmishing, fighting in Gwent was limited during the early stages of the war. The king raised his standard at Nottingham on 22nd August 1642 and then marched to Shrewsbury to collect his Welsh infantry. Among the Welsh commanders who joined him was William Herbert of Cogan, the member of Parliament for Cardiff. The royalist army then moved toward London, the key objective for the king. On the way, however, they were intercepted by a parliamentary army led by the earl of Essex. The ensuing battle at Edgehill was bloody and indecisive with heavy casualties among the Welsh infantry. William Herbert was among those killed. In the aftermath, the royalist army was able to proceed to the outskirts of London, but then it was forced to withdraw to Oxford where Charles established his capital. Several early administrative decisions were taken including naming the marquis of Hertford as lieutenant-general of the western counties including south Wales. Hertford moved into Wales, securing Newport, Caerleon and Cardiff before returning to Oxford at the end of the campaigning season of 1642.[3]

One consequence of the campaign of 1642 was that Worcester and Lord Herbert took exception to the position of Hertford who they regarded as an intruder in their domain. Such tensions did not help circumstances in 1643, although the king remained in a strong position and was still hopeful of taking London. There were also key royalist targets in the west with Gloucester and Bristol being the most important objectives. If these cities could be taken, the west, providing access to the important recruiting grounds of Gwent and Glamorgan, would be secure. Lord Herbert raised a force and advanced on Gloucester. On March 24th, however, the army, untrained and armed in part with only scythes and sickles, was attacked and scattered at Highnam in the Forest of Dean. The royalist historian Clarendon was particularly critical of Lord Herbert over the incident, arguing that if the money spent on this force had been delivered directly to the king the war might have been won. The argument is a doubtful one, apparently not shared by the king. Certainly Charles had decided that the support of Lord Herbert and his father was vital and that the key regions of south Wales would have to be administered as a separate entity. As a consequence the king made Lord Herbert his lieutenant-general in south-east Wales and Herefordshire and then proceeded to lay siege to Gloucester himself. Eventually the city was relieved by the earl of Essex and the king was forced to withdraw. In the meantime, however, his forces had gained an important success by taking Bristol on July 26th. A less favourable development was that a parliamentary force commanded by Sir William Waller tested Worcester's strength, passing through Monmouth, Usk and Chepstow before withdrawing. [4]

In September, Parliament agreed the Solemn League and Covenant with the Scots, promising to introduce presbyterianism in return for military support. In January 1644, the Scots crossed the Tweed and the situation became critical for the king. In an attempt to consolidate his vital Welsh base, Charles made Prince Rupert supreme commander in Wales with Sir Charles Gerard as his adjutant in the south. A vigorous recruiting campaign was mounted but disenchanted Welshmen rallied much more slowly than before. One reason was that there was less enthusiasm for following Rupert's 'foreign' professionals than there had been for the known quantity of Lord Herbert and other members of the local gentry. Even more important was the awareness of heavy casualties suffered in previous campaigns. Recruiters sent into Wales by Rupert offended the gentry and failed to move the common men. One of the officers sent to raise forces was Sir Thomas Dabridgecourt who recruited in south-east Gwent. Writing to the king from St. Pierre near Chepstow, he pleaded, 'if your Highness shall be pleased to command me to the Turk, or Jew or Gentile, I will go on my bare feet to serve you; but from the Welsh, good Lord deliver me'. While these local difficulties were being faced, however, disaster met the royalist cause at Marston Moor on July 2nd. Cromwell, in concert with the Scots, defeated the king and claimed the whole of the north of England for Parliament. There was a parliamentary reverse, however, as Essex was defeated in Cornwall. In the aftermath, Cromwell obtained the Self-Denying Ordinance which led to Sir Thomas Fairfax assuming command of the New Model Army. After the defeat at Marston Moor, Raglan grew in importance. The king hoped to build his support in the south-west and what might be described as a Raglan-Bristol axis was critical in his planning. Raglan and other strong points in south Wales were supplied from Bristol and there was always the possibility of reinforcing Bristol from Raglan. As a consequence, Beachley became an important objective for both sides because of its key position in controlling the Severn approaches. In September 1644, Prince Rupert sent some 500 men to fortify the Beachley peninsula; they attempted to secure it by building defences which in part incorporated Offa's dyke. Sir Edward Massey, the parliamentary commander, tried to disrupt the crossing first by burning passage boats at Aust and then by attacking Beachley itself. On 22nd September, Massey and some 600 men stormed the defences and captured the peninsula. Having taken it, however, Massey decided that it was impossible to hold it, especially since it was vulnerable to naval gunfire. The parliamentarians attempted to dismantle the fortifications and then moved on to Monmouth.[5]

Early in 1645, Shrewsbury fell and then in June the royalist army was crushingly defeated at Naseby. Charles lost half of his forces including much of his Welsh infantry. Many of the captured Welshmen were taken as prisoners to London where they were preached to, receiving a sermon in Welsh delivered by Walter Cradock of Llangwm, a man of Gwent who opted for Parliament at the outset of the conflict. Cradock tried to convince the men to transfer their loyalties and take up arms with the parliamentary forces. Many did so. In the aftermath of the disaster at Naseby, Charles withdrew to Raglan. For several weeks, the castle was the king's headquarters as he tried to raise a new army. The task was not an easy one. Heavy casualties and a dissatisfied gentry combined with resentment of the activities of some royal troops in Wales to make recruitment difficult. Charles found that it was impossible to raise additional Welsh troops without guaranteeing that they would be led by Welsh officers. There were, however, some bright spots for the king. Traditionally, when Charles visited Monmouth, for example, he was presented with a contribution of £30 on a pewter platter. The king travelled through Usk, Caerleon and Newport, staying at Tredegar House where he conferred with Rupert who was charged with holding Bristol. The two men had a second meeting at Crick, apparently discussing the wisdom of the king going to Bristol. In the event, Charles stayed in Wales, moving to Cardiff where he was forced to deal with the grievances of the discontented men calling themselves the 'Peaceable Army'. As these moves were taking place in south Wales, Charles despatched Lord Herbert, recently created earl of Glamorgan, to Ireland in a desperate attempt to raise Irish troops. It was thought that Lord Herbert would have an advantage in gaining support from his co-religionists. Having done what he could in Wales, Charles went to Oxford. He then returned to Raglan before moving on to Chester where his last army was defeated at Rowton Heath on September 24th. Even that disaster, however, paled into insignificance when on September 10th, Rupert surrendered Bristol.[6]

With these reverses, Raglan inevitably became one of the parliamentary force's prime objectives. After the surrender of Bristol, one of the few remaining centres of significant royalist support outside beleaguered Oxford was the triangle of land controlled by Raglan, Monmouth and Chepstow. The attack against this last bastion was led by Thomas Morgan, the diminutive governor of Gloucester who had gained a reputation in Europe for conducting sieges during the Thirty Years War. In October 1645, Morgan attacked Chepstow taking the town and demanding the surrender of the castle. The garrison initially refused the demand, but when artillery was set up and the castle bombarded, they surrendered. Monmouth soon followed suit making the situation for Worcester at Raglan a desperate one. The 76-year-old Worcester held his castle with a force of about 800 men. He tried to re-gain the initiative by sending part of this force in an attempt to re-capture Monmouth but they were beaten back after a battle on the Monnow bridge. Soon the vice tightened as Morgan surrounded Raglan with about 1500 men. This was not a large enough force to take the castle or even to press the siege as closely as Morgan would have hoped; sallies were made from the castle which had been well provisioned for a long siege. In the event, it was the final collapse of the royalists in England which sounded the death knell for Raglan. In June of 1646, Oxford fell and a substantial number of troops were sent to Raglan. Morgan's force was swelled to about 3,500 and the siege was tightened. Throughout July trenches and gun positions were pushed closer and closer to the castle and at the beginning of August, Fairfax himself arrived to take personal charge of the siege. Fairfax carried on negotiations with Worcester by correspondence as the encircling trenches were pushed closer still to the castle. By 14th August, parliamentary earthworks were within 60 yards of the walls and Worcester recognized that the position was hopeless. Finally, on 19th August, Worcester surrendered the castle which had earned its description as 'first fortified and last rendered'. The fall of Raglan was a desperate blow to the elderly Worcester who was taken to London as a prisoner of Parliament. In the following winter, he sickened and died. The parliamentary forces assured that this bastion of royalist support, which had been the focus of power in Gwent for some 200 years, could never pose a threat again. Raglan was rendered uninhabitable, the great Tŵr Melyn Gwent was undermined, and one of Britain's great libraries was destroyed in the process. [7]

A short, peaceful lull settled over Gwent in the aftermath of the fall of Raglan. This ended in the second civil war which began with disgruntled parliamentary troops in Pembrokeshire. Cromwell led an army into south Wales, arriving in Monmouth only to learn that Sir Nicholas Kemeys of Llanfair Discoed had seized Chepstow for the king. In May 1648, Cromwell diverted his force to Chepstow, taking the town. He demanded the surrender of the castle but this was refused. Anxious to lead the main force into Pembrokeshire, Cromwell left a regiment to reduce the castle. Artillery pieces were set up and the castle was bombarded. Battlements were knocked off some towers and a breach was made in the wall. Many members of the demoralised garrison fled through the breach but Kemeys still refused to surrender. As a result, the parliamentary forces were ordered to storm the castle and Kemeys was killed, whether in the fighting or after having been captured is unclear. [8] This second fall of Chepstow marked the end of the conflict in Gwent.

NOTES

[1] For a general background to the period, see Davies, Godfrey, *The Early Stuarts* (Oxford: 1959). The Welsh dimension can be found in Dodd, A. H., *Studies in Stuart Wales* (Cardiff: 1952) and Williams, David, pp. 95-109. Gwent is discussed in Clark, A., *The Story of Monmouthshire* Vol. I. (Monmouth: 1980). Dodd points to Lord Herbert's seat on the Council of Wales and the deputy lieutenancy of the county as a demonstration of the rising influence of Raglan. He argues that as Raglan's star rose, Ludlow's declined as the de facto capital. See pp. 54-55 and 64-65.

[2] Williams, J. Gwynne, 'Wales and the Civil War' in Roderick (ed.) II pp. 62-69; Williams, David, pp. 95-97; and Clark, pp. 174-175.

[3] Williams, J. Gwynne, pp. 63-64; Williams, David, pp. 99-100; Clark pp. 175-176; and Jones, G. E., pp. 90-91. Hertford's army was mauled at Tewksbury on the way to Oxford.

[4] Williams, J. Gwynne, pp. 64-66; Williams, David, pp. 100-101; and Clark, pp. 177-180. Waller's withdrawal was not without incident. His horse lost its footing and plunged him into the Severn in full armour.

[5] Davies, pp. 136-141; Williams, J. Gwynne, pp. 66-67; Williams, David, pp. 104-105; Perks, pp. 12-13; and Waters, I. *Beachley between the Wye and the Severn* (Chepstow: 1977) pp. 7-10. There was a second attack at Beachley in October of 1644 as Sir John Wintour attempted to fortify the peninsula again, partially to secure the royalist supply line and partially to protect his own house at Lydney. Massey led a wild cavalry charge through the defensive hedge lined with musketmen. Unhorsed, faced with a pistol which misfired at point-blank range, and having his helmet clubbed off his head, Massey managed to survive and win an important victory.

[6] Williams, J. Gwynne, pp. 66-67; Williams, David, p. 105; and Jones, G. E., p. 90-91.

[7] Taylor, pp. 17-22 and 55-56; Clark, pp. 190-198; Kissack, County Town, pp. 36-42; and Perks, p. 12. See also Clark, A., *Raglan Castle and the Civil War in Monmouthshire* (Chepstow: 1953) especially pp. 56-64. There were other pockets of resistance; Harlech did not surrender until March 1647. Raglan, however, was of unique importance.

[8] Perks, pp. 12-13; and Clark, Monmouthshire, pp. 199-202.

Commonwealth and Restoration

With the victory of Parliament, there were inevitably major changes in the lifestyle of Gwent. An important consequence of the war was an acceleration of the introduction of puritanism into the region. As has been seen, there had been puritans before the war. Several emerged during the reaction to the policies of William Laud who became archbishop of Canterbury in 1633. The pomp of Laud's tenure and his attempt to impose uniformity through a revived Court of High Commission produced a puritan backlash. Among those who fell foul of Laud and the Commission was William Wroth, the elderly vicar of Llanfaches. Wroth was summoned before the commissioners along with William Ebery, a young Cardiff vicar. Ebery had already been admonished by the bishop of Llandaff who had deprived his curate of his license. The curate was none other than Walter Cradock of Llangwm who, as has been seen, played an important role during the civil war. The cases against Wroth and Ebery dragged on for well over two years. Finally, in 1638, Wroth submitted and Ebery was forced to resign. In the aftermath, however, in November of 1639, the pastor of the first independent church in London was sent 'to help old Mr. Wroth, Mr. Cradock and others'. The others probably included Morgan Llwyd and Vavasor Powell. The result was a 'gathered' church at Llanfaches which became the first independent church in Wales. [1]

Despite this early initiative, at the outbreak of war puritanism was not strong enough to have much influence in Gwent. Wroth died in 1642 and while Ebery had established an independent church in Cardiff, at the outset of war both he and Cradock fled to England. As the war proceeded, Parliament struck upon the idea of increasing puritan sympathy by appointing itinerants to preach in the Welsh language throughout south Wales. The three named, who commenced their duties in the autumn of 1646, included Cradock, Henry Walters of Piercefield near Chepstow and Richard Symonds from Abergavenny. An additional impetus was provided by John Miles who returned to Wales in 1649 after having been baptised in a baptist chapel in London. Soon baptist churches emerged including one in Abergavenny. In February 1650, Parliament passed the Act for the Propagation of the Gospel in Wales which delegated authority to a Commission which has been described as the only attempt to grant Wales a measure of self government before the twentieth century.[2] Any five commissioners, from the total of 70, could examine ministers and eject them from their livings if they were found to be unsuitable. Reasons for ejection included an inability to preach in Welsh, use of the Book of Common Prayer, pluralism or scandal in their private lives. Within three years, 278 ministers had been ejected including 45 from the county of Monmouthshire. The act also named 25 Approvers, including Cradock, any five of whom could approve preachers and appoint school masters. The latter is interesting because it represented the first provision for education to be made by the state. A total of 59 schools were established. There were schools at Monmouth, Usk, Magor, Newport, Abergavenny, Caerleon and Chepstow. Less successful was the provision of puritan ministers who were difficult to find. As a consequence the Approvers were forced to rely on itinerant preachers, many of whom were ill-suited to the task although Approvers like Cradock and Walters performed good service as itinerants themselves. The act was passed for a three year period and might have been extended in 1653. In that year, however, Crowmell expelled the Long Parliament and declared himself Lord Protector. As a consequence, there was no further funding and the provisions of the Propagation Act lapsed. Some itinerants settled into parishes. Cradock, for example, stopped at Usk, remaining there until his death in 1659.[3]

The county committee was an important element in local administration during the Commonwealth. The Monmouthshire committee, which included Herberts and Morgans, was a powerful one which, along with the Glamorganshire committee, provided over a sixth of the total commission established by the Propagation Act. Cromwell himself, along with his son Richard, was on the Glamorgan committee by virtue of his being granted the lordships of Raglan, Chepstow and Gower by Parliament in 1648. By the end of the Commonwealth, however, the Roundhead nucleus of the committee had given way to a very different body of men. In the later stages of the Protectorate, the Monmouthshire county list was headed by Sir Trevor Williams of Llangibby who was making his first appearance in public affairs since being excluded after the second civil war. Other members included Thomas Morgan of Machen who had also been in retirement for most of the interregnum and another Thomas Morgan, a man of Gwent who had served as Monck's lieutenant in Scotland. Another member was Walter Rumsey of Llanover who had been a south Wales judge under Charles I. As a consequence, the county of Monmouthshire was uniquely set for the Restoration. One Roundhead observer lamented that the committee had been taken over by 'cavaliers or at best neuters who will never engage against the enemy'.[4]

The Restoration in 1660 saw a reaction against the puritans. Some, like Vavasor Powell, were arrested and a number of puritan ministers were removed to make way for the former incumbants who they had replaced. John Miles, with most of his baptist congregation, sought the safety of America and others followed their lead. Despite persecution, however, the indulgences of 1672 and religious census of 1676 demonstrate that puritanism survived. More than 4,000 dissenters, a number certainly lower than the actual total, were identified in Wales. Of that number, over half lived in the south-eastern counties of Breconshire, Glamorganshire and Monmouthshire. Clearly dissent had become sufficiently well rooted to resist official opposition. Religious opponents, however, were not limited to puritans. In 1676, approximately 1,000 Roman Catholics were identified in Wales and fully one half of them were in the county of Monmouthshire. Persecution of priests was more ferocious than that of puritan ministers and the Jesuit David Lewis, a native of Abergavenny, was hanged at Usk in 1679. The death of Lewis and other priests was a severe blow to catholicism which largely disappeared in Gwent until the nineteenth century when it was re-introduced by Irish workers coming into the industrial centres.[5]

Politically, the Restoration saw the re-establishment of the Council of Wales although its power was limited and it survived only until 1688. Before that, however, the Council played a role in the even more important restoration of the royalist gentry. In Gwent, of course, that meant the successors to Worcester. Lord Herbert of Raglan was disqualified from office by his catholicism. His son, however, who succeeded in 1667, had become a protestant during the Protectorate. As a consequence, in 1671 he became president of the Council realizing a long-standing ambition of the house of Raglan. Raglan itself was uninhabitable but in 1673, Worcester built Great Castle House in Monmouth. Worcester saw his main task as securing Welsh support for the succession of the king's catholic brother. He was successful enough in the task to be rewarded by being created duke of Beaufort in 1682. In order to consolidate his position and discourage political discontent, in 1684 Beaufort, as president of Wales, made a tour of the entire principality. The tour proved a great personal success; it became a triumphal procession. In the short term, it may also have helped stifle discontent. Remarkably, there is evidence that had James II been less incompetent as king, Beaufort might actually have raised a Welsh army to oppose William of Orange. In the event, the king's actions were such that Beaufort found himself supporting his cause virtually single handed and losing the presidency as a consequence. Beaufort was not the only loser as the Council itself was disbanded in the aftermath. This did not, however, mark the end of the family fortunes as among those throwing their support behind William was Beaufort's son, the marquis of Worcester. The duke himself was later at least outwardly reconciled to William and Mary. The whole of Wales accepted the change with one or two exceptions, notably the burgesses of Abergavenny who refused the Association Oath of 1696.[6]

By this time, however, there were fundamental changes in the social scene and the political power structure in Gwent. One important symptom of the change was that Beaufort had built Badminton which became the principal family seat.[7] Circumstances in Gwent, which had been dominated from Raglan from the time of William ap Thomas through the civil war, changed dramatically by the beginning of the eighteenth century. The dukes of Beaufort continued to own vast tracts of Gwent and, as will be seen, to dominate local politics. The nature of that domination, however, was new.

NOTES

[1] Williams, J. Gwynne, 'Wales and the Commonwealth' in Roderick (ed.) II, p. 70; Williams, D., pp. 113-114; and Jones, G., p. 120. The basis for the study of this period was provided by Richards. See Richards, T., *Religious Developments in Wales, 1654-1662* (London: 1923); *Wales Under the Penal Code, 1662-1687* (London: 1925); and *Wales Under the Indulgence* (London: 1928). A general background to the period is in Clark, G., *The Later Stuarts* (Oxford: 1956).

[2] Williams, D., pp. 114-115.

[3] Ibid. pp. 115-118; and Jones, G. E., pp. 121-122. The educational background is provided in Williams, J. and Hughes G., *The History of Education in Wales* (Swansea: 1978). A localised study of schools is Davies, E. T., *Monmouthshire Schools and Education* (Newport: 1957).

[4] Dodd, pp. 125, 145, and 169-70.

[5] Williams, D., pp. 118-122.

[6] Dodd, pp. 72-75, 229-232; Taylor, pp. 22-23; Dodd, A. H., 'The Landed Gentry After 1660' in Roderick (ed.) II, pp. 78-85; and Dodd, A. H., *Life in Wales* (London: 1972) pp. 96-97. There is a valuable contemporary account of Beaufort's tour; Dineley, *Progress of the first Duke of Beaufort* (1684).

[7] See Taylor, pp. 22-23.

Education and Politics

The Revolution of 1688 provided toleration for dissenters but it also confirmed the position of the anglican church and established an unchallengeable alliance between the gentry and that church. This relationship did nothing to improve the religious welfare of parishioners. There were, for example, serious problems with appointment of bishops. These difficulties had been obvious from the reign of Charles II when some highly idiosyncratic appointments were made to Welsh sees. None was more so than that of William Beaw as bishop of Llandaff. Beaw had been a soldier in the royalist army and in exile served as a cavalry officer under the czar. He then took service with the king of Sweden and fought in Poland. At the Restoration he returned, deciding to take orders as a means of advancement. His reward was the bishopric at Llandaff in 1679. He remained in the post for the remaining 26 years of his life, much of it spent campaigning for a better appointment. When Beaw died at the age of 97 in 1706 he left a legacy of neglect which was typified by the palace at Mathern which had been allowed to deteriorate to such a state that it was unoccupied for over 100 years.[1] In succeeding years there was little improvement. In fact, the situation became even worse after the Georgian succession when support by the bishops in the House of Lords became vital to the government. Loyalty was assured by initially appointing new bishops to poorer sees and then offering hope of advancement to ensure continuing support. Since the Welsh bishoprics were the poorest in the kingdom, transient bishops became the norm. During the reigns of George I and George II, there were six bishops of Llandaff, four of whom were transferred to richer bishoprics. Moreover, the remoteness of the Welsh sees and the political demands of London, meant that most bishops spent little time in Wales. At least Llandaff faired better than Bangor with bishop Hoadly. Hoadly was appointed bishop of Bangor in 1716 and held the post for six years. During that period he achieved the dubious distinction of never having set foot in the diocese. With these transient bishops, nepotism was rife and pluralism became the norm. Moreover, as virtually all these political appointees were English, they had little sympathy for the language of the parishioners for whom they were responsible. In many cases this was simply a matter of indifference combined with a desire to give preferment to friends, families and hangers-on. With a few, however, there was an active desire to eradicate the Welsh language as quickly as possible. [2]

The malaise within the established church created the need for a new approach to revive religion. Soon, Methodism offered an alternative which was widely acceptable to disillusioned parishioners. As early as 1715, Griffith Jones, vicar of Llanddowror, was attracting huge congregations and resisting censure for preaching outside his own parish. Soon the home grown reforming zeal of Jones was fuelled by outside influences. In 1729, John Wesley formed his 'Holy Club' and by 1735, the year when the Wesley brothers departed on a missionary visit to Georgia, the pattern of Methodism was emerging clearly. It was also in 1735 that the young Howell Harris was converted after hearing the vicar of Talgarth preach on a Palm Sunday. In the following year, Harris conferred with Griffith Jones and began to collect converts. From his home base at Treveca he expanded his scope; dissenting ministers invited him into, among other regions, Gwent. It is likely that in his meeting with Jones, Howell Harris learned of the Oxford Methodists. It was not until 1739, however, that Harris met John Wesley. By this time a split was developing between the Calvinist and Arminian traditions within the movement. Harris was Calvinist in his approach and Wesley Arminian, but the difference did not prevent cooperation between the two in Welsh regions and by the end of his life Wesley had made no fewer than 46 visits to Wales. Many of these were to Gwent. [3] Wesley's first visit to Wales, for example, saw him arrive in Chepstow by the New Passage from Bristol. Almost immediately he set off on a preaching circuit, beginning with a sermon on Devauden Green that afternoon. A crowd of between 300 and 400 people heard Wesley preach on 'Christ our wisdom, righteousness, sanctification and redemption.' The congregation was drawn from the whole of the surrounding area, with some travelling six miles or more. After preaching, Wesley held an evening singing service in a home near Devauden before moving on to Abergavenny next day. Many of those who heard him were obviously moved by his message. One woman, for example, followed him on foot to each of his successive meetings in Abergavenny, Usk, Pontypool and Cardiff. [4] Other preaching circuits followed. For example, in February 1748, he again arrived in Chepstow after sunset on a snowy evening. Nevertheless, he pressed on in the direction of Abergavenny and Brecon, staying the night at the Star, 'a good though small inn' at Llanfihangel-tor-y-

Mynydd. Wesley's journal entries are instructive as an indication of the state of religious knowledge in the region. He found the people 'ripe for the gospel' and suggested that they were:

> earnestly desirous of being instructed in it (the gospel) and as utterly ignorant of it they are as any Creek or Cherokee Indians. I do not mean they are ignorant of the name of Christ. Many of them can say both the Lord's Prayer and the Belief. Nay, and some all the Catechism. But take them out of the road of what they have learned by rote, and they know no more . . . either of gospel salvation or of that faith whereby alone we can be saved than Chicali or Tomo-cachi.[5]

The religious revival sparked by Methodism had a profound impact on many people. So too did a related theme which attracted the attention of the revivalists—education. The Puritan schools provided for by the Propagation Act were of short duration. The void which they left, however, was filled by the Welsh Trust established by an ejected puritan minister, Thomas Gouge. The trust began to found schools in Wales in about 1672 and by 1675 there were schools at Chepstow, Monmouth, Usk, Llantrisant, Llangybi, Caerleon, Newport, Abergavenny, Pontypool, Bassaleg, Machen and Michaelstone-y-Fedw. Mathern was added to the Gwent list by 1678. These schools were conducted in English and one of the objectives of the Trust was to teach the English language to the children of Wales. The Trust did, however, distribute devotional works in Welsh to those strongly Welsh-speaking areas where this was the only way to reach the majority of adults. It is instructive to see where Welsh books were considered necessary in the county of Monmouthshire. A 1678 report shows that 248 books were distributed in the county including 4 to Llantrisant near Usk, 23 in Newport, 4 in Bassaleg, 12 in Mynyddislwyn, 46 in Bedwellty and Henllys and no fewer than 103 in Abergavenny. Significantly, a number of books were sent to the extreme east of the county including 13 to Llanishen near Trelech and a remarkable 43 to Mathern.[6]

Gouge died in 1681 and the schools came to an end almost immediately. Before long, however, there was a new educational movement, the S.P.C.K. (Society for Promoting Christian Knowledge) and in many cases its schools were established where Welsh Trust schools had been previously. A teacher in the S.P.C.K. school at Laugharne in 1708 was none other than Griffith Jones and he became the founder of the next important educational movement—the circulating schools. Itinerant teachers were used, remaining in one place for about three months which was considered long enough to establish basic literacy. Jones was convinced that the schools should be free, conducted in Welsh, and limited to the absolute basics of reading and the catechism. Moreover, adults made up the majority of the scholars. In 1738, the first of the circulating schools were established in Gwent. Initially the schools were concentrated in the west although over the next 30 years they extended all the way to the Wye.[7]

As the religious revival spread and educational provision improved to a degree, the political scene also changed. The swashbuckling maintenance of influence by force, which had typified Gwent practice, gave way to a more genteel practice of politics. It is true that members of the old Gwent catholic families, notably Richard and William Vaughan of Courtfield, joined Prince Charles Edward, Bonnie Prince Charlie, in the ill-fated rising of 1745. That was, however, atypical. Politics in the county of Monmouthshire followed an eminently predictable pattern as the old gentry families maintained their hold. Political interests were dominated by the duke of Beaufort and the Morgans of Tredegar. Because the county had two members of Parliament a system emerged with the duke naming one member and the Morgans the other. From the creation of Monmouthshire, a member of the respective families, or one of their nominees, represented the county for over 250 years. Nor were the Morgans content with power in Gwent. By the end of the eighteenth century, the Morgans of Tredegar had emerged as one of the wealthiest houses in Wales with estates not only in Tredegar and Machen but also at Dderw in Breconshire and Ruperra in Glamorgan. The income from these holdings has been estimated at almost £30,000 and their influence extended to the control of three Parliamentary seats—Breconshire, Brecon borough and the second Monmouthshire seat.[8] There was an attempt to break this mould of politics in Monmouthshire in 1771. Valentine Morris had acquired Piercefield house near Chepstow and used his substantial wealth acquired in the West Indies to turn it into a showpiece of national renown. He caused an uproar, however, when he defied convention and stood for Parliament against the Morgan candidate in 1771. His opponent John Morgan, shocked at opposition in the family preserve, attacked Morris as an upstart and an American foreigner to boot. Morris for his part enjoyed some Beaufort support. Even that, however, wasn't enough to change the entrenched pattern and Morgan won by 743 votes to 535. The campaign was a disaster for Morris who spent an estimated £6,000 in the contest. His ensuing indebtedness forced him to return to the West Indies in a vain attempt to recoup his fortunes.[9] The main lesson was that only national reform would alter the local political structure.

NOTES

[1] Williams, D., pp. 127-128, 133.

[2] Ibid. pp. 132-135; and Jenkins, Geraint, *Literature, Religion and Society in Wales 1660-1730* (Cardiff: 1978) pp. 3-4, 7. One cause of poverty in the Welsh Church was that so many tithes were in the hands of lay owners and were not applied to religious purposes at all.

[3] Jones, E. D., 'The Methodist Revival' in Roderick (ed.) II, pp. 101-109; and Williams, D., pp. 142-149.

[4] Williams, A. H., (ed.) *John Wesley in Wales 1739-1790, Entries from his Journal and Diary* (Cardiff: 1971) pp. 1-4.

[5] Ibid. pp. 5-6, 31-32. Tomo-Chachi and Chicali were American Indian chiefs Wesley met in Georgia.

[6] Roderick, Alan, 'A History of the Welsh Language in Gwent' in *Gwent Local History*, 50, Spring 1981, pp. 26-27; and Williams, D., pp. 122-123.

[7] Clement, Mary, 'The Campaign Against Illiteracy' in Roderick (ed.) II, pp. 86-93; Davies, E. T., Schools, pp. 59-65; and Williams and Hughes, various references. For details of the work of the S.P.C.K. see Clement, M., *The S.P.C.K. and Wales, 1699-1740* (Cardiff: 1954).

[8] Thomas, P. D. G., 'Eighteenth Century Politics' in Roderick (ed.) II, pp. 96-98; and Williams, D., pp. 161-165. The transition from political violence to stability was not without incident, especially in the late seventeenth and early eighteenth century. For a discussion, see Jenkins, Philip, 'Party Conflict and Political Stability in Monmouthshire 1690-1740', *The Historical Journal*, 29, September 1986, pp. 557-575.

[9] Waters, I., *Piercefield* (Chepstow: 1975), pp. 14-18. The fullest account of Morris' life is Waters, I., *The Unfortunate Valentine Morris* (Chepstow: 1964). A late eighteenth century history was Williams, D., *History of Monmouthshire* published in 1796. For a biography of the author, see Jones, Whitney, *David Williams—the Anvil and the Hammer* (Cardiff: 1986).

Early Industrialization

A gentry-dominated political system and the religious revival were significant factors in defining the structure of life in Gwent during the eighteenth century. During that century another dimension, industrialization, became progressively more important. As has been seen, there was a long-standing industrial tradition typified by the Hanbury works in and around Pontypool. Somewhat incongruously to modern minds, however, a major early centre of local industrialization was Tintern. In the mid-sixteenth century, Britain imported substantial quantities of wire which was important, especially for the carding combs used in preparing wool for spinning. As a consequence, William Humfrey, the assay master of the Royal Mint in London, established a wire works at Tintern in 1566. A company, the Society of Mineral and Battery Works, was formed to control the Tintern operation. The original intention was to make brass and brass wire so an expert in these processes, Christopher Schutz, was brought from Saxony to supervise production. On his arrival, however, Schutz found that he did not have the necessary equipment and began to draw iron instead. Eventually the decision brought financial success; one estimate is that by 1597, some 5,000 people were employed throughout the country in making goods from Tintern wire. Demand for wire became so great that in about 1600, the company built a second wireworks at the nearby village of Whitebrook. In the early stages, the Tintern works received iron from the Hanbury forges at Monskwood and Pontypool. Disagreements, however, caused the company to build their own furnace and forge at Tintern, possibly as early as 1630. The area was ideally suited to iron production because the substantial forests produced a ready supply of the charcoal required for smelting. By 1690 there were two forges in Tintern and a third at Pont y Saeson on the Angidy brook which joins the Wye at Tintern. By the middle of the eighteenth century, the region had become an industrial complex extending for some two miles up the Angidy Fechan, Angidy Fawr and Fedw brooks. By 1821 there were at least 18 water wheels powering the works as well as an extensive system of dams and leats. [1]

The main thrust of industrialization, however, was shifting to the west and the coal fields of Gwent and Glamorgan. Pontypool continued to be an industrial centre. The iron works there remained in the hands of the

Hanbury family and in the early eighteenth century, John Hanbury mastered the technique of using mechanical rollers to produce thin sheets of good quality iron which were then coated with tin to make tin-plate. Some of the tin-plate was decorated and, as it resembled Japanese lacquered wood, was called Japan-ware. It was used in making a variety of small containers and led to a brief boom beginning in about 1728. The real key to the shifting emphasis of industry, however, was the process developed by Abraham Darby at Coalbrookdale in Shropshire in 1709. Darby successfully smelted iron with coke by increasing the strength of the blast in his furnace. Despite the implications of the discovery, however, the widespread application of the technique was slow; it was increased demand for iron during the Seven Years War which stimulated new production using coke smelting in south Wales. In 1759 Thomas Lewis and partners including Isaac Wilkinson leased land belonging to Lord Windsor on Dowlais brook near Merthyr Tydfil. Lord Windsor had inherited the Herbert estates in Glamorgan through his mother. In 1760 the Lewis partnership employed John Guest to manage operations and he began experiments using coal. By 1763 Guest, in partnership with Wilkinson, began his own venture nearby. Meanwhile in 1765, Anthony Bacon went into partnership with William Brownrigg and established the Cyfarthfa Furnace at Merthyr. These furnaces and forges were successful, but depression followed the Seven Years War temporarily inhibiting further expansion. The American War which began in 1776, however, created new demand with Bacon expanding his gun casting at Cyfarthfa and extending his operations further by leasing the Plymouth Furnace near Merthyr in 1777 and the Hirwaun Furnace in 1780. When Bacon died in 1786, Cyfarthfa was leased to Richard Crawshay. Within eight years, the operation had become so prosperous that Crawshay was able to buy it outright. By this time, there was also significant iron production in the Sirhowy valley. Production began at the Sirhowy Ironworks, the first coke furnace in Gwent, in 1778.[2] Inevitably, the industrial focus of Gwent shifted to the western coalfield. Moreover, industrial development of Gwent and Glamorgan became inseparably linked. Soon there was a proliferation of iron works. In 1782 John Guest became a partner at Dowlais and although he died within three years his descendants eventually acquired a controlling interest in the works. Meanwhile, Francis Homfray leased land from Bacon for a forge at Cyfarthfa. He held the lease for less than two years but then, with his sons Jeremiah and Samuel, he leased land for a furnace at Peny-darren near particularly rich iron deposits. At about this time, expansion was further accelerated by new technological developments. Watt's steam engine not only provided an efficient power source, it also increased the demand for iron. More significant in the short term, however, was the perfection of the puddling process. Previously, brittle iron from the furnaces had been worked into wrought iron by being beaten with tilt hammers. In 1783, however, Henry Cort in Hampshire developed a method for stirring the molten iron so that carbon impurities could be removed. The iron was then passed through rollers at a welding heat. With the new process, speed of production was increased approximately 15 fold and the quality of the iron was also improved. While Cort was developing his process, Peter Onions was working on a similar technique at Cyfarthfa and litigation followed over the patent. Wherever the technique began, puddling became so commonplace in south Wales that it came to be described as the 'Welsh method'. Its application further accelerated the expansion of the iron industry along the rim of the coal-field. In 1803 Richard Crawshay acquired the Rhymney works which, in 1810, passed to his son-in-law Benjamin Hall. In 1794, Richard Fothergill took over the Sirhowy works. An even more important Gwent works was located lower down the Sirhowy valley where the Tredegar iron works was begun by Richard Fothergill and Samuel Homfray. The land was leased from Homfray's father-in-law, Sir Charles Gould Morgan who had married the heiress of Tredegar Park and adopted the family name; the new works were named after the family seat. The works at Ebbw Vale were acquired by Jeremiah Homfray in 1789 and then by James Harford in 1796. Harford also obtained an interest in the Nantyglo furnaces but large scale production there dates from 1810 when the works were bought by Joseph and Crawshay Bailey, nephews of Richard Crawshay. On the Afon Lwyd, Thomas Hill and his partners started the Blaenafon works in 1789. The growth in industrial activity was remark-able and the works concentrated in south Wales were soon of national importance. The heart of this iron industry was a narrow stretch of land approximately eighteen miles long and not much more than a mile wide running from Blaenafon to Hirwaun. In a sense the proximity was deceptive since the works were located in narrow valleys, frequently at the head of the valley, with ranges of hills dividing them from each other. Nevertheless, they shared the same basis of prosperity—a concentration of easily worked coal, rich iron deposits, limestone for smelting and stone for lining furnaces all readily at hand. Some of the works emerged as industrial giants with concerns like Ebbw Vale expanding through the purchase of bankrupt works nearby. Nevertheless, an increasing number of smaller works grew up around the larger ones. Investment was impressive. It was suggested that in 1816, for example, some £250,000 had been expended at Blaenafon. In the following year it was decided to increase the capital of the Tredegar Works from £100,000 to £120,000 by allowing the accumulation of profits. In 1820-21 the capital of the Ebbw Vale Company was £62,440 14s. 9d.; it increased substantially soon afterwards.[3]

In a related development, expansion of the iron industry led to a gradual but continuous increase in coal mining. Through much of the eighteenth century, the southwestern rim of the coalfield was most heavily exploited for export because it was there that the coal measures touched the sea. As a result, trade in coal developed from Swansea. Elsewhere difficulty in transport meant that for the most part coal was used only locally. This was especially true in Gwent where the road system was notoriously bad. When giving evidence to support application for a Turnpike Act in 1754, Valentine Morris was asked how people travelled in the county of Monmouthshire. His response was 'in ditches'. The situation was improved through the building programme of several turnpike trusts, but even then road transport was ill suited to heavy loads of coal and iron on horse drawn vehicles. The answer to that problem was the canal and between 1790 and 1800 there was a spate of construction in south Wales. The Monmouthshire Canal was completed from Newport to Pontnewynydd above Pontypool in 1796 with a branch to Crumlin opened shortly after. In 1797, the Brecknock and Abergavenny Canal was begun, eventually extending the Pontypool branch to Brecon. Of course much of the coal field was unsuitable for canals so less accessible areas were served by a system of tram roads. Since the iron works were generally at the heads of the valleys, it was relatively easy to move heavy loads down hill and then draw the empty trams back. This system linked Blaenafon to the Monmouthshire canal at Pontypool and works like Ebbw Vale to the branch at Crumlin. Since there was no canal in the Sirhowy valley, Samuel Homfray had a tram road built to Newport linking Sirhowy and Tredegar. He also built a nine mile tramroad to link his works at Penydarren to the Glamorgan canal. The line earned a special place in industrial history when, in February 1804, Richard Trevithick successfully ran the world's first steam locomotive along it. The canals eased shipment of iron but also opened new avenues for coal export. First in the queue to capitalize on the possibilities was the Monmouthshire Canal company which managed to gain an exemption from coastwise duties on coals shipped at Newport and carried east of the Holme islands. The privilege was established in a parliamentary act of 1797 and almost immediately gave Newport a monopoly of the coal trade to the Bristol Channel ports. When the privilege was extended to include coals for Bridgwater in 1802, Newport began to surpass Swansea as a coal port. By 1820, Newport had ousted Swansea and within another ten years was the largest coal port in Britain with the exception of the ports on Tyne and Wear. Cardiff lagged well behind. In 1830, for example, Cardiff shipped only about a quarter of the coal moved from Newport. Interestingly, the trade of 'sale coal' from Newport was not controlled by the ironmasters but instead was in the hands of local entrepreneurs. Most notable among them were Thomas Prothero, a Newport attorney, and Thomas Powell, a local timber merchant. The two formed an association to control prices at Newport and in the process created the first 'coal ring' in south Wales.[4]

The ironmasters themselves had little time for coal as they were busily concerned with expanding production to keep up with rapidly increasing demand. Technological innovations made their task easier. Steam engines began to be used widely in south Wales for pumping water from the mines, crushing ore for smelting, and strengthening the blast to increase the heat in the furnaces. The widespread use of the hot blast in iron manufacture provided considerable advantages. One was that raw coal could be used instead of coke. Improved production techniques allowed the ironmasters to take advantage of the increasing demand resulting from national industrial expansion. Particularly significant was the rapid rate of construction of tramroads and then the railways. The rails for the Stockton to Darlington railway, for example, were made at Ebbw Vale and Nantyglo enjoyed a world-wide reputation for iron rails. This rapid expansion of local industry had a dramatic demographic impact. The population of Monmouthshire in 1801 was 45,568. By 1831 the total had risen to 98,126; between 1801 and 1841 the population of the county increased by 117 per cent, the highest percentage in any shire in Britain. This population explosion brought an influx of non-

Welsh workers, but in the first decades of the century the population remained predominantly Welsh. Whether indigenous or immigrant, however, the growing labour force found working and social conditions apalling. The geography of the mining valleys presented special problems. Houses in the valleys were inevitably built in long, narrow ribbon developments. Serious difficulties with drainage and sanitation were intensified since as population increased houses were built in terraces one above the other. In many cases, overhanging coal tips dominated the whole development. Overcrowding was common and disease became inescapable. The valleys were fertile breeding grounds for epidemics including, after 1831, cholera. Another problem growing from the geography of the valleys was the relative isolation of the industrial centres. Employers provided the houses and as a result the threat of eviction placed permanent pressure on employees. Moreover, truck shops run by the company provided a major source of grievance. The well established 'long pay' system meant that workers were payed monthly, often receiving wages in the form of vouchers which could only be used in the company shop. Because these shops had a virtual monopoly, they generally charged up to 30 per cent above the rates in the towns. Trapped in the system, workers found themselves constantly in debt to the shops and, as a consequence, more easily controlled by the employers. Arguably even greater problems arose from working conditions. Work in the forges was long and dangerous, but conditions in the mines were worse. An almost total lack of safety devices in an environment where explosion and flooding were commonplace frequently led to death and disability.[5] Such conditions inevitably led to discontent and as a consequence social unrest became a dominant theme in the history of Gwent in the early nineteenth century.

NOTES

[1] Pickin, J., 'The Ironworks at Tintern and Sirhowy' *Gwent Local History*, 52, Spring 1982, pp. 3-9; Williams, D., pp. 92-93; Tucker, D. G., 'The Wireworks at Tintern and Whitebrook' (a paper presented to the Historical Metallurgy Group, Cardiff, September 1972). A useful nineteenth century account is Llewellin, William, 'The Iron and Wireworks of Tintern' *Archaeologia Cambrensis*, October 1853. See also, Davies, D. J., *The Economic History of South Wales prior to 1800* (Cardiff: 1933). For the impact of the works on local employment patterns, see Howell, pp. 42-45. Hanbury gained a stake in the Tintern works in 1569 but that did not prevent a major row over supply of inferior iron. The matter is discussed at some length in Clark, II, pp. 25-36.

[2] John, A. H., *The Industrial Development of South Wales* (Cardiff: 1950), especially pp. 24-40; Pickin, and Williams, D., pp. 185-188. Lord Windsor's daughter and heiress married the marquis of Bute. It should be noted that there were other tinplate works, notably one in Caerleon. An account of Japan ware is Nichols, R., *Pontypool & Usk Japan Ware* (Pontypool: 1981).

[3] Williams, D., pp. 185-188 and John, pp. 35-36. The literature on the industrial revolution is immense. A good concise introduction to the topic is Ashton, T. S., *The Industrial Revolution 1760-1800* (Oxford: 1968).

[4] John, pp. 39-40, 116-117; Williams, D., pp. 193-195; and Hadfield, C., *The Canals of South Wales and the Border* (Cardiff: 1967) pp. 127-183. See also Gladwin, D. D. & J. M. *Canals of the Welsh Valleys and their Tramroads* (Oakwood: 1974) especially pp. 11-15 and 21-27; and Hadfield, C. *The Canal Age* (London: 1968). Principal subscribers to the Monmouthshire canal included Josiah Wedgwood, Sir Charles Morgan and the duke of Beaufort. In 1809, some 141,742 tons, representing two thirds of the total coal shipped from Newport, went to Bristol and Bridgwater.

[5] John, especially pp. 58 and 87-97; and Williams, D., pp. 229-231.

Social Discontent and the 'Scotch Cattle'

Social strains and economic hardship inevitably led to discontent in the industrial valleys. This was especially true during and after the Napoleonic wars which artificially increased demand for iron. The result was over-production and alternating periods of high wages followed by unemployment. The ensuing agitation produced an official reaction which expressed itself in the Combination Acts of 1799 and 1800 prohibiting the association of workmen in attempting to increase wages, reduce hours or otherwise ameliorate conditions. Not surprisingly, frustration produced outbreaks of violence with Merthyr in particular being a centre of discontent; there was rioting there in 1800 and again in 1810. The end of the war temporarily threw the iron industry into decline with forges idle and wages reduced. Serious rioting resulted with violence beginning at the Tredegar iron works in October 1816. The rioters then crossed over the mountain to Dowlais where special constables fired into the crowd, killing one of the rioters. The death was the cause of more widespread rioting which struck all the iron works from Merthyr to Blaenafon. The unrest was so widespread that the employers relented and withdrew notices of reduction of wages. The rioting ceased almost immediately. By 1817 the iron trade had revived sufficiently for Crawshay to raise wages and discontinue the hated company shop. Unfortunately for the coalfield, however, other owners did not follow his lead in abolishing truck which continued to be a major cause of discontent. There were, of course, other factors leading to ferment in the valleys, particularly the widespread demand for parliamentary reform. These factors came to a head in Merthyr with a dramatic escalation in the level of violent confrontation. Anti truck meetings had been held in Merthyr from 1830 and in 1831 news of the failure to carry the first Reform Bill arrived at about the same time that coal owners were attempting to reduce miners' wages. The result was an explosion popularly described as the Merthyr Rising. Crowds attacked and sacked the local debtors court in Merthyr and the magistrates called in troops. A detachment of the Argyll and Sutherland Highlanders arrived from Brecon on the 3rd of June only to be confronted by an angry crowd, some of whom rushed the soldiers. The troops panicked, bayonetting and firing on their assailants; at least sixteen people in the crowd were killed and some seventy were seriously injured. Approximately twenty soldiers were also wounded. The casualty toll did not, however, stop the confrontation. On the following morning, a crowd outside the town turned back additional troops trying to deliver ammunition from Brecon. Later in the day the Swansea yeomanry, who were advancing on the town, were attacked and disarmed. A commitment of substantial troop reinforcements, however, then ended the confrontation without further fighting. In the aftermath, the presumed leaders of the rising were arrested and eventually several were transported. Two were condemned to death although one of these, the haulier Lewis Lewis (Lewsyn yr Heliwr), who undoubtedly was a leader, was reprieved. The second man, Richard Lewis, who was better known as Dic Penderyn, was a 23 year old collier accused of wounding a soldier. Despite considerable doubt about the evidence against him and petitions of support by local people, Dic Penderyn was hanged. The episode at Merthyr did have at least one important national consequence as anti-truck legislation came into effect in January 1832. It was, however, only partially successful and did nothing to stop the 'long pay' system which in itself assured that employees continued to depend on credit. Moreover, the company shops remained and the legislation was ignored to such an extent that truck continued to be a major grievance.[1]

Such continuing grievances fueled the most persistent and violent expression of protest in the Gwent valleys—the Scotch Cattle. A strike in 1822 marked the first appearance of the Cattle who continued to re-emerge until as late as 1858. This secret colliers organization was described as having 'naw mil o blant ffyddlon', nine thousand faithful children, and seems to have had cells, or herds, in every industrial valley. The leader was styled the Bull, Tarw Scotch, and meetings were held at night, sometimes with the accompaniment of drums, horns and guns. Men would frequently black their faces and dress in animal skins. The Cattle can only be described as a terrorist group and intimidation was their most effective weapon. A typical threatening letter warned 'we are determined to draw the hearts out of all the men above named, and fix two of the hearts upon the horns of the Bull; so that everyone may see what is the fate of every traitor'. These were not idle threats as the bands destroyed company property worth thousands of pounds and attacked contractors, agents, bailiffs and the keepers of the truck shops. In 1822 and 1830 when the colliers wanted to stop supplies of coal from reaching either the iron works at the heads of the valleys or Newport, the Cattle tore up miles of tramroad and also burned wagons and barges. Attacks were not, however, confined to such obviously industrial targets. Strike-breakers, better paid workers from the ironworks, Irish immigrants or any other workers willing to take lower wages or opposing the tactics of the Cattle could all be 'scotched'. Attacks became ritualized. In April 1832, for example, between 250 and 300 members of the organization marched three abreast down the Bute or Rhymney rail line. Their leaders, who wore horns on their heads, were armed. Warning notices with the red bull's head adopted as a symbol of the Cattle were posted in Blackwood before the band went on the rampage breaking the windows in some 100 homes. Men who ignored the warnings and worked during a strike could expect a second visit with the Cattle breaking into their houses, attacking the occupants and destroying property. The Cattle were active throughout industrial Gwent with the suggestion in 1834 that law and order had broken down completely between Dowlais and Abergavenny. Pontypool and other peripheral industrial centres did not escape the activities of the Cattle. Despite their tactics, it is obvious that there was widespread support for the Cattle because even with the intro-duction of troops and concerted efforts by the magistrates, in the early stages it was almost impossible to penetrate the organization. Finally, however, the authorities managed a breakthrough of sorts and in 1835 Edward Morgan was hanged at Monmouth gaol for Cattle activities which included murder. Nevertheless, the Cattle re-emerged on the coalfield in 1836-9, 1842-3, 1847-50 and 1857-8.[2]

The Scotch Cattle imposed a solidarity on the coalfield through intimidation and assured that there would be a simmering undercurrent of violence in social protest. There was certainly continuing cause for protest. The continuation of the truck system despite the legislation of 1832 was one cause of complaint. So too was the collapse of Robert Owen's dream of a Grand National Consolidated Trades Union with the arrest of the Tolpuddle agricultural labourers in March 1834. In the same year, the Poor Law Amendment Act produced another major cause of discontent. It has been argued that the Poor Law replaced truck as the chief grievance of industrial workers. Moreover, there was profound disappointment that the Reform Act of 1832 had not brought the degree of democracy which many of its supporters had expected. It is true that the franchise was extended and the worst evils of the pocket borough system ended, but the Act fell well short of democracy as modern readers would define it and which supporters of reform had hoped it would bring. An expression of this dissatisfaction was published in May 1838 in the People's Charter which called for universal manhood suffrage, equal electoral districts, annual parliaments, vote by ballot, abolition of the property qualification for election to parliament and payment of members of parliament. The demands of the Charter found a ready body of adherents among the discontented workers of the industrial valleys. Consequently, Chartism provided a new focus which would further intensify the level of violent confrontation in Gwent.

NOTES

[1] The fullest account is Williams, Gwyn, *The Merthyr Rising* (London: 1978). There are concise summaries in Williams, D., pp. 232-234 and Evans, G., pp. 353-355.

[2] Jones, D. J. V., *Before Rebecca, Popular Protests in Wales 1793-1835* (London: 1973), pp. 86-113.

[3] Williams, D., pp. 236-237 and Jones, G. E., pp. 235-237. There are a number of good general studies of this period including Woodward, Ll., *The Age of Reform 1815-1870* (Oxford: 1962) and Briggs, A., *The Age of Improvement 1783-1867* (London: 1959). General Chartist studies include Briggs, A., (ed.) *Chartist Studies* (London: 1959) and Cole, G. D. H., *Chartist Portraits* (London: 1965). Basically, the Poor Law of 1834 required the able-bodied poor to seek relief in a workhouse where conditions were to be as uncongenial as possible. It was argued that the threat of the workhouse would be sufficient to banish poverty and unemployment through fear. The effects of the act were mitigated by the establishment of a Poor Law Board in 1847 which made the law work more humanely.

The Newport Rising

As has been seen, the Morgans of Tredegar and the duke of Beaufort controlled politics in the county of Monmouthshire with the two county seats and the seat for the boroughs of Monmouth, Newport and Usk virtually appointed by one or the other. Between 1816 and 1820 an unsuccessful attempt was made to break this stranglehold by a radical alliance including Thomas Prothero, the town clerk of Newport; John Hodder Moggridge, a lesser industrialist; and John Frost, a tailor-draper. Soon the radical coalition collapsed in acrimony and Frost, who had returned to Newport from London in about 1806 and established himself in Mill Street, emerged as the most forceful radical spokesman in the county. Working with the printer Samuel Etheridge he launched a series of printed broadsides against corruption by the gentry families and also by his former colleagues, especially Prothero. The conflict between Frost and Prothero became so acrimonious that in 1823 Frost was gaoled for libel. This did not, however, dampen his enthusiasm for the radical cause and in 1831 he was instrumental in establishing a Newport branch of the Political Union of the Working Classes committed to manhood suffrage. Frost and his fellow radicals were desperately disappointed with the Reform Act of 1832; arguably Monmouthshire fared worse than any other county under the act. Despite dramatic population growth, parliamentary representation remained the same. To make matters worse, the county had one of the lowest percentages of electors in the country. Frost's conclusion was that the 'Reform bill was a humbug'.

This disappointment, however, only encouraged Frost and like minded men to become even more active. Among leaders who emerged at this stage was Zephaniah Williams, geologist and former mineral agent who eventually kept the Royal Oak between Blaina and Nantyglo. Williams' friend, the schoolteacher John Thomas, and Morgan Williams also began production of an Owenite journal, *Y Gweithwr/The Workman* at about this time.[1] With such radical activity, the cosy traditional approach to politics could not be sustained and campaigns became highly charged. For instance, in 1835 Benjamin Hall defended the Monmouth boroughs seat which he first won in 1832. Hall was the son of the proprietor of the Rhymney ironworks but he advocated radical causes such as election by ballot and enjoyed considerable non-conformist support. He was also a friend of the Welsh language. In the election he was opposed by the land-owning Tory industrialist Joseph Bailey who, in an attempt to restore the old order, gained both Morgan and Beaufort support. The contest was a close one and before Hall won a narrow victory, his supporters had taken their case on to the streets, rioting in Newport. It was in this charged atmosphere that Frost began to make a significant mark in local politics. In 1836 he was made a magistrate and in November of that year became mayor of Newport. A shift in the balance of power on the council prevented Frost's re-election but radical politics continued to gain adherents. In the summer of 1838, for example, a Working Men's Association was formed in Newport by William Edwards who was soon supported by others including Samuel Etheridge and William Townsend. By the Autumn of that year, Frost had become an active advocate of the People's Charter and in November was chosen at a public meeting of the Working Men's Association to act as the delegate for Newport, Pontypool and Caerleon at the Chartists' National Convention of the Industrial Classes in London.

The growth of Chartism in Gwent was rapid. By January 1839 there were already over 400 active Chartists in Newport. Their leaders, in addition to Frost, included Edward Thomas, a grocer who was also a Welsh poet of note; John Dickenson, a butcher; Thomas Wells, a corn merchant; and James Horner, a shoemaker. This nucleus attempted to spread the message through a series of lecture tours with Newport to Abergavenny being their most popular route. Speakers attacked the vested interests of both the large gentry families and the industrialists. In the early stages support was drawn largely from the middle classes with little effort to gain converts to the Charter in the coalfields. That changed at the beginning of 1839 with the arrival of Henry Vincent who had been appointed as a sort of roving ambassador by the London Working Men's Association. On January 1st, Vincent with Frost present, drew a crowd of about 1,000 to his first meeting at Pontnewydd. His work rapidly produced dividends since by February, when Vincent and Frost departed for the convention in London, some 20 new Chartist branches had been established and the number of active supporters had risen to perhaps as many as 20,000. At the convention, Frost played a major role and was chairman at the Crown and Anchor meeting where threats were made against the government. That was too much for the home secretary who removed Frost from the list of magistrates. Among the decisions taken by the convention was one to send representatives to gain signatures for the Chartist petition—a monster petition which they had hoped to present to Parliament in May. As a consequence, Vincent was again sent into south Wales, arriving in Monmouth and then embarking on a hectic programme which saw him speaking to four meetings in two days at Newport with some 3,000 present at one of his meetings. Vincent stirred the crowd by suggesting that if the petition were rejected, 'every hill and valley of Wales should send forth its army'. His visits to the valleys sometimes took on the appearance of a triumphal procession. Up to 100 flag waving girls, for example, preceded him to a meeting at Blackwood which was followed by an evening of penillion singing. The results were impressive. Within days, over 15,000 signed the petition at Merthyr and Blackwood. By this time there were active coalfield lodges in Blackwood, Pontllanfraith, Tredegar, Ebbw Vale, Beaufort, Blaina, Brynmawr, Dukestown, Abersychan and Llanhilleth. Additionally, there were smaller branches or cells. In the Blackwood district alone, for example, there were branches at Maesycwmer, Gelligroes, Fleur de lis, Argoed and Croespenmaen. The focus for most of these groups was a local public house, or better still an unlicensed beer house. Radical centres included the Star in Dukestown, the Miner's Arms near Nelson, and the Navigation Inn at Crumlin. In the coalfield branches, there was a strong Welsh dimension; meetings were opened and closed with prayers in Welsh and much of the business was transacted in Welsh. Some groups also introduced secret oaths and there can be little doubt that there was a strong Scotch Cattle dimension in many of the branches.

The rapid rise of Chartist power gave considerable concern to the civil authorities and industrialists. In an effort to stem the Chartist tide, attempts were made to ban meetings and stop Vincent. In May troops were brought into Newport, Abergavenny and Monmouth and warrants were issued for the arrest of several Chartist leaders including Vincent. He was soon arrested in London and brought to Newport. The arrest led to disturbances in the streets of Newport and Frost seems to have played a role in calming the situation. Impossibly high bail was set and Vincent was transferred to Monmouth gaol to stand trial. Interestingly, while the arrest and arrival of soldiers increased tensions, it also presented a new opportunity to some Chartists who tried to convert the soldiers to their cause. They succeeded with over a dozen who deserted. Meanwhile many meetings were held through south Wales with crowds of 5,000 to 8,000 at Hirwaun and Penreolgerrig and smaller meetings at Nantyglo, Blackwood, and Pontypool. The monster meeting, however, was the Whit Monday gathering at Blackwood which was attended by up to 30,000 people. Despite such popular reaction, however, Vincent was found guilty and sentenced to one year's imprisonment. Also sentenced were William Edwards, to nine months, and John Dickenson and William Townsend, to six months each. These August convictions would have been bad enough in Chartist minds but the situation was made worse by the fact that in July the House of Commons had rejected the National Petition.

With these reverses the activities of the Chartists became more frenetic. It is difficult to know precisely what intentions were, assuming that objectives had been clearly defined at all. There was certainly a desire to apply pressure to obtain the release of Vincent and there had already been much talk of 'physical force' to obtain the charter. There was, however, another undercurrent in Chartist circles. Some attempted to revive the old notion of a regional revolt which seemed a possibility at the time of the Merthyr rising. A number of Chartists certainly discussed the possibility of workers seizing south Wales and setting up a Chartist state. Vincent himself had helped give credibility to the idea. On his first visit to Pontllanfraith, for example, he had argued that 'a few thousand of armed men on the hills could successfully defend them. Wales would make an excellent Republic. ' There was certainly a violent and revolutionary strain in the coalfield. The Glamorganshire Chartist Dr. William Price was one of the most colourful eccentrics of nineteenth century Wales and his recollections must be treated with some caution. Nevertheless, his account of a discussion between David Davies, a delegate from Abersychan and Frost seems a reasonable reflection of attitudes in some branches. Davies, a veteran of Waterloo, told Frost:

Abersychan Lodge is 1,600 strong; 1,200 of them are old soldiers; the remaining 400 have never handled arms, but we can train them into fighting men in no time. I have been sent here to tell you that we shall not rise until you give us a list of those we are to remove—to kill. I know what the English army is, and I know how to fight them, and the only way to success is to attack and remove those who command them

—the officers and those who administer the law. We must be led as the children of Israel were led from Egypt—through the Red Sea.

Whether such accounts are strictly accurate or not, there is evidence that general attitudes, organization and even personnel changed significantly in the autumn of 1839. Moreover, there is also a suggestion that the reconvened Chartist convention was at least considering the possibility of a coordinated national rising.

In October, Zephaniah Williams and William Jones, a Pontypool watchmaker, were sent to rally the various Chartist branches; each was to lecture in his native tongue—Welsh with Williams and English with Jones who had originally come from Bristol. At this stage intense pressure was placed on waverers to join the Chartists. Payment of 5d. meant that a person received a card and it was widely suggested that the card would be the only guarantee of safety after the rising which now seemed inevitable. That was more particularly the case as smiths at Pillgwenlly and Beaufort, as well as other makeshift forges, began turning out hundreds of pike heads. Guns and bullet moulds were also collected. The pace of preparation quickened amidst an air of secrecy. There could be no doubt that some sort of major action was planned but it is likely that until the last minute, most of the Chartist supporters didn't know what. There was, however, consensus among the leadership that their first objective was to take Newport.

The march on Newport took place on a wet Sunday night, November 3rd. There were three main contingents — Frost led the group from Blackwood, Williams the men from Ebbw Vale and Nantyglo and William Jones the Pontypool marchers. The men with Williams gathered on the mountain above Ebbw Vale before moving down the valley, some in commandeered trams. They came from the works around Ebbw Vale, Brynmawr, Nantyglo and Blaina. The Blackwood men with Frost were swelled by contingents from Tredegar, Sirhowy and some from Rhymney. Both the column led by Frost and that under Williams converged on Risca. Some paused there to try to dry out weapons while others pressed on to the assembly point, the Welsh Oak near Pontymister. The Pontypool group did not arrive at the rendezvous and instead stayed to the north of Newport, apparently waiting for news of Frost's assault on the Westgate. This has led to questions about the commitment of Jones and some of those with him. There was, however, considerable activity between Pontypool and Blaenafon and it is plausible that the Pontypool men were being held in reserve to wait for the fall of Newport and then prevent troop reinforcements from arriving. They might then march on Monmouth and perhaps Abergavenny, Usk and even Brecon.

As the marchers advanced on Newport, the authorities there were preparing for conflict. Thomas Phillips, the mayor, had summoned a substantial number of special constables and also warned Capt. Richard Stack, in charge of the 70 infantrymen in the workhouse on Stow Hill, to be ready for an attack. The soldiers were billeted in the workhouse which was thought to be one of the main targets of the Chartists. Phillips eventually decided to go to the Westgate hotel with most of the constables and the Westgate inevitably became a key objective for the Chartists. As morning dawned, Phillips was told that between 4,000 and 5,000 Chartists were on the outskirts of the town. He immediately called for military help and one officer, two sergeants and 28 privates were moved from the workhouse to the Westgate where they joined 60 or more special constables. In addition, several Chartists who had been arrested during the night were also taken to the hotel. This concentration meant that any thoughts of a two pronged attack on the hotel and the workhouse were abandoned and Frost concentrated all of his force on the Westgate. At about 9.20, the Chartists marched into Commercial Road with at least the leading ranks in good order, five abreast. Frost and Charles Waters, the secretary of the Newport radical association were near the front as the marchers arrived. Inevitably, there is some confusion about the attack. What is clear is that a shot was fired and the Chartists in the front ranks rushed towards the Westgate. There was more firing as they forced their way into the hotel and more shots were exchanged in the lobby at which point several of the special constables fled. It has been estimated that some 80 shots were fired by the Chartists, many in the direction of the fleeing constables. As this fighting was going on inside, Chartists outside were using their pikes to pound on the shutters and break in windows of the hotel. By this time, several had been wounded on both sides. Up to this point, however, the troops had been held back in the long public room of the hotel. As the situation deteriorated, the soldiers opened fire, filing past windows and firing in sequence into the crowd in the street. This steady fire inflicted heavy casualties and the Chartists fell back to the nearest cover. Having forced back the main body, the troops then turned their attention to the attackers in the hotel.

Ordering the constables clear, they began firing volleys into the crowded hall of the hotel. By this time there was a cloud of heavy smoke through the hotel and under its cover some of the Chartists tried to launch counter attacks against the soldiers. In all, the battle at the Westgate probably lasted about 25 minutes. In the fighting several soldiers were injured, one of the sergeants miraculously surviving six slugs in his head. Phillips and several of the constables also received gun shot wounds. Although casualties on both sides were, and continue to be, disputed, it is probable that some 22 Chartists were killed with over 50 injured, some seriously. Among the dead was one of the soldiers who had deserted to the Chartists. As David Jones observes, the battle saw 'greater casualties on the civilian population than at any other time in the nineteenth or twentieth century.'[2]

In the aftermath, the Chartists withdrew in confusion. Frost was reported to have left the scene of devastation dazed and tearful. For some time after the conflict, there were widespread fears of further attacks but these did not materialize. Many of the Chartist leaders fled, some to America. The principal leaders, however, were arrested. Frost along with Waters was found in the house of the printer John Partridge in Newport. Jones was taken in a field near the Navigation Inn at Crumlin. Zephaniah Williams came closest to making his escape; he was arrested at Cardiff docks, actually on board a ship due to sail for Oporto. The three were tried in Monmouth on charges of high treason with proceedings beginning on the 31st of December 1839. They were convicted and on the 16th of January all three were sentenced to death. After almost three weeks in the condemned cell, however, their sentences were commuted to transportation for life. Almost immediately, on the 3rd of February, they were taken under heavy guard to Chepstow where they began the long journey which ended in Van Dieman's Land. Eventually all three were pardoned but only Frost returned, coming home in 1856.[3]

There are significant interpretative problems with these events at Newport. Some contemporary observers saw the conflict as an abortive nationalist revolt which would lead to a 'Silurian Republic'. They stressed the similarities with the Rebecca unrest and the Merthyr rising and made much of the 'conspiratorial' quality of the Welsh language. Certainly there is no question that the industrial valleys had been centres of alienation for a considerable period. Continuing violence on the coalfield, albeit on a reduced scale, seemed confirmation of endemic unrest in the region. Moreover, there was also a view that a successful rising in Newport was to be a signal for more widespread Chartist revolts in other regions. Coordinated risings were certainly discussed and there was an atmosphere of revolution on the continent which affected thinking.[4] The Merthyr rising, for example, came hard on the heels of 1830, a year of revolution in Europe. Events in Newport occurred mid way between that year of upheaval and the next of Europe's years of revolution—1848. The conspiratorial interpretation, however, has not found universal favour. In fact, the most widely accepted view, put forward by Professor David Williams, is that the events in Newport should be seen simply as a demonstration of strength by the Chartists. It is possible that the attack on the Westgate was the result of another monster meeting which became uncontrollable. It is difficult to avoid the conclusion, however, that the preparation, organization and armaments of the Chartists suggests something rather more. This view has recently been put forcefully by David Jones who sees Newport as an organized insurrection. When Newport was taken and secured, the Pontypool men would march on Monmouth and free Vincent and his colleagues. In Gwent, at least, the Charter would be won by force. The view of historians on these matters is reflected in the terminology which they use to describe the events in Newport. One school prefers to write simply of the march on Newport. Jones, on the other hand, characterizes events as the Newport rising and accepts the implications of that description.[5] On balance, it seems likely that Jones is correct. Whatever the case, the Chartist era marks a highly significant episode in the historical development of modern Gwent.

NOTES

[1] Robert Owen from Newtown in Powys had established the showplace New Lanark mill and argued strongly that social environment determined an individual's character. Committed to cooperatives, Owen became a driving force in the attempt to set up a national trade union movement. As has been seen, his Grand National Consolidated Trades Union collapsed in 1834.

[2] Jones, David J. V., *The Last Rising* (Oxford: 1985), p. 156. Benjamin Hall was first elected for Monmouth boroughs in 1831, but was unseated on petition by his opponent. He was returned in 1832. See Kissack, County Town, pp. 104-105.

[3] A variety of sources including contemporary press reports have been consulted. In the main, however, this chapter is drawn from Jones, David J. V., a challenging new account; Williams D., *John Frost: A Study in Chartism* (Cardiff: 1939), the standard authority; and Wilks, Ivor, *South Wales and the Rising of 1839* (London: 1984). It should be noted that some men were literally press ganged onto the march and others fled to avoid it.

⁴ See especially Jones, D. J. V., pp. 199-229. The rising of 1839 has an assured place in the folklore of Gwent. In 1933, unemployed men from the valleys marched on Newport to present their grievances to councillors because 'the Chartists were fighting for bread and life: so were the modern Monmouthshire men'. During the miner's strike in 1984, thousands of miners and their families also marched on Newport as their 'forebearers, the Chartists' had 145 years previously. The events continue to fascinate even in regions only peripherally involved with the rising. See for example, Wiles, Eric, *Chepstow and the Chartists* (Chepstow: 1985).

⁵ Wilks also describes events as a Rising, suggesting that the most useful term is Y cyfodiad—the rise. See Wilks, p. 183. Among the interesting points stressed by Wilks is the role of John Rees of Tredegar. Better known as Jack the Fifer, Rees is credited with leading the attack on the Westgate. Rees had emigrated to the United States and in 1835 he moved to Texas where he became involved in the revolution against Mexico. After taking part in the storming of San Antonio, Rees had been captured and was one of the few prisoners to escape the massacre at Goliad. After the revolt, he returned to Wales where he was caught up in the Chartist agitation. After the Newport rising, Rees eluded capture and eventually returned to Texas where he took a commission in the army of the Texan Republic and a grant of land near the Colorado river. Wilks believes that the military expertise of Rees is further confirmation that the Chartists at Newport were determined on an armed military confrontation. See Wilks, p. 139, 186-187 and 200; and Wilks, Ivor, 'Insurrections in Texas and Wales: the Careers of John Rees', in the *Welsh History Review*, 11, 1 (1982) pp. 67-91.

ZEPHANIAH WILLIAMS.　　JOHN FROST.　　JONES, THE WATCHMAKE

The attack on the Westgate hotel

The ironworks at Blaenafon
(Welsh Industrial and Maritime Museum)

Crawshay Bailey's ironworks at Nantyglo
(Welsh Industrial and Maritime Museum)

William Philby, 13-years-old, (left) on his first day as a miner at Big Pit, Blaenafon.
He died of pneumoconiosis in 1974

(Welsh Industrial and Maritime Museum)

The South Wales Borderers at Rorke's Drift

(Major R. P. Smith)

Piercefield, today a shell but once a house of world renown

Lady Llanover

(National Museum of Wales)

Construction of the Newport transporter bridge which opened in 1906

(Welsh Industrial and Maritime Museum)

The Farming Scene

While the significant, and at times stormy, process of industrialization accelerated, farming continued to be the main interest in many parts of Gwent. It is true that industry became a magnet drawing men into the valleys and that in the early stages much of the workforce came from Gwent or other parts of south Wales. It was, however, farm labourers who were being attracted to the industrial centres and not farmers. Had there been more farms available there would undoubtedly have been more farmers; the forge and pit face were second best options for most. Industry did, however, serve as a limited safety valve not only by offering alternative employment but also, as a consequence, by keeping agricultural wages relatively high. This was a factor reducing agricultural unrest which was intense in many regions. There was widespread distress in rural Britain following the Napoleonic wars. The end of the conflict brought a dramatic fall in agricultural prices and even farmers on productive land found themselves farming at a loss. Much arable land returned to waste and labourers were dismissed. By 1818 there were reports of 'great, unexampled and increasing distress' in Monmouthshire which was one of the more favoured counties in Wales. Fluctuation in prices continued to be a problem which by 1830 led to widespread revolt among agricultural labourers in the south and southeast of England. This disturbance eventually reached Gwent where 'swing' letters appeared and there were threats to hay ricks and the hated threshing machines which destroyed winter employment. These problems were most intense among corn producers, but prices of stock and dairy produce were also depressed. Nevertheless, Gwent was less affected than many regions. It was not, for example, caught up in the Rebecca agitation which saw attacks on toll gates in west Wales beginning in 1839.[1]

By mid-century, there was general improvement. The repeal of the Corn Laws in 1846, for example, did not cause immediate calamity for corn producers although many expected the worst at the time. In the event, there was relative prosperity largely as a result of accidents which insulated British farmers, at least until the end of the American civil war. Moreover, livestock farmers did even better with an era of prosperity lasting from 1853 until the late 1870s. In many cases, however, farmers in Gwent were less able to capitalize than some of their counterparts in other areas—the pace of innovation was slow by the standards of English farming. Nevertheless, changes came. Turnips and rape, for example, were fairly common in southeast Gwent from the beginning of the nineteenth century and crop rotation was well established on many farms. The rate of parliamentary enclosure was also slow with the 1776 Ifton enclosure being the only example in the county prior to 1797. At the beginning of the nineteenth century, the number of enclosures accelerated with acts like the large 1810 Trelech enclosure which involved the parishes of Trelech, Penallt, Mitchel Troy, Cwmcarfan, Llandogo, Tintern and Llanishen. [2]

In the early decades of the nineteenth century, rent levels were unrealistic and the additional burden of rises in local rates and taxes presented serious problems for tenants. With the improvement in farming fortunes in the 1850s, however, many tenant farmers began to do reasonably well. This was especially true for those with larger holdings. Moreover, Gwent farmers were especially well placed since the mining valleys provided a ready market for produce ranging from beef and mutton, through dairy products, to clover-hay and wheat straw. The fortunes of tenants is of prime importance because the vast majority of farm land in Gwent was in their hands. In 1887, 88.9 per cent of cultivated land in Wales, including Gwent, was farmed by tenants and only 11.1 per cent by owner-occupiers. These statistics are virtually identical to those for England and Scotland. Most land lords wished to avoid long-leases with fixed rents and the crisis years of the 1820s provided opportunities to establish annual tenancies. Within this system, large landowners like the duke of Beaufort continued to dominate the rural scene. A particularly iniquitous aspect of the system was that until the secret Ballot Act of 1872, tenants could be evicted for voting against their landlord's choices. In the 1870s, and probably generally throughout the nineteenth century, some 43 per cent of Gwent consisted of estates of over 3,000 acres and 22 per cent were estates over 10,000 acres. A large proportion of this land was occupied by tenants with rents representing a vital source of profit for the gentry. In parts of Gwent, royalties from mineral deposits could become even more important to the large land owners. Some members of the gentry did retain an active interest in farming and were instrumental in introducing innovation. Sir Charles Morgan of Tredegar was a case in point as he was an enthusiastic stock breeder on his farm in the 1840s. He also tried to encourage agriculture through the annual Tredegar show. In 1851, for example, Morgan provided 16 silver cups for winning entries to his show.[3]

Despite gentry domination, tenancy of a farm conferred status and farmers generally considered themselves to be a cut above the gwyr y tai bach, people of the little houses, who included farm labourers and other non-farming cottagers. Even when a farmer failed and was forced to become a labourer himself, he seems to have retained a measure of his prior status. It has been argued, however, that this gradation of status was not a difference of class and that there was a marked absence of class division between tenant farmers and their labourers on farms west of Offa's dyke.[4] One reason for the blurred distinction was that there was some scope for social mobility. Many labourers, while working for a wage on one farm, would acquire a small-holding of their own and thus gain a foothold in the farming community. On most Welsh farms, men were not assigned special work but were expected to adapt to every farm task. This notion of the 'all-round' labourer contrasted to the English model where the tendency was for men to be categorized as shepherds, stockmen, carters, spademen, etc. Additionally, nineteenth century occupational boundaries in Gwent have been demonstrated to have been particularly fluid both in agriculture and in other activities. Short-time work in the building trade, for example, forced stone masons to go jobbing as carpenters. The necessity of taking on a variety of tasks was especially pronounced with agricultural labourers. A Royal Commission on labour found that farm labourers in the county of Monmouthshire in 1892 undertook a wide range of additional employment. Three-quarters spent part of their time engaged in wood-cutting, quarrying and mine work. The practice was so widespread and the application of time so variable that it was 'difficult to determine whether they may be styled wood-cutters and quarrymen coming to the land for hoeing, harvesting and sundry piece work, or whether they are in the main agricultural labourers going to the woods, quarries and mines in the winter months.' Whatever type of work done, the working day was excessively long. A labourer could expect to earn something like 10s. per week at mid century with an average working day which would begin at 5 a.m. and end at 8.30 p.m. Indoor servants worked indefinitely from early morning till late at night with no real control of hours or working conditions. Nevertheless, this was the dominant employment pattern for the large majority of residents of rural Gwent throughout the nineteenth century.[5]

Slowly technological innovation changed farming practices. Through the first half of the nineteenth century farm implements in general use were limited to the plough and harrow. By mid-century, the iron swing plough had come into common use in Gwent. Seed was broadcast by hand throughout the century as corn drills were too expensive for all but the largest landowners. Nevertheless, sowing seems to have been done skilfully with seeds sprouting evenly on most farms. Until the end of the 1870s, hay was mown with a scythe and this was common practice on small farms into the 1890s. The scythe was also used for cutting oats and barley; a reaping hook was the implement used for cutting wheat until the 1890s. The traditional approach to threshing was by flail although by the 1870s even most small farms had introduced threshing machines driven by horse or water power. The benefits of mechanisation to the farmer were obvious. In mowing, for example, one man with a machine could outperform six men using scythes and the scythe was two or three times as fast as the reaping hook or sickle. Moreover, while adoption was slow, by the 1880s, all the modern machine harvesting aids with the exception of the combine harvester were already in production. The self-sheaving reaper-binder, for example, was available. Horse powered mowers, swathe turners for tossing and turning the hay, horse-rakes, stacking machines and elevators were coming into general use.[6]

Despite innovation, however, the relative prosperity which British farmers enjoyed until the early 1870s gave way to declining fortunes during the last quarter of the century. The artificial protection from the full impact of the repeal of the Corn Laws ended; the elevator system, the railways and widespread use of ocean-going steam ships permitted substantial import of foreign produce at low costs. This was especially significant with the recovery of the economy in the United States creating scope for massive grain production in the American middle-west. Naturally, in the early years it was corn producers who were hardest hit. From the mid-1880s, however, refrigeration techniques allowed importation of frozen and chilled meat. Not only that, dairy farmers began to face increased competition from imported European butter, cheese, bacon and eggs as well as from cheese brought from the United States. The impact of the ensuing agricultural depression was severe with marginal holdings being abandoned. Moreover, the farming decline came at the same time that mechanisation was already reducing the demand for manpower. The combined effect of the two factors was a wholesale exodus from the countryside. Rural workers were inevitably drawn into the industrial centres in a search for work and cottages and small farms were abandoned even in the traditionally most productive agricultural regions of Gwent. [7]

NOTES

[1] Howell, David, *Land and People in Nineteenth Century Wales* (London: 1978), pp. 1-6, 107; Williams, D., pp. 197-209; and Jones, D. J. V., *Before Rebecca* p. 59. At the beginning of the century there were instances of corn riots with bands of people near Chepstow seizing grain from farms and over 500 attempting to seize a corn barge in the Wye. The incidents are described in Jones, D. J. V., p. 26. See also Williams, D., 'Rural Wales in the Nineteenth Century' in Roderick (ed.) II, pp. 147-154. For the background to the Rebecca unrest see Williams, D., *The Rebecca Riots* (Cardiff: 1955).

[2] Howell, D., pp. 6-9, 16-17; Clark, A., 'Enclosures in Monmouthshire' in *Severn and Wye Review*, 2, No. 1, Summer 1972, pp. 27-31.

[3] Howell, D., pp. 2-23, 36-37, 58-59. Some 43% of Gwent, excluding waste, was occupied by estates of 1-1000 acres. Of this total, 12% were 300-1000 acres, 15% were 100-300 acres, and 16% were 1-100 acres. Percentages are drawn from Bateman, J., *The Great Landowners of Great Britain and Ireland* (London: 1883).

[4] Ibid. p. 93.

[5] 'Village Labour' in Samuel, R., (ed.) *Village Life and Labour* (London: 1975) pp. 3-26; and Howell, D., pp. 93-101. For village employment patterns in east Gwent, see Howell, R., pp. 42-45. See also Colyer, R., 'Conditions of employment amongst the farm labour force in Nineteenth Century Wales' in *Llafur*, Vol. 3, No. 3, pp. 33-41.

[6] Morgan, David H., 'The Place of Harvesters in Nineteenth Century Village Life' in Samuel (ed.) pp. 29-72; and Howell, D., pp. 128-132.

[7] Howell, D., pp. 7-9; Williams, D., 'Rural Wales' pp. 151-152; and Howell, R., p. 63 and n. 4, p. 92.

The Wye Valley Tour

Division into multiple tenancies was clearly a major feature of the management of large estates and the home farms of some members of the gentry did provide a setting for innovation. There was, however, another approach to land use and that was to establish large formal gardens with carefully contrived vistas. Tredegar Park with its oak avenue offers an example. Another was Piercefield near Chepstow which brought one corner of Gwent to national prominence and sparked a fledgling tourist boom which was sustained through much of the nineteenth century. Part of the appeal of the house and grounds was the close proximity of spectacular vistas over the Lower Wye Valley, especially the dramatic views from the summit of the Wyndcliff. A further bonus was the fact that the imposing ruins of Tintern abbey were nearby. As has been seen, in the mid-eighteenth century Piercefield was acquired by Valentine Morris and the innovative Morris decided to enhance the natural appeal of his estate. He engaged William Knowles, a Chepstow builder who had cleared the ruins of Tintern abbey for the duke of Beaufort, to lay out the grounds. Then Charles Howells, an innkeeper in Pont y Saeson, was made foreman for an ambitious plan to lay out walks in the grounds along the ridge overlooking the Wye. These walks, which can still be followed today, were punctuated by a series of vantage points. The first of these, following the route from the Chepstow end, was the Alcove which gave walkers a view of the Wye and Chepstow castle. The second viewing point was the Platform which offered impressive vistas from a raised platform, once enclosed in ornamental railings. Winding through the Alcove wood, walkers next came to the Grotto near the ramparts of the hillfort in the Pierce Wood. The Double View, which was the next stopping place, overlooked the great horseshoe of the Wye encircling Lancaut. Next, visitors would move on to the Halfway Seat which had been placed on levelled ground shaded by a large beech tree. Having rested there, walkers then pressed on through the Druid's Temple to the Pleasant View before entering the Giant's Cave. In the eighteenth century, the entry to the cave actually featured a guardian giant, at least to the more imaginative walkers. Sadly, the giant has since weathered away. Morris had swivel guns placed nearby to impress his visitors with the echo. From the cave, a lower path led to the Cold Bath, a stone building fed by a spring. The main walk, however, rose to the top of the cliff where another seat had been placed near two large beech trees on the edge of the precipice. The next stop was at the even more impressive drop at Lover's Leap, a sheer fall of about 180 feet protected by iron railings. After that was the Temple, a turret with an observation platform. The Temple was demolished in about 1800 but an even more impressive vista remained — the top of Wyndcliff which was literally the high point of the walks.[1]

The significance of these walks lies in the fact that they attracted international renown. An early nineteenth century 'gardening' entry in the Encyclopaedia Britannica, for example, featured Piercefield and described the view from the top of the Wyndcliff as 'astonishing sight! the face of nature probably affords not a more magnificent scene . . . ' Many were convinced to come and see for themselves. Among them were Thomas Gray and William Gilpin. The Russian ambassador, Count Alexei Pushkin, also visited. Turner painted Tintern abbey and Wordsworth composed his famous lines nearby. Coleridge was impressed enough with the Wyndcliff to see 'the whole world imaged in its vast circumference'. Another visitor was Joseph Banks who came to Piercefield for a second time in 1767, the year before he embarked as the botanist on Captain Cook's circumnavigation of the world. He wrote in his journal, 'I am more and more convinced that (Piercefield) is far the most beautiful place I ever saw'.[2]

Morris' enjoyment of his creation was cut short by his disastrous attempt to break the Morgan strangle-hold on local politics. His ensuing indebtedness led to the sale of Piercefield in 1784. This did not, however, mark the end of the house's great days. Lt. Col. Mark Wood, a member of Parliament and former chief engineer in Bengal, acquired the estate in 1794 and in 1798 virtually rebuilt the house adding a doric portico and wings. He maintained the walks which continued to be a major attraction. They were actually enhanced in 1828 when the duke of Beaufort had 365 steps built from the new Tintern turnpike road to the top of the Wyndcliff. He also built Moss Cottage, a thatched rest haven for visitors, replete with stained glass windows, at the base of the cliff. As late as the 1850s, visitors were advised to visit Piercefield and its celebrated walks. At about the same time, there were suggestions that Piercefield would be the ideal residence for the prince of Wales. In the event, it was not the prince, but John Russell, the owner of collieries in

Risca who acquired the mansion and grounds in 1856. Eventually, Piercefield passed to the Clay family and in 1926 the grounds became Chepstow racecourse.[3]

NOTES

[1] Howell, R., pp. 39-40; Waters, I., Piercefield, pp. 7-11. A useful record is the Piercefield Sale Particulars, 1819. See also 'Sketches in Monmouthshire' in Edwards, O. M., *Wales*, Vol. I. (Wrecsam: 1894) pp. 260-261.

[2] Howell, R., pp. 41-42; Waters, I., Piercefield, pp. 13-14; and Sale Particulars, 1819.

[3] Howell, R., pp. 41-42, 51-52; Waters, I., Piercefield, pp. 16-29; and *Taylor's Six Penny Guide to the Banks of the Wye* (London: 1854). See also Lucas, P., *Fifty Years of Racing at Chepstow* (Tenby: 1976) and Kissack, pp. 245-256. Moss Cottage was razed in 1962 but the 365 steps survive.

Industrial Dominance

Through the nineteenth century, industrial activity became progressively more dominant in shaping the character of Gwent. A particularly significant factor in this process was the advent of the railways. As has been seen, a network of canals and tramroads had formed a transportation system adequate for the early phases of industrialization. Soon, however, increasing demand required a new approach and steam locomotion seemed to offer the best solution. It is true that the first locomotive in Gwent, purchased by Samuel Homfray of the Tredegar Ironworks, had an uninspirational debut. It was intended to run on the company's tramroad, covering over twenty miles to Newport, and a test run was made in December 1829. It was an eventful journey — the nine ton locomotive was so heavy that it broke a succession of tram plates. The time required to repair the damage and replace the engine on the rails was such that the journey lasted virtually all day. Worse, however, was that a low tree branch in Tredegar Park knocked the chimney off and it was necessary to call in horses to tow the engine away. Despite these problems, however, in the following year the route was repaired and strengthened and the engine began a lengthy working life, eventually cutting freight costs by some 35%. The obvious appeal of such cost reductions led to a national explosion of railway construction which reached a peak in the 1840s. By 1843, this 'railway mania' gripped Gwent and local men, complaining of excess charges on the canal, began moves to establish a railway. The Canal Company, however, recognized that change was inevitable and pre-empted them by obtaining an act of Parliament empowering them to enter the railway stakes themselves in 1845. In 1848, a new era was heralded as the company changed its name to become the Monmouthshire Railway and Canal Company. By 1850, horse traction had virtually disappeared in Gwent and in August 1852, Dock Street station opened in Newport as the terminus for passenger trains connecting to Blaina and Ebbw Vale. A line also connected Pontypool to Newport and in 1854 passenger trains began to run from Blaenafon to Mill Street station in Newport. In that year, the Newport, Abergavenny and Hereford railway also began operations. Through the 1850s, the system expanded with connections eventually extending through the whole of the coalfield. These rail links to the industrial valleys were very important. Even more significant, however, was Brunel's south Wales railway and its link to the Great Western and important markets in England. The line from Chepstow to Swansea was opened in 1850 and in 1852 the Chepstow railway bridge was completed, providing the final vital link with the Great Western.[1]

This railway development stimulated Welsh industry in two ways. In the first place, the rate of expansion created a substantial and increasing demand for iron. In addition, it became easier for manufactured goods to be conveyed to wider markets. Furthermore, industrialists were able to import quantities of ores; Ebbw Vale and Dowlais were in the forefront of works exploiting the unusually rich ore deposits of northern Spain. Increasing demand also stimulated development of new production processes. An especially significant innovation was the perfection of the Bessemer process in 1856. Puddling was made obsolete by the new technique in which molten pig iron was poured into a pear shaped converter where hot air was blown at high pressure through pipes. Carbon and manganese impurities were burnt out and the purified metal was then poured into ingot moulds. The implications were far reaching because for the first time, steel could be produced on a large scale cheaply. Ebbw Vale and Dowlais quickly began producing Bessemer steel, largely for steel rails. Before long, Bessemer converters were also in operation at Rhymney, Blaenafon and Tredegar. The scene was not, however, one of universal expansion as these developments came hard on the heels of a crisis in the iron industry. By the end of the 1860s most of the British railway system had been completed and the demand for iron rails plummeted. To make matters worse, many of the leases, which had been granted for ninety-nine years in the mid eighteenth century, expired. Landowners were keen to gain a greater share of the profits and re-negotiated leases accordingly. The Dowlais lease, for example, which had been granted by Lord Windsor at £31 per annum, was renewed by the marquis of Bute, his great-grandson, for £30,000 per year. Such massive increases, combined with the expense of converting old plant to new processes, caused many works to close or, as at Nantyglo, to rely on coal and iron royalties. The crisis in iron production, however, did not extend to steel and plants which converted were able to exploit increasing demands from foreign railway development, especially in the Americas and India.[2]

The new steel making processes put high grade foreign ore at a premium although one technique did slightly reduce dependence on imports. In 1879, Percy Gilchrist, who was a chemist at the Blaenafon works, and his London-Welsh cousin, Sidney Gilchrist Thomas, devised a process for removing phosphorus by lining the converter with limestone or a similar material. There were highly significant implications as this process opened the door for exploitation of the substantial phosphoric iron beds in the United States and in Lorraine. Soon American and German industries flourished and foreign competition became intense. In the short term, however, the process did allow Welsh ore to be used in steel production. Even with this development, however, demand meant that dependence on imported supplies continued to grow. By the end of the century, some 340,000 tons of ore per year were imported into Newport. This reliance on imported material placed the works at the heads of the valleys at a marked disadvantage; it was not cost effective to move vast tonnages of ore twenty or thirty miles inland by rail. Inevitably there were casualties. In 1890, for example, the plant at Rhymney was dismantled and the company began to concentrate exclusively on coal production. In the following year, the Dowlais works was largely moved to East Moors at Cardiff. Firms like Ebbw Vale did not relocate but their competitive position was weakened as a consequence. New iron-using industries inevitably sought coastal locations. Another local industry which favoured locations with easy access to the coast was tin-plate manufacture. By the mid 1870s, south Wales enjoyed a virtual monopoly in production of tinplate with 18 tinworks in Gwent. Soaring demand created largely by the food canning industry in the United States led to fifteen years of boom in the industry. When large American tin deposits were discovered, however, there was a protectionist reaction. In 1890, the McKinley tariff effectively closed the American markets with severe consequences. Nevertheless, alternative markets allowed many firms to survive and in 1914 works were able to convert to production of shells and other armaments.[3]

Against this background of fluctuating fortunes in iron and steel, the other major element in the south Wales economy, coal, became progressively more dominant. Coal production statistics for the second half of the nineteenth century are remarkable. In 1854, 8½ million tons were produced; by 1913 that total had soared to 56.8 million tons with almost two-thirds of that total going abroad either as export or for fuel in ocean-going ships. In good times, wages in the mining industry were high and the demand for manpower seemed insatiable. As a consequence, a veritable army of men went down the pits and whole new social structures emerged in Gwent. With little alternative employment, sons followed their fathers as colliers and mining communities developed distinctive economies and life styles. Inevitably, the work underground was difficult and dangerous. Collapse, flooding and explosion took a heavy toll with a series of major disasters. For example, an explosion killed 268 men at Abercarn in 1878. Even more disastrous was the loss of life at Senghenydd where 439 were killed in 1913. It is not surprising in view of such disasters that militancy developed in the coalfield and that the miners were in the forefront of the new trade union movement. Depression in coal prices and a related attempt by owners to reduce wages provoked strikes in the early 1870s. In the aftermath, the sliding scale which tied wages to prices was introduced. Wages and prices were adjusted every six months by a joint committee of five employers and five representatives of the miners. The miners' leader, who acted as vice-chairman of the committee was William Abraham, better known as Mabon, from Cwmafan. Mabon was a prominent non-conformist leader and an active supporter of the eisteddfod. He was also a master orator in both Welsh and English. A strong advocate of conciliation and arbitration, Mabon dominated the Welsh miners' organizations. In 1885, he was elected to Parliament, eventually becoming a privy counsellor in 1911. Despite Mabon's influence, however, the sliding scale was opposed by many from the outset. This is hardly surprising since the price of coal fell in each of the first four years that the scale was in operation. It was only in 1882 that wages returned to the level of 1869. As a consequence, many miners began to agitate for a minimum living wage independent of prices and to campaign at the same time for an eight hour day. The leader of this agitation was William Brace from Risca who attacked not only the mine owners but also Mabon. The increasing dissatisfaction eventually led to a strike in April of 1898 for a ten per cent increase on the basic rate for calculation of the sliding scale. The strike failed after some six months, but it was important because defeat stimulated unity and there was an amalgamation of the seven miners' unions, including the Cambrian Miners' Association led by Mabon. The new, more unified grouping was styled the South Wales Miners' Federation which became affiliated to the Miners' Federation of Great Britain. Interestingly, Mabon's stature was such that he became the first president of the South Wales Federation with Brace as vice-president. The sliding scale ended in 1902 and the eight hour day was won in 1909 but unrest continued with major strikes in 1910 and 1912. [4]

It is obvious that the processes of industrialization, particularly the huge labour demands of coal production, had a profound impact on the economy and social structure of Gwent. By the end of the nineteenth century the Gwent and Glamorgan coalfield area was an industrial centre of world-wide importance. Inevitably, aspects of the traditional lifestyle of the region disappeared in the flood of thousands flocking into the valleys in search of work. The demographic changes were dramatic. At times during the century, the county of Monmouthshire had the fastest growth rate in Britain with Glamorgan close behind. The hundred years between the Napoleonic wars and the First World War saw the population of Wales almost quadruple. This growth was strikingly uneven as eventually nearly four-fifths of the people of Wales were concentrated in Gwent and Glamorgan. In the early years, much of this population influx was from other parts of Wales. By the time of the Scotch Cattle and the Newport rising, however, there was already substantial Irish immigration into the coalfield and as industrialization accelerated, immigration from the English regions also increased. The process was a protracted one. During the decade 1901-1911, the coalfield attracted a net total of 129,000 people, most of them from England. There were many consequences. Studies show, for example, that the lifestyle in the coalfield came to be dictated by industrial factors to a startling degree. From the 1870s, for example, Welsh marriage rates mirrored the price of coal. Perhaps the most significant of the changes, however, was that Welsh speaking communities were overwhelmed by the influx of non-Welsh industrial immigrants. [5]

NOTES

[1] A summary of railway development in Gwent can be found in Clark, II, pp. 145-151. See also Llewellyn-Jones, Frank, 'Wales and the Origins of the Railway Revolution' in the *Transactions of the Honourable Society of Cymmrodorion*, 1983, pp. 115-131; and Smith, L., 'The Broad Gauge Story' in the *Journal of the Monmouthshire Railway Society*, Summer 1985, pp. 36-49. There is considerable literature on railway development. For an introduction, see Barrie, D. S. M., *South Wales*—Vol. 12 in *A Regional History of the Railways*; MacDermot, E. T., *History of the Great Western Railway*, 2 vols. revised by C. R. Clinker. A 150th anniversary offering is Whitehouse, P. & St. John Thomas, D., (eds.) *The Great Western Railway* (London: 1984). For the construction of the Severn Tunnel, 1872-1886, see Walker, T. A., *The Severn Tunnel, Its Construction and Difficulties* (London: 1891). For a summary of coaching services preceeding the railway boom, see *Pigot's Directory for Monmouthshire*, 1835. A summary of east Gwent services is in Howell, R., p. 67.

[2] Williams, D., pp. 218-221; and John, pp. 164-165.

[3] Morris, John, 'Coal and Steel' in Roderick (ed.) II, pp. 177-184; Williams D., pp. 221-226; and Jones, G. E., pp. 169-170. For tinplate see Minchinton, W. F., *The British Tinplate Industry* (Oxford: 1957) and Stephens, T. (ed.) *Wales To-Day and To-Morrow* (Cardiff: 1907) pp. 361-368. Among other examinations of industrial developments in Wales are Thomas, Brinley, *The Welsh Economy, Studies in Expansion* (Cardiff: 1962); Humphreys, Graham, *Industrial Britain: South Wales* (Newton Abbott: 1972); and Minchinton, W. F. (ed.), *Industrial South Wales 1750-1914* (London: 1964). See also *Llafur*, the journal of the Welsh Labour History Society. When John Lysaght Ltd., showed interest in establishing a sheet steel rolling works on the east side of the Usk at Newport in 1896, moves were made to provide a crossing in Pillgwenlly. The result was one of Newport's best known land marks—the transporter bridge opened in September 1906.

[4] Williams, D., pp. 239-245; and Evans, G., pp. 408-409. The most comprehensive account of the Miners' Federation is Francis, Hywel and Smith, David, *The Fed: a History of the South Wales Miners in the Twentieth Century* (London: 1980). For detailed studies of the development of the coal industry see Jevans, H. S., *The British Coal Trade* (London: 1915); Morris, J. H. & Williams, L. J., *The South Wales Coal Industry, 1841 to 1875* (Cardiff: 1958); and Jones, P. N., *Colliery Settlement in the South Wales Coal Field 1850-1926.* (Hull: 1969). See also Evans, E., *Mabon* (Cardiff: 1959). Brace was elected to Parliament in 1906.

[5] Williams, Gwyn, *When Was Wales?* pp. 173-181; Williams, D., p. 245; and Thomas, Brinley, 'The Growth of Industrial Towns' in Roderick (ed.) II, pp. 185-192. For a detailed study of income variations in relation to industrialization, see Thomas B., *Migration and Economic Growth* (Cambridge: 1954). See also Jones, Ieuan, *Explorations and Explanations, Essays in the Social History of Victorian Wales* (Llandysul: 1981), especially pp. 222-225,

Schools and the Blue Books

The nineteenth century was clearly a period of rapid social change. Among the factors accelerating this change, while at the same time ameliorating its worst effects, was education. The circulating schools along with a number of charity and Sunday schools offered some basic educational provision at the end of the eighteenth century. In general, however, schooling was minimal. The situation improved marginally at the beginning of the nineteenth century as a result of two movements. Joseph Lancaster was a Quaker educator who began the Royal Free Schools of Borough Road in London. Under the patronage of George III, he pioneered a system of non-sectarian education available to the whole community. The monitorial system, in which older pupils drilled younger ones, was developed and young men and women were trained to start new schools.[1] Schools based on the system which Lancaster preferred to call the British system, but which was widely known as Lancasterian, soon began to spread. In 1806-7, Lancaster toured south Wales and in the aftermath several schools were established including one at Abergavenny. Slightly later, in 1812, steps were taken to set up a school at Usk where a local committee hoped to accommodate 150 boys, 100 of whom were to be sons of the labouring poor who would be educated free. James Davies was appointed headmaster and was sent to the new school at Abergavenny for a crash course in school mastering. Davies is an interesting example of an early nineteenth century schoolmaster. Born in Grosmont, he had been a weaver for some 15 years. An unhappy marriage, however, seems to have been a factor in causing him to leave and become a pedlar before opening a small shop in Usk. It was with this unpromising background that he was selected to undertake his new role as schoolmaster.[2]

Nationally, the Lancasterian schools soon faced serious competition. Dr. Andrew Bell, an Anglican clergyman, was highly critical of the non-sectarian approach of Lancaster. Claiming that he was the real originator of the monitorial method which he had used at Madras in India, Bell was instrumental in the establishment of the 'National Society for Promoting the Education of the Poor in the Principles of the Established Church' which began to establish 'Madras schools' throughout the country. The ambitious aim of the group was to ensure that every parish in England

and Wales had a school to educate the poor under the watchful eye of the established church. Significantly, the financial resources of the church provided backing for the plan. Soon existing church schools entered into union with the National Society and new schools were established. In Wales, the diocese of Bangor was the first to avail itself of grants from the National Society with a school opening in 1812. The diocese of Llandaff was slower off the mark but in June 1814, the first National School opened at Devauden with James Davies as schoolmaster. Davies' new appointment was something of a personal gamble as he gave up the guaranteed stipend at Usk. He may have anticipated the growing financial difficulties at Usk which caused that school to fail as a Lancasterian venture and, 'due to a lack of funds' become a National School in 1823. Whatever his reasons, the move seems to have suited him, because Davies remained at Devauden until 1848. Then, at the age of 83, he left to take over another school at Llangattock Lingoed where he remained until his death in the following year. One of the most interesting and slightly surprising aspects of Davies' long career is that despite his unpromising background and a reputation as an autocratically stern disciplinarian, he was a success as a schoolmaster. Many others who became teachers with similarly unlikely backgrounds proved to be singularly unsuccessful in the task.[3]

Partially because of poor teaching, educational provision in many parts of Gwent remained woefully inadequate. Moreover, there was considerable opposition to the National Society from the large number of non-conformists throughout the county who objected to their children being taught the catechism and having to attend church on Sundays. On the other hand, most were too poor to bear the cost of establishing a Lancasterian school. Not surprisingly, education continued to be erratic and was frequently below standard. The poor quality of education was a factor in the government's decision to send inspectors to report on the educational conditions in Wales in 1847. Regrettably, however, the three-man commission turned their investigation into a vendetta against the Welsh language. Their inspection has been colourfully, and accurately, described as an 'ego-trip of three arrogant and ignorant barristers probably buttonholed by some militant clergymen'.[4] The commissioner who investigated parts of the county of Monmouthshire, Jellinger Symons, was particularly venomous in his hatred of the language. He reported that 'it is not easy to overestimate its (the language's) evil effects' and confidently proclaimed that 'there is no Welsh literature worthy of the name'. This assessment was made on the strength of no knowledge of the Welsh language at all. There is no doubt, however, that English speaking clergymen supported the commissioners. The incumbent of Trevethin, for example, concluded with respect to the language that 'the sooner it becomes dead the better'. The reports of the commissioners, now known as 'Brad y Llyfrau Gleision' (treachery of the Blue Books) caused a storm of protest through Wales. Not only was the language attacked, but also the morality of the common people was impugned. Symons described the people as repulsively rude and savage and, while excepting Newport, found industrial regions teeming with grime and 'evil rampant in every shape'. Not surprisingly, non-conformists who prided themselves on an upright lifestyle nurtured through regular attendance at chapel reacted indignantly. Nevertheless, the government was happy to accept the report and when the compulsory Education Act of 1870 required all parents to send their children to school, it was already clearly established that English should be the only language in those schools.[5]

The consequence of these developments was that education, while becoming more widely available and generally of a higher standard, emerged as an important factor undermining the Welsh language. It is possible that the language could have survived the onslaught of the Blue Books but it could not withstand the double blow of compulsory English language education and the overwhelming demographic changes associated with industrialization.

NOTES

[1] Williams, J., and Hughes, G., *The History of Education in Wales* (Swansea: 1978), especially pp. 28-44, 83-104. See also Davies, E. T., *Monmouthshire Schools and Education to 1870* (Newport: 1957).

[2] Ibid. pp. 83-104. Davies prompted two interesting studies. One was by Sir Thomas Phillips, the mayor of Newport wounded in the Westgate hotel, who wrote *The Life of James Davies, a Village Schoolmaster* in 1850. See also, Society for Promoting Christian Knowledge, *Davies of Devauden* (London: 1841).

[3] Ibid. pp; 92-93, 105-126; and Powell Jones, T., *The Contribution of the National Society to Welsh Education, 1811-1870* (doctoral thesis, University of London: 1967), especially pp. 23-24.

[4] Williams, Gwyn, *When Was Wales?* p. 208.

[5] Ibid. pp. 208-209; Williams, D., pp. 254-257; and Davies, E. T., Schools, pp. 105-106. See also Probert, W. J., 'The Blue Books of 1847 and a Tredegar Minister' in *Gwent Local History*, No. 59, Autumn 1985, pp. 10-22. This is a good account of Ieuan Gwynedd, a leading critic of the commissioners. Williams Forster's Education Act was a first step to compulsion although a decade was required before the objective was fully achieved.

The Welsh Language

The decline of Welsh was clearly very important in the historical development of Gwent. The rate and nature of the decline is, however, difficult to trace with confidence. As has been seen, Gwent was strongly Welsh in speech through the seventeenth century. There are suggestions that at least in some regions a fairly rapid decline set in during the following century. On the other hand, there are counter indications which demonstrate that the language continued to thrive in many parts well into the nineteenth century. There was certainly a strong base for the language as the eighteenth century began. A demand for Welsh books, for example, was reflected in a decision by Thomas Jones, who had emerged as a major distributor of Welsh books. In 1695, he engaged Samuel Rogers, an Abergavenny bookseller, to supervise distribution of books to shop keepers through south Wales. His competitors were forced to follow suit and John Rhydderch soon began distribution from Pontypool.[1] Books were not only being purchased, some were being written and published in Gwent. In 1740, one of the first printing presses in Wales was established in Pontypool; among the books published there was a collection of hymns by Morgan John Lewis of Blaina and Edmund Williams from Cwm Tyleri. The real test of strength of the language, however, was its persistence among the ordinary people of Gwent and there is considerable evidence to suggest that its use was widespread. In the 1750s, for example, English newcomers to Caerleon were forced to organise their own Baptist chapel because services in the town were conducted in Welsh. In the 1770s, bilingual services were held in St. Woolos church in Newport and, in the following decade, a row broke out between Bishop Barrington and Sir Charles Morgan over the incumbent of Bassaleg. The bishop disputed Morgan's right to nominate a candidate for the position and particularly objected to the fact that the suggested candidate was unable to speak Welsh. The eventual compromise was for the Morgan candidate to be accepted but only on the condition that he would agree to learn Welsh. When Viscount Torrington visited Gwent in 1781, he found that in the town of Monmouth 'Welsh is as much understood and spoken as English'. A Trelech inn keeper told Torrington that while English was spoken in that village, six miles distant people 'understood it no more than my dog.' Six years later, Torrington paid a second visit to the region, and reported that as much Welsh as English was spoken in Newport. There was certainly an awareness of Gwent's Welsh traditions in and around Newport. At the end of the century, for example, Evan Evans, curate of Bassaleg, commemmorated the ancient traditions of that place with his Welsh classic 'Llys Ifor Hael' (court of Ifor Hael).[2] He wrote:

Llys Ifor Hael, gwael yw'r gwedd yn garnau	The court of Ifor Hael, sad its aspect, a heap of stones
Mewn gwerni mae'n gorwedd,	lying within the meadow,
Drain ac ysgall mall a'i medd,	a blight of thorns and thistles has taken it,
Mieri lle bu mawredd.	brambles where there was grandeur.

At the beginning of the nineteenth century, Iolo Morgannwg claimed that the highest percentage of monoglot speakers in Wales was to be found in Monmouthshire. Iolo's observations must be treated with caution but there seems to be an element of truth in the claim. Certainly William Coxe, in the celebrated account of his travels through Monmouthshire published in 1801, reported a substantial use of Welsh. He suggested that natives of the western parts of the county 'unwillingly hold intercourse with the English, retain their ancient prejudices and still brand them with the name of Saxons'. In many cases, Coxe needed the services of an interpreter and near Croespenmaen found himself sorely in need of one. Seeking food for himself and his horse, Coxe could at least manage the key word, cwrw (beer) but could proceed no further until a bi-lingual labourer chanced by.[3] Coxe's discomfort is not surprising; in 1815, for example, half of the population of Blaenafon spoke no English at all. At about the same time, even in areas like Trevethin Welsh was the sole language of the parish church. In 1829, the *Monmouthshire Merlin* complained of the 'doggedness with which the lower class of inhabitants' clung to the Welsh language. Moreover, in the 1820s Welsh is known to have been spoken even in Llandogo on the banks of the Wye. As has been seen, Welsh was thought by many to be an important factor in the Newport rising. It was the pace of industrialization, however, which undermined this obviously strong attachment to the language. By 1841, while 61% of the population of Blaenafon continued to be Welsh speaking, only 21 out of a population of 5,115 were unable to speak English. In areas like Pontypool, the process of Anglicisation was proceeding even more rapidly. Nevertheless, there were many who resisted the trend. There was in fact a literary flowering in the western valleys from about 1830 to 1870. There were a succession of eisteddfodau which produced poets of note like John Davies, Brychan, who lived in Tredegar. Davies worked as a miner but then became a bookseller and publisher. Among his publishing ventures was a series of anthologies of songs and ballads of Gwent and Glamorgan including the Llais Awen Gwent a Morgannwg (the voice of the Muse of Gwent and Glamorgan) which appeared in 1852. A particular impetus to the Welsh cultural renaissance in Gwent was provided by the Abergavenny Cymreigyddion Society which was founded in 1833. The Society encouraged literary activity and campaigned for Welsh medium education. Among the important members of the group was Thomas Price, Carnhuanawc, the vicar of Cwmdu near Crickhowell, who was a historian and expert on Breton culture. Others included T. E. Watkins of Blaenafon and Thomas Watkins, Ynyr Gwent. The Cymreigyddion actively encouraged Welsh literature in Gwent and produced several books on history and literature. Among the books and periodicals published in Gwent were those of Robert Ellis, Cynddelw, a Baptist minister in Sirhowy who adjudicated at eisteddfodau and edited several Welsh periodicals. Another editor was William Roberts, Nefydd, also a Baptist minister. He set up his own press in Blaina where he produced *Y Bedyddiwr*. Other names of note include Aneurin Jones, Aneurin Fardd, an expert on Welsh classical metres, and William Williams, Gwilym Gwent, the Tredegar born blacksmith who became one of the most popular Welsh composers of his era. Interestingly, both Jones and Williams eventually emigrated to the United States where they continued to write in Welsh.[4]

Of all the Welsh literati of Gwent, the best known is undoubtedly William Thomas, Islwyn. The poet was born in Ynysddu in 1832 and attended schools in, among other places, Tredegar and Newport. Reputedly, the language of the home in Islwyn's childhood was English but this did not prevent him from establishing a lasting reputation as a Welsh poet. His grief over the death of the girl he intended to marry, led to the epic poem 'Y Storm' which is regarded as his masterpiece despite the fact that it was written when he was only 21 years old. In later life Islwyn, who was ordained in 1859, concentrated his talents on the fixed topics of various eisteddfodau where he won several bardic chairs.

Islwyn has been described as the greatest Welsh poet of the nineteenth century and Saunders Lewis, who argued that Islwyn's importance was on a par with that of Wordsworth, described 'Y Storm' as one of the leading achievements of nineteenth century European literature.[5]

The nineteenth century flowering of Welsh culture in Gwent enjoyed backing from some unlikely quarters. Among supporters of the Cymreigyddion of Abergavenny was the Dowlais iron master Sir Josiah Guest and his wife Charlotte. She gained a special place in Welsh literary history for her translation of the tales of the Mabinogi, although her misunderstanding of the plural has enshrined the work as the Mabinogion. Perhaps even more important were the activities of Lord and Lady Llanover. As has been seen, Lord Llanover, Benjamin Hall, was member of Parliament for Monmouth boroughs and as commissioner of works he gave his name to Big Ben, the world famous clock. He and his wife learned Welsh and became patrons of Welsh culture, encouraging eisteddfodau and campaigning for Welsh language education. Lady Llanover, who took the name Gwenynen Gwent (the honey-bee of Gwent), became an active patron of Welsh culture and it was she who institutionalized the now widely recognized Welsh national dress for women.[6]

Influential patrons and a deep seated tradition were not, however, sufficient to stem the irresistable tide of population movement into Gwent which eventually all but swamped the language. It is true that even in the middle 1890s over 60% of the population in the western valleys were Welsh speaking. Nevertheless, the decline was striking. Symptomatic was that a progression of Anglican churches abandoned Welsh in their services including Llanfoist in 1850; Cwmyoy, 1854; Mamhilad, 1860; Llanfair Cilgedin near Llanover, 1860; Llanfihangel Pontymoel, 1870; Llanellen, 1877; Goytre in the 1880s; and Trevethin, 1890.[7] Two points are clear, one is that the flood of industrial immigration in the last half of the nineteenth century and the first decade of the twentieth century overwhelmed the Welsh language in most parts of Gwent.[8] Equally obvious, however, is that there was a strong Welsh tradition in Gwent throughout the nineteenth century. Works from Gwent were important in the broader literary history of Wales, and the Welsh language and culture were vital formative influences on the people of Gwent.

NOTES

[1] Jenkins, G., pp. 248-249.

[2] Roderick, Alan, 'A History of the Welsh Language in Gwent' in *Gwent Local History*, No. 50, Spring 1981, pp. 28-36.

[3] Coxe, William, *An Historical Tour Through Monmouthshire* (London: 1801), pp. 1, 213-222. See also Evans, G., p. 357.

[4] Roderick, Welsh Language, II, 51, Autumn 1981, pp. 2-11; and Humphrey, E., pp. 132-133. See also Howell, R., pp. 49-51 and Thomas, Mair, *Afiaith yng Ngwent* (Cardiff: 1978). The latter study, in Welsh, is an excellent overview of the Abergavenny Cymreigyddion.

[5] Lewis, Saunders, *Meistri'r Canrifoedd* (Cardiff: 1973) pp. 357-371. The leading works on Islwyn are in Welsh and include Jones, D. Gwenallt, *Bywyd a Gwaith Islwyn* (Liverpool: 1948) and Gruffydd, W. J., *Islwyn* (Cardiff: 1942).

[6] Evans, G., pp. 378-379 and Williams, D., pp. 272-273.

[7] Roderick, Welsh Language, II, pp. 17-24. See also Southall, J. E., *Wales and Her Language* (Newport: 1892).

[8] There was a residual Welsh dimension encouraged in part by the National Eisteddfod which was held at Newport in 1897, Abergavenny, 1913, Pontypool in 1924 and Ebbw Vale in 1958. The language survives in places to the present day and has enjoyed a limited revival in the 1980s. A pocket of retention in eastern Gwent is described in Howell, R., pp. 50-51. An excellent recent study of the language in industrial districts is Williams, Sian, *Agweddau Cymdeithasol ar Hanes yr iaith Gymraeg yn ardal ddiwydiannol Sir Fynwy yn y Bedwaredd Ganrif ar Bymtheg* (Ph.D. Aberystwyth: 1985).

The 'Myth of Monmouthshire'

Late Victorian Britain was a confident and aggressive society. Confidence grew from the economic success which greeted the world's first industrial nation. As has been seen, the industrial might of Gwent and Glamorgan were key contributors to that success. By the last two decades of the nineteenth century, foreign competition was eroding Britain's trading position, but not enough to produce self-doubt. Aggressive competition in the industrial sphere, also extended into politics and foreign policy. Here too, Gwent played a role. The Usk-born naturalist, Alfred Russel Wallace, devised a theory of the origin of the species through natural selection independently of Charles Darwin. The evolutionary model was first made public in a joint paper read by Wallace and Darwin at the Linnean Society in July 1858. Intense intellectual controversy followed and soon non-scientists began to try to apply the idea of 'survival of the fittest' to nation states themselves. The application of 'social-Darwinism' helped to provide psychological justification for Empire. Obviously there were other factors with economic and strategic questions generating an imperial mentality which became a dominant theme in the late Victorian era. It is perhaps not surprising, given the emphasis on Empire, that many men from Gwent found themselves involved in military campaigns in a series of remote outposts through the world. In 1879, for example, the 24th Regiment of Foot, soon to be styled the South Wales Borderers, lost 21 officers and 581 men in the disaster at Isandhlwana during the Zulu war. Shortly afterwards, however, men from the regiment earned a lasting place in military history by defending the mission station at Rorke's Drift where a force of 140 men, 30 of them incapacitated, fought off over 4,000 Zulu warriors. Among the 24th Regiment there were a disproportionate number of men named Williams and Jones, five of each at Rorke's Drift. Two of these Joneses, Robert and William, held one end of the embattled makeshift hospital as the Zulus attacked the mission station. At the other end of the hospital was John Williams, the son of an Abergavenny policeman. Williams, supported by Henry Hook, who held off the Zulus, pickaxed his way through the internal walls of the burning building and dragged most of the patients into the room held by the Joneses and then away to safety. All four men were among the eleven recipients of the Victoria Cross; the highest number of VCs ever awarded for a single action. [1]

The imperial ideal had wide appeal in the jingoistic '80s and '90s. The idea of being a part of a great imperial system struck a responsive cord and people in Gwent were not immune. Moreover, the desire to be counted among the imperial Britons fueled inclinations which were already strong in some quarters. With the gentry there had been a long process of anglicisation with some, like the dukes of Beaufort, establishing family seats in England and abandoning their Welsh roots completely. Many industrialists came to Gwent from England and remained English in their outlook. For these and others with social aspirations all things English became desirable while those things Welsh were not. As a consequence, there was an attempt to refine what might best be described as the myth of Monmouthshire—the notion that the administrative anachronisms in the Act of Union had in some way made the county non-Welsh. The distinction implied in the description Wales and Monmouthshire was nurtured. For these people Wales was a place apart— frequently beginning somewhere in the county but always at a place apart from wherever they happened to be. The influence of this 'Saesraeg' mentality was such that a degree of official sanction was given to the notion. An important example was the Welsh Sunday Closing Act of 1881 which was a specific response to pressure from Welsh non conformists. Significantly it was the first time that an act of Parliament established a separate legal principle for Wales as distinct from England. The attorney-general, however, negated, wrongly in law, the inclusion of Monmouthshire within the operation of the act. It was not until 1921 that the provisions were extended to the county. [2]

In the event, however, it was impossible to sustain the myth. Quite apart from its cultural and historical traditions, Gwent's economic structure was so intertwined with that of Glamorgan that the two could not be separated realistically. This point was stressed in the Welsh Intermediate Education Act of 1889 which included Monmouthshire. The act was particularly important since by the First World War, Wales was covered with a network consisting of some hundred 'county' secondary schools. As a consequence of the act, secondary education in Wales was significantly better developed than that of England. [3] Another uniquely Welsh question was disestablishment. With some three quarters of the population being non conformists, there was widespread opposition to the established church. Disestablishment finally became law in 1914 but provisions of the act were postponed until after the war. The church in Wales finally came into existence in 1920; the disestablished church was entirely separate from Canterbury with its own archbishop. Re-organization followed with the creation of the new diocese of Monmouth in 1921 and the diocese of Swansea and Brecon in 1923.[4]

Special legislation for Wales was a reflection of growing national awareness which in the early 1890s found expression in Cymru Fydd, the Young Wales movement. Gwent had a key, albeit negative, role in the movement's later stages. In its infancy, Cymru Fydd stressed education and culture. Soon, however, it became more political and this produced conflict between two leading Liberal M.Ps. who had helped to form it — David Lloyd George and D. A. Thomas, later Lord Rhondda. From the outset, there was suspicion of the nationalist intentions of the movement in the southern industrial ports of Swansea, Barry, Cardiff and Newport and this scepticism was manipulated by Thomas in his conflict with Lloyd George. When Lloyd George attempted to bring his message into the south, the opposition was mobilized. The climax came at Newport in January 1896. The meeting was packed with a large delegation from Glamorgan and Lloyd George was shouted down. The rift proved irreparable and helped institutionalize tension between north and south.[5]

As these developments were unfolding, politics within Gwent changed slowly but dramatically. The election of 1868, the first under the provisions of the second reform act, is frequently seen as a political watershed. Its effects, however, were limited, especially in rural constituencies where the Ballot Act of 1872 was needed to lift the threat of eviction. The Reform Act of 1884 was also particularly significant in extending electoral reform into rural regions and increasing the numbers of constituencies; the county of Monmouthshire gained a fourth MP. The general trend in the county under the changed system was obvious when, in the election of 1885, three of the four seats were taken by the Liberals. South Monmouthshire, however, was won by F. C. Morgan. Remarkably it was not until the Liberal landslide of 1906 that Colonel Ivor Herbert captured the seat and ended the centuries old domination by the Morgans of Tredegar. Within the county, another important change emerged from the Local Government Act of 1888. On 1st April 1889, the Monmouthshire County Council came into being with 48 councillors and 16 aldermen. The Council was, however, reduced in size by Newport's decision to exercise its right, based on a population in excess of 50,000, to become a County Borough in 1891. The 1894 act governing Parish Councils further extended the system of local government.[6]

With the Morgan stranglehold on parliamentary politics broken and a system of elected local government established, Gwent had taken on a much more modern aspect during the first decade of the twentieth century. That was also true of another pursuit — rugby. Lloyd George may have overstated the case when he complained that south Walians had sunk into a 'morbid footballism'. There is no doubt, however, that the game had come to hold a special fascination. There was even a nationalist dimension to the game, especially after a first 'triple crown' was won in 1893. The Edwardian era saw a 'golden age' in which, between 1901 and 1912, the triple crown was captured six times. The climax to these glorious days was undoubtedly the victory over the previously unbeaten New Zealand All Blacks by 3—0 in December 1905. Gwent clubs were in the fore-front of this era of success; Welsh rugby was dominated by the big three teams — Newport, Cardiff and Swansea. Pontypool, too, emerged as a major force. It is important to understand that rugby had quite literally become more than a game. In contrast to the other home countries, Welsh rugby was not a public school monopoly. Instead it was one of the few pursuits which crossed class barriers. The team which beat the All Blacks, for example, included miners and tin-plate workers playing side by side with professional men like Dr. Teddy Morgan who scored the winning try. Of the great players during this era, none made a greater impact than Arthur Gould of Newport. On Gould's retirement, a grateful Newport honoured him with no less than a house as a testimonial. Uproar ensued as the other home unions cried professionalism and a temporary breach occurred as Wales continued to uphold the decision. While the position was virtually untenable in terms of the rules of amateurism, the Welsh stance was widely supported in Wales as an expression of self determination. When the other unions relented, the feeling of vindication transcended sport.[7]

NOTES

[1] The fullest account of the Zulu war is Morris, Donald, *The Washing of the Spears* (London: 1973). Joseph Williams died covering the retreat of John Williams and the hospital patients.

[2] Morgan, K. O., *Wales in British Politics 1868-1922* (Cardiff: 1970) pp. 42-43; and Morgan, K. O., *Rebirth of a Nation: Wales 1880-1980* (Oxford: 1981) pp. 36-37.

[3] Williams, D., pp. 278-280; Morgan, K. O., Politics, pp. 98-104; Morgan, K. O., Rebirth, p. 37. Monmouthshire miners agreed to a 1/- levy to support the National Library of Wales.

[4] The disestablishment controversy was protracted. See Morgan, K. O., Rebirth, various references but especially pp. 184-185; and Williams, D., pp. 266-267.

[5] Morgan, K. O., Rebirth, pp. 112-122; Williams, D., pp. 280-283; and Evans, G., pp. 411-418. See also Coupland, R., *Welsh and Scottish Nationalism* (London: 1954) especially pp. 226-232 and William, George, *Cymru Fydd: Hanes y Mudiad Cenedlaethol Cyntaf* (Liverpool: 1945).

[6] Morgan, K. O., Politics, especially p. 219; Williams, D., p. 262; and Clark II, p. 203. Councillors were elected to a three year term, aldermen, making up a quarter of the total, were chosen by the councillors—for details see Ambrose, G. P., *Monmouthshire County Council 1888-1974* (Newport: 1974) and Warner, John, *Local Government in Newport 1835-1935* (Newport: 1935). Background material is presented in Wallace, R., 'Wales and the Parliamentary Reform Movement, 1866-68' in *The Welsh History Review*, Vol. II, Dec. 1983, No. 4, pp. 469-487. See also Clark, J. H., *Reminiscences of Monmouthshire* (Usk: 1908) pp. 142-143.

[7] Morgan, K. O., Rebirth, pp. 73, 133-134; and Smith, David and Williams, Gareth, *Fields of Praise: the official history of the Welsh Rugby Union* (Cardiff: 1981).

War and Decline

The great turning point of modern history was the First World War. The conflict certainly heralded changed circumstances for Gwent; an era which began with death and disequilibrium, ended in widespread decline. The first major upheaval was of course the war itself. The horrors of the conflict are well known but it is important to remember that men from Gwent were involved from the outset in the worst of the fighting and continued to be engaged in all theatres throughout the war. In 1914, for example, men of the South Wales Borderers were involved at Mons where they prevented a major breach in the British line before joining with the Welsh Regiment, recruited largely from Glamorgan, in a costly counter attack. At the first battle of Ypres, the Borderers attacked the village of Poelcappelle and then grimly held their position as the German army counter attacked and broke the line. Eventually the gap was closed but that was possible only because the Borderers had held their trenches. In 1915, the Borderers were caught up in the second battle of Ypres; by this time the casualty toll had reached such levels that territorial units were also heavily involved. Among them were men from the Monmouthshire Regiment, some of whom held a position along the front of the Frezenberg ridge. They were in shallow trenches because in places it was only possible to dig some three feet before becoming hopelessly water logged. In this death trap, they underwent some of the heaviest bombardment yet seen in the war and were wiped out virtually to a man. Further along the line, the First Monmouthshire stubbornly refused to surrender when surrounded. The hundreds killed as a consequence added to the approximately 60,000 British casualties in the battle. At about the same time as the fighting around Ypres, other men from the South Wales Borderers were involved in the even more disastrous and futile Gallipoli landing. On April 25th, a battalion of the Borderers went ashore from trawlers and took the cliffs at Morto Bay. They then attacked and captured Turkish trenches across flat, open ground and held their advances against two fierce counter attacks. In the end, however, the whole hopeless enterprise was abandoned as a costly failure. The Borderers who survived the devastation at Gallipoli returned to the western front only to find themselves leading an advance into the carnage of the Somme. By this time there was a full Welsh division at the front with many men from Gwent making up its numbers. Later in 1916, other Borderers and men from the Royal Welch Fusiliers led a major advance in Mesopotamia.[1]

The human cost of such fighting was immense. The lengthy lists of the dead which are found in virtually every church and chapel in Gwent still bear testimony to a loss of life on a scale which is barely comprehensible. Because of the enormity of the losses, it is easier to understand the human tragedy in terms of individuals. A particularly poignant example of the sorts of sacrifices being demanded was a soldier who survived. Cliff Price was a championship distance runner who many expected to achieve international mastery on the track. Holder of the Welsh record at one and two miles, this Newport Harrier was Welsh champion at one and four miles and in 1913-14 he became Welsh senior cross-country champion. The times which he recorded suggested that he was poised on the brink of international dominance. Sadly, however, he was unable to develop his potential. When the war came, he enlisted and was sent to France. Wounded in battle, he was invalided home. As soon as he was able, however, he returned to the front. Once again Cliff Price returned home to the village of St. Arvans, but this time having lost a leg in the fighting.[2]

With large numbers of young men killed and maimed, there was serious social disequilibrium in Gwent. One consolation, however, was that there was economic prosperity since the basic industries of coal and steel were vital to the war effort. Moreover, artificially stimulated industries continued to thrive briefly after the war since steel was needed for rebuilding and coal mines in Belgium and France had been destroyed in the fighting. This short-lived boom also applied to agriculture where prices rose steadily from 1918 through 1920. An important consequence of these high prices was that many of the gentry took advantage of the situation by selling off their estates and a new pattern of owner occupation emerged. The halcyon days of boom, however, collapsed dramatically in the early 1920s and Gwent was among the hardest hit regions. The problem was an over reliance on the basic industries of coal, iron, steel and tin-plate. When these industries faltered, there was no alternative employment and localised depression became inevitable. Steel manufacturing in the valleys away from the coast was among the first casualties. The works at Blaenafon closed in 1922 with the blast-furnace section following two years later. Tredegar followed suit and in 1929 steel making stopped in Ebbw Vale. The decline in tin-plate manufacture was slower but was nevertheless pronounced.[3]

This decline in the metal industries was serious but depression in coal was devastating to the economy of Gwent. The contraction in demand for coal was marked. During the war, the United States captured many traditional markets for Welsh coal including Canada and Latin America. The best alternative markets were France and Italy but they were receiving large amounts of German coal as a part of reparation payments. When the government decontrolled the mines in March 1921, a three month strike ensued. In the aftermath, coal owners reacted to declining markets by making savage cuts in wages—in some areas by as much as 75%. These reductions, combined with rising mass unemployment, engendered deep bitterness in the coalfield. An expression of that hostility was the General Strike in May 1926. The strike, however, collapsed after nine days. Nevertheless, the miners remained solid for months before being, quite literally, starved back to work. The overall decline of coal production during this period was dramatic. When the First World War began, the south Wales coalfield was producing 56.8 million tons and employing 234,000 miners. A quarter of a century later, as the Second World War broke out, production had fallen to 35.3 million tons by only 136,000 miners. In 1923, a total of 6,769,493 tons of coal were exported from Newport. Only two years later, that total had already been reduced to 4,850,364 tons. By 1936 exports through the port had fallen to just 2,555,713 tons.[4] This serious decline in the economy of Gwent through the 1920s was intensified by the world depression which began in 1929. By the end of 1930, unemployment in the Rhymney-Tredegar area stood at 27.4% while in Newport it was 34.7%.[5] Nor did the situation improve. By 1935 the unemployment rate in Merthyr Vale had soared to over 50%.

While depression in industry continued, there was a similar decline in agriculture. The decision taken in 1921 to repeal the Agriculture Act and end state subsidies providing guaranteed prices for wheat and oats was a blow to cereal farmers. It is true that sheep farmers did relatively well in the middle 1920s but livestock prices generally fell. Since many freeholders had acquired their farms fairly recently by taking out large mortgages, the situation rapidly became critical. The only hope for many farmers was to turn to milk production and an increasing use of motor transport, allowing collection from farms, helped to make this option a viable one. The establishment of the Milk Marketing Board in 1933 was also particularly important. The Board acted as an intermediary between the farmers and the milk companies and paid a 'pool price' for milk. Subsidies allowed production to increase and prices to rise. It must be stressed, however, that profits for producers were small. Furthermore, milk production required less manpower than arable farming and increasing mechanisation put additional farm labourers out of work. As a consequence, the drift from the land which had been pronounced before the war continued through the inter war period. [6]

Government intervention mitigated the agricultural crisis. Eventually there were similar attempts to bolster industrial areas. In December 1934 portions of the coalfield were declared 'special areas' where new industries would be encouraged. The most important example of government intervention was at Ebbw Vale. In 1935, Richard Thomas and Company announced their plan to open an American style strip mill at Redbourn in Lincolnshire. The idea was to concentrate the processes in the production of steel and tin-plate on a single site. A vigorous lobbying campaign, however, applied pressure to bring the plant to Wales instead. An argument advanced was that the industry had a social obligation and that the plant should be placed in an area of industrial decline. As a consequence, the company acquired the derelict steel works at Ebbw Vale and began production there in 1938. A number of other smaller alternative industries were also introduced including the Northern Aluminium Company plant at Rogerstone, the Pilkington Brothers glass making works at Pontypool, and the Weston Biscuit Company at Llantarnam. Firms like the Saunders Valve Company and Metalitho, tin box manufacturers, were established in Cwmbran. [7] Such developments mitigated the effects of depression to a small extent. For many people, however, there was no option but to seek work in less depressed areas. For example, as the world-wide depression began to bite more deeply in 1931, the county of Monmouthshire, which had been such a magnet for work-seeking immigrants, showed a net loss of 22,000. [8]

The political beneficiary of the discontent arising from this industrial decline was the Labour party. In 1918, the county had been divided into six parliamentary constituencies including Newport, Abertillery, Bedwellty, Ebbw Vale, Monmouth and Pontypool. Before the war, the Liberals had dominated the politics of the region. At Pontypool in 1918, however, an Asquith Liberal stood against the Lloyd George Liberal who was pledged to the national government. The ensuing split gave victory to Labour and presaged a new political era. As industrial discontent grew, the support for Labour intensified. By 1923 Labour was polling over half the votes in the county and the industrial valley seats soon became among the safest Labour bastions in the country. At the County Council level, too, many seats became virtual sinecures for Labour councillors.[9] In the end, however, neither a political re-orientation nor limited government intervention could reverse the industrial decline which dominated the inter war years. Regrettably, the event which finally broke the depression was another war.

NOTES

[1] There are numerous accounts of the war. A good introduction can be found in Taylor, A. J. P., *English History* (Oxford: 1965), pp. 1-114. In addition to the official histories, Hammerton, Sir J. A. (ed.) *A Popular History of the Great War* (London: 1934) offers a detailed, if over glorified, account. See especially II, pp. 414-416 and VI pp. 474-480. The Welsh dimension is central to Nicholson, Ivor and Williams, Lloyd, *Wales: its part in the war* (London: 1919). The Welsh Guards were formed in 1915.

[2] Howell, R., p. 66.

[3] Williams, D., pp. 286-287; Morgan, K. O., Rebirth, pp. 216-217; and Davies, John 'The End of the Great Estates and the Rise of Freehold Farming in Wales' *Welsh History Review*, Vol. 7, No. 2, Dec. 1974.

[4] Williams, D., pp. 287-288; Morgan, K. O., Rebirth, pp. 283-288; and Clark II, p. 176.

[5] Morgan, K. O., Rebirth, p. 212-215.

[6] Ibid. pp. 219-220 and Williams, D., p. 289.

[7] Williams, D., pp. 292-294; and Clark II, pp. 179-181.

[8] Williams, D., pp. 290. See also Williams, G., *When Was Wales?*, pp. 252-260.

[9] Morgan, K. O., Rebirth, pp. 272-303; Clark, II, p. 173; and Jones, J. G., 'Welsh Politics Between the Wars: The Personnel of Labour' in *Transactions of the Honourable Society of Cymmrodorion*, 1983, pp. 164-183.

Modern Gwent

During the Second World War, men from Gwent were again involved on all fronts. There was, however, a new dimension to this war since aerial bombardment brought civilian populations into the front line. The industrial centres in Gwent were more fortunate than other parts of south Wales with Swansea, Cardiff and Pembroke docks being particularly hard hit. Nevertheless, there were attacks and loss of life. Stress became an important factor; in Newport there were no fewer than 480 air raid warnings during the first year of the air war. On 26th June 1940, a single bomber made the first actual attack on Newport, dropping a string of bombs which damaged an oil depot. Even when attacks were directed against other targets, there were still dangers. For example, in September 1940 a bomber crashed into a house on Stow Park Avenue killing two children. Residential areas were sometimes targets of the blitz. Houses in Lewis street, Albion street and Capel street were hit by bombs in one attack. In another, a total of 37 died in Newport; some 30 of whom were killed when bombs hit houses on the corner of Eveswell street and Archibald street. [1] Other parts of the county were less directly threatened although even rural districts were never totally immune. For example, in October 1939, Chepstow race course was converted to a landing strip and aircraft maintenance facility. As a consequence, it became a potential target and badly directed bombs were later dropped into woods nearby. [2] During the war, a total of 51 people were killed during air attacks on Newport with 63 seriously injured. [3] The war had other consequences in Gwent. Air defence batteries dotted the landscape. Additionally, evacuees were moved into rural districts and land girls were introduced into several villages, some marrying and staying after the war. [4]

Despite these difficulties, there was significant economic expansion during the war years. With large numbers of men in the forces and local industries caught up in the war effort, unemployment, the scourge of the thirties, disappeared from the valleys. This industrial activity was carefully controlled. The Essential Work Order of 1941, for example, directed work into plants with important defence contracts like the Royal Ordnance Factory at Glascoed near Pontypool. Arguably the most significant industrial development, however, was the decision of the government to take over operational control of the coal mines in

1943. The changes were implemented by Gwilym Lloyd George, the minister for fuel and power. A National Coal Board was established to control production targets and conduct collective bargaining. A consequence of nationwide wage bargaining was the incorporation of the South Wales Miners' Federation into the National Union of Mineworkers in January 1945. The NUM formulated a Miners' Charter calling for the abolition of piecework methods of payment and the establishment of a national day-wage system. Nationalization was of course a key feature and one which was important in the election manifesto of the Labour party which swept to victory in 1945.[5]

Nationalization had been presented as a panacea but there were many who cautioned that more was needed if the depression which followed the First World War was to be avoided after the Second. An important body in planning for post-war re-structuring was the Welsh Advisory Council of the Ministry of Reconstruction. Particularly important in the view of the Council was broadening the industrial base so that south Wales would no longer be over-dependent on the old traditional industries like coal, steel and tinplate. That concern was a well-founded one since the major Welsh industries had actually declined despite the economic expansion caused by the war. Tinplate production, for example, dropped; in 1939 there were 26,000 workers in the industry, in 1945 only about 10,000. Even more strikingly, coal production had fallen from 35.3 million tons to 22.4 million. In 1938 there were 136,000 miners employed in the south Wales coalfield but by 1944 that number had fallen to 112,000. In an effort to rejuvenate the economy and to broaden the industrial base, the Board of Trade was given coercive powers to restrict the expansion of industry in the south-east and in the Midlands and to encourage it to move into less favoured areas like south Wales. Some significant results were achieved like location of Girlings' car components with a workforce of some 3,000 in Cwmbran. Other successes included Monsanto Chemicals in Newport, the Alfa-Laval milking machine factory in Cwmbran, and British Nylon Spinners at Pontypool. Cwmbran was particularly well placed to attract new industry since it was established as a new town under the 1946 New Towns Act. In 1949, the Cwmbran Development Corporation was set up to integrate the almost five square miles which included old Cwmbran, Pontnewydd and Croesyceiliog into a new town.[6]

Development of new industry helped promote a boom. Even the traditional industries — coal, steel and tinplate — enjoyed some prosperity as did the docks. On 1st January 1947, the mines were nationalized to great rejoicing in the valleys where public ownership was seen as the realization of a dream of fifty years standing. There was also important investment in pits like Hafod-yr-ynys. Soon, however, it was recognized that the National Coal Board approached its task like any other large corporation and by the mid 1950s there were problems with production norms and fears of pit-closures in the geologically difficult south Wales coalfield. Nevertheless, there were other major nationalizations, notably, though temporarily, through the creation of the Steel Board in 1951. This development came at the end of a post-war boom which lasted from 1945 until 1952. Throughout this period, unemployment was relatively low and by 1951, the Board of Trade's controller for Wales was able to report proudly that unemployment had been largely conquered save for a few 'small pockets'. Significantly, however, one of those pockets was the region between Blaenafon and Merthyr.[7]

In agricultural districts, wartime shortages stimulated food production and the farmers' improved circumstances were sustained by the 1947 Agriculture Act which provided guaranteed prices. Increasing production, steady price levels and expanding markets allowed even upland farmers to prosper. Production of both milk and breeding sheep, for example, doubled between 1947 and 1968. This relative prosperity, however, did not stabilize rural communities in Gwent and the pattern of movement away from the land continued. There were several contributory factors. One was that farm holdings became progressively larger as farmers tried to be more competitive; farms of twenty acres or less virtually disappeared. Furthermore, mechanization accelerated, further reducing the demand for agricultural labourers. The scale of the exodus is reflected in the fact that full-time male farm workers in Wales declined from 31,301 in 1951 to 14,237 in 1968. Derelict cottages throughout Gwent stand as testimony to this demographic revolution in the countryside.[8]

If the change in rural regions was dramatic, the transformation of industrial districts was even more so. By the mid-1950s, there was widespread concern in the coalfield and the 1960s justified that concern. The Welsh mining industry declined from 106,000 men employed in 1960 to only 60,000 in 1970. By 1979 the workforce had plummeted to only about 30,000. It is true that the decline was not a steady one. The oil crisis of 1974 placed a premium on coal at a time when militancy in the coalfield was growing. There were national miners' strikes in 1972 and 1974. In the aftermath, there was acceptance, reluctantly in the south Wales coalfield, of a productivity scheme. Investment followed in projects like the 'linked pits' programme of north Gwent. Nevertheless, over the next decade the general pattern of contraction continued with the protracted strike of 1984 fought largely over the issue of pit closures. There was a similar decline in the steel industry despite an air of optimism in the early 1960s. Particularly important in stimulating optimism was the massive new strip mill at Llanwern which began production in 1962. By the end of 1963, the plant was producing at a rate of 1,400,000 tons of crude steel per year and had a potential of almost two million tons. Nevertheless, by the late 1960s, the steel industry, re-nationalized in 1965, was in decline. World demand contracted and foreign competition intensified. As the industry declined intense pressure was put on Ebbw Vale. Despite its rescue in 1938, the plant remained at a severe competitive disadvantage because it was far from the sea and there was no room to expand on the site. As a consequence, the long history of steel making at Ebbw Vale finally ended in 1975-6 creating large scale redundancies. Problems continued and in the early 1980s, even Llanwern was threatened by rationalization schemes although its future was made to appear more secure by investment in 1985.[9]

As K. O. Morgan has demonstrated, the decline in the traditional industries has been a key feature in the recent history of south Wales. He suggests that another is the fact that economic and employment opportunities have tended to become concentrated in an increasingly narrow coastal strip. Again, the interaction between Gwent and Glamorgan is obvious as the new industrial centre extended from Barry to Llanwern, including Newport and Cardiff. Both Newport and Cardiff increased in population by about 40% in the fifties and sixties, a period in which the growth rate in the rest of south Wales was only about 5%. The drift of industry toward Newport and Cardiff was accelerated by the completion of the Severn bridge which was opened in September 1966. Despite tolls and increasing repair costs to the bridge, it and the M4 became an industrial lifeline for south Wales. The Heads of the Valleys road along the northern rim of the coalfield helped to link the old industrial centres but this could not check the predominance of the coastal belt.[10] It was certainly in this area that the silicon chip boom, with a variety of computer software companies, began. In the early 1980s, there were hopes that this new technology would offer a bright and secure industrial future for Gwent. Difficulties with several firms, however, soon suggested that these early expectations had been overly optimistic.

There were other important implications for Gwent in the development of the M4 and other improvements in the road system. The Beeching Report on the railways in 1963 led to the sad devastation of rural rail services. For the more fortunate, however, there was soon an increasingly available alternative means of transport; the rapid growth in ownership of private motor cars dramatically increased mobility. The implications were far-reaching for rural Gwent. Villages which had always been largely self-contained agricultural communities were transformed by the process best described as 'commuterization'. Large new estates sprang up, especially in scenic areas like the Lower Wye Valley, and employment patterns changed out of all recognition. Villages with easy access to the motorway began to attract residents who were employed in what would previously have been unthinkably distant places like Newport, Cardiff, Bristol and, in a few instances, even London.[11]

During the post war period, political patterns remained largely unchanged with Labour retaining its grip on the industrial heartlands of Gwent. Among the M.Ps. returned for the valleys was the member for Ebbw Vale, Aneurin Bevan, who earned a secure place in history as the principal architect of the National Health Service. In the 1980s, safe Gwent seats produced successive leaders of the Labour Party, Michael Foot and Neil Kinnock. At the county and district level too, Labour continued to dominate despite occasional shocks in the valleys of Gwent and Glamorgan like a Plaid Cymru majority on the Rhymney district council in 1976. While voting patterns remained largely unchanged, however, the institutional framework of politics did not. A significant development, for example, was the creation of a secretary of state for Wales. The Welsh Office, which was established in 1964, was initially given powers over housing and local government, road transport and aspects of local planning. In 1969 these powers were extended to include health and agriculture with education being added shortly thereafter.[12] This limited degree of devolution was important; so too was the reorganization of local government. Provisions which came into effect in 1974 established a new county pattern in Wales. In the southeast, there were only minor adjustments to boundaries but there was a particularly significant symbolic change — the county once again officially became Gwent. This adoption of the new, old name represented a recognition of the historical and cultural traditions of the region.

NOTES

[1] Western Mail, *Bombers Over Wales* (Cardiff: n.d.) pp. 25-28. Stress factors are considered in Morris, J. 'Morale Under Air Attack: Swansea, 1939-1941' *Welsh History Review*, Vol. 11, June 1983, No. 7, pp. 358-387.

[2] Howell, R., pp. 66-67.

[3] Western Mail, Bombers, p. 45.

[4] Howell, R., pp. 66-67.

[5] Morgan, K. O., Rebirth, pp. 299-301.

[6] Ibid. pp. 307-317; and Clark, II, pp. 185-187, 195-196.

[7] Morgan, K. O., Rebirth, pp. 311-313. Steel was nationalized in 1951, denationalized in 1953, and re-nationalized in 1965.

[8] Ibid., p. 326; and Howell, R., pp. 63, 92 n4.

[9] Morgan, K. O., Rebirth, pp. 315, 317-322.

[10] Ibid. pp. 322-326.

[11] Howell, R., pp. 67-69. See also Rees, G. L., 'Passenger Transport in Wales' in *Transactions of the Honourable Society of Cymmrodorion*, 1976, pp. 82-101.

[12] Morgan, K. O., Rebirth, pp. 388-389, 401. For a detailed study of the referendum campaign and devolution debate, including the significant negative role of the county councils, see Foulkes (ed.), *Welsh Veto: The Wales Act and the Devolution Referendum* (Cardiff: 1982). See also Foot, Michael, *Aneurin Bevan* (London: 1975).

Conclusions

Gwent presents a rich historical pageant. Throughout the millenia, strong cross cultural contacts have been at work; invasion, conflict and population movements have shaped the region. From the ancient Beaker People to the industrialists of the eighteenth century, social change has resulted from the introduction of new ideas and innovative economic techniques. Nevertheless, there has also been a strong element of continuity. The Romans, for example, clearly transformed Gwent, but a native tradition survived to reassert itself with the emergence of the kingdom of Gwent. The Normans created a dominant new cultural synthesis which flourished within marcher society. Traditional lifestyles, however, were sustained, at times even in the shadow of the Norman castles. The native Welsh dimension in the tripartite power structure of the March not only survived, but in a sense, eventually triumphed through men like William ap Thomas.

The most comprehensive transformation in local society was caused by the industrialization of the late eighteenth and early nineteenth century. The large population movements associated with the emergence of Gwent-Glamorgan as a centre of the industrial revolution, undermined traditional culture to an unprecedented degree; rapid industrialization created the new cultural synthesis which shaped lifestyles right into the twentieth century. Moreover, problems of de-industrialization continue to be dominant themes in the 1980s as Gwent attempts to find a new role and a modified economic base. Even within the upheavals associated with industrialization, however, a thread of continuity can be traced and there are elements in the historical patchwork which link ancient past to present. It has been noted that the re-adoption of the name Gwent for the region was symbolically important. That is a point which should be stressed because one conclusion which is inescapable from an examination of the history of Gwent is that the underlying Welsh tradition has frequently been decisive. Even in the wake of an upheaval on the scale of the Norman conquest, native culture endured. Similarly, in the industrialized nineteenth century Gwent remained closely linked to Glamorgan and, even as the language declined, both were strongly influenced by a common Welsh cultural inheritance. At times there has been a reluctance to recognize the legacy of this common experience. However, whether or not agencies like the modern County Council support the National Eisteddfod or accept a role in communal activities like the Royal Welsh Show, there is no escaping the fact that Welsh influences have shaped the history of Gwent. It is true that there were times at which Gwent was a focus of English history, particularly when powerful marchers asserted themselves against the king. In such instances, as in later periods like the civil war and the Newport rising, local developments in Gwent were important in shaping the general course of British history. Nevertheless, despite the refinement of the 'myth of Monmouthshire' by some elements in the population, Gwent remained an important part of Wales. At times, occurrences in Gwent were critical in the course of Welsh history. Similarly, Welsh influences were often decisive in the course of history in Gwent. Welsh traditions were a major factor shaping marcher society, dictating the nature of cultural institutions in Gwent into the nineteenth century, and influencing the social response to industrialization. As a consequence, it is only within the broader context of Welsh history that the development of Gwent can ever be fully understood.

Appendices

'Arthurian' Gwent

One of the most persistent literary themes has been Arthur and the tales of Camelot. From Malory to Walt Disney, the Arthurian legend has continued to fascinate. Since in several instances the tales of Arthur have focused on Gwent, it is interesting to see what, if any, actual connection can be demonstrated. Inevitably, the first question which must be considered is the historicity of Arthur and the paucity of evidence makes the matter a difficult one. The most important source is the British Museum holding identified as Harleian MS 3859 which is popularly described as Nennius' History of the Britons but which Leslie Alcock prefers to identify as the British Historical Miscellany. Within this miscellany is an Easter annal with a cycle ending at the death of Rhodri ap Hywel Dda. Easter annals were tables showing the date of Easter over a number of years. Their significance lies in the fact that marginal entries frequently recorded contemporary events. In year 72 of the miscellany cycle, which would be AD 518, there is an entry for the battle of Badon 'in which Arthur carried the cross of our Lord Jesus Christ on his shoulders for three days and three nights and the Britons were victors'. Another entry, for year 93 or AD 539, refers to 'the strife of Camlann in which Arthur and Modred perished'. There can be little doubt that in the first entry, scuid (shoulder) was a scribal error for scuit (shield). These entries in the Easter annals are particularly significant because the large number of other names appearing—including popes, kings, saints and princes—are all genuine. Consequently, Arthur and Modred must be accepted as historical characters or presented as the only two fictitious entries among a hundred or so verifiable ones. Moreover, there is additional material which supports the historicity of Arthur. A separate section of the miscellany is a battle listing poem which describes the battles of Arthur against the invading Saxons. In them his status is explained in a passage which says that he fought 'with the kings of the Britons but he himself was leader (duke) of battles'. To many minds, this suggests that Arthur should be viewed as the leader of a mobile cavalry force who had adopted the Roman title dux bellorum. Other evidence complements this picture. Early Welsh poetry lends support to the existence of a leader called Arthur. In the Gododdin, for example, Gwawrddur is praised as a warrior although his exploits could not compare with those of Arthur who was clearly viewed as a standard. We are told that 'he glutted black ravens on the wall of the fort, though he was not Arthur'.[1] Another interesting bit of circumstantial evidence from the Welsh material is that the name Arthur is unknown among the Welsh ruling houses before about 600. There is then a spate of Arthurs including Athrwys ap Meurig in Gwent.[2] The implication of this evidence is that there was indeed a military leader named Arthur who resisted the Saxon advance in the early sixth century.

Assuming therefore that Arthur was an historical figure, the second question which must be considered is whether he had links with Gwent. Superficially, there is evidence to suggest that he could have done, notably in the romances appended to the tales of the Mabinogi. These stories are quite specific in identifying Caerleon as Arthur's court. 'Owein, or the Countess of the Fountain', for example, begins, 'The Emperor Arthur was at Caer Llion ar Wysg'. Similarly in the story 'Peredur Son of Efrawg' we find that 'Arthur was in his chief court at Caer Llion ar Wysg'. The story of 'Gereint and Enid' begins:

> Arthur was accustomed to hold court at Caer Llion ar Wysg and at one time he did so through seven Easters and five Christmases. Once he held it there at Whitsuntide, for it was the most accessible spot in his kingdom, whether by land or by sea.'[3]

Similarly in the Welsh triads, the three principal courts of Arthur are identified as 'Caerleon-on-Usk in Wales, and Celliwig in Cornwall, and Penrhyn Rhionydd in the North'.[4] The ninth battle in the battle listing poem is also placed at Caerleon.[5]

In view of this material, the Arthurian link with Caerleon would appear clear. It has certainly been persuasive to some including Tennyson who travelled to Caerleon in search of inspiration for his 'Idylls of the King'. Local tradition also pointed to the ruined amphitheatre as the original model for the Roundtable. Before the Tourist Board leaps to a campaign presenting Caerleon as Camelot, however, it must be noted that there are serious problems with taking any of this material as historical evidence. The single most significant problem is Geoffrey of Monmouth. Geoffrey must be seen as one of Gwent's leading literary figures as his *History of the Kings of Britain* enjoyed immense success and was the prime influence in launching the Arthurian legend. However, while as

literature, Geoffrey's work was a classic, as history it was virtually use-
less. Nevertheless, because of wide-spread influence, the myths of
Geoffrey became institutionalized as history. This is important because
while the tales of the Mabinogi were based on ancient oral traditions,
they were probably not written in their present form before about 1300
—well after Geoffrey. Geoffrey localized his hero in Caerleon and the
later romances followed his lead. Even in the description of the principal
courts in the triads, earliest versions seem to favour Aberffraw to Caerleon.[6] The simple fact is that none of this material can be taken as evidence for any Arthurian link with Gwent.

There is a temptation to leave the matter at this, simply concluding
that any Arthurian connection with Gwent is unproved and unprovable.
On the other hand, there is a small seed of evidence which requires
further thought. As we have seen, Giraldus Cambrensis was an astute
observer who can, as a rule, be taken as a reliable source. In general, he
was no admirer of Geoffrey of Monmouth who he openly derided.
Nevertheless, he happily accepted that 'the great Arthur's famous court'
had been at Caerleon. This would at least suggest that local tradition
claimed Arthurian links, something not surprising since many regions
made similar claims. The description of Caerleon by Giraldus, however,
is of considerable interest. He wrote:

Caerleon is of unquestioned antiquity. It was constructed with great
care by the Romans, the walls being built of brick. You can still see
many vestiges of its one-time splendour. There are immense palaces,
which, with the gilded gables of their roofs, once rivalled the magnif-
icence of ancient Rome . . . There is a lofty tower, and beside it
remarkable hot baths, the remains of temples and an amphitheatre.
All this is enclosed within impressive walls, parts of which still
remain standing.[7]

For some time, it has been fashionable to reject this description as an
uncharacteristically inaccurate piece of reporting by Giraldus. Because
it was assumed that Caerleon had been dismantled by the Romans before
their withdrawal, it followed that there could be no buildings on the
scale described by Giraldus. The recent excellent archaeological work
done by David Zienkiewicz, however, has now demonstrated that the
massive Roman baths at Caerleon were still standing at the time that

Giraldus visited the town. The discovery justifies confidence in Giraldus as an observer and confirms that impressive structures stood in Caerleon for centuries after the departure of the Romans. None of this, of course, pertains directly to the question of Arthur. What we are left with, however, is an indication that there was a twelfth century folk tradition that placed Arthur in Caerleon. Moreover, we now know that Caerleon remained an impressive site at the time that the historical Arthur was conducting his mobile campaigns against the Saxons. It is, therefore, conceivable that Caerleon could have served as one of a series of Arthurian foci. There is no confirmation of this association with Gwent, or with any other purported Arthurian sites, but the possibility cannot be rejected out of hand.

NOTES

[1] There are numerous books which deal with the historical Arthur — some in a fairly fanciful fashion. The best serious study is Alcock, Leslie, *Arthur's Britain* (London: 1973). See especially, pp. 29-88.

[2] Davies, Wendy, Miscellany, p. 67.

[3] A readily obtainable translation is Jones, G. & Jones, T., (tr.) *The Mabinogion* (London: 1949). Also widely available is Gantz, Jeffrey, (tr.) *The Mabinogion* (London: 1976).

[4] Bromwich, Trioedd, p. 211.

[5] Alcock, p. 63.

[6] Bromwich, p. 211. References to Aberffraw may not be particularly important since the bards of Gwynedd were as keen as Geoffrey to localize Arthur. For a concise discussion of Geoffrey's impact, see Jarmon, A. O. H., "Geoffrey of Monmouth and the 'Matter of Britain' " in Roderick (ed.) I, pp. 145-152.

[7] Journey Through Wales, 1, 5.

The Kings of Gwent

The main line of the Kings of Gwent can be traced with some confidence from the charters in the Book of Llandaff. Inevitably, the dates during which any king was active must be highly approximate. As has been discussed in the text, the reigns of kings sometimes overlapped.

King	Approximate dates
Main Ergyng Dynasty	
Erb	c525—55
Peibio ap Erb	c555—85
Cinuin ap Peibio	c585—615
Gwyddgi ap Peibio	c585—615
Gwrgan ap Cinuin	c615—45
The Kings of Gwent (Main Dynasty)	
Tewdrig	?—c625
Meurig ap Tewdrig	c620—65
Athrwys ap Meurig	c625—55
Ithel ap Athrwys	c655—705
Morgan ap Athrwys	c670—710
Ithel ap Morgan*	c710—45
Ffernfael ap Ithel ap Morgan**	c745—75
Rhodri ap Ithel ap Morgan	c748—70
Meurig ap Ithel ap Morgan	c748—70
Rhys ap Ithel ap Morgan	c748—70
Gurgauarn ap Ffernfael	c770—805
Athrwys ap Ffernfael	c770—805
Hywel ap Rhys***	c856—86
Arthfael ap Hywel	c886—916
Cadell ap Arthfael	c916—42
Gruffydd ap Owain ap Hywel	c916—35
Cadwgan ap Owain ap Hywel	c920—50
Morgan ap Owain ap Hywel (Hen)	c930—74
Idwallon ap Morgan	c974—1005
Rhys ap Owain ap Morgan	c1005—1035
Hywel ap Owain ap Morgan	c1010—1043

Meurig ap Hywel	c1035—1065
Cadwgan ap Meurig	c1055—1072
Gruffudd ap Llywelyn****	c1055—1063
Caradog ap Gruffudd	c1065—1081

Kings of Gwent Iscoed

Nowy	c950—60
Arthfael ap Nowy	?—c980
Rhodri ap Elised ap Nowy	?—c1005
Gruffydd ap Elised ap Nowy	?—c1005 [1]

* Sub kings appear to have disappeared by the reign of Ithel.

** Ffernfael had strong Gwent links and his brothers may have concentrated their interests in the west.

*** The gap preceding Hywel results from a break between the Second and Third sequences in the Llandaff Charters. For a portion of this period a different branch of the ruling family was represented by Meurig ap Arthfael, c848—74; and Brochfael ap Meurig, c870—910.

**** As is discussed in the text, Gruffudd ap Llywelyn incorporated Gwent into a Welsh nation state.

NOTES

[1] This chronology is drawn largely from Davies, Wendy, Charters, pp. 73-80; and Miscellany, pp. 66-73.

The Castles of Gwent

There is a remarkable concentration of castles in Gwent. In addition to massive ruins like Chepstow and Raglan, there are numerous smaller sites, often only overgrown mounds from an early motte and bailey castle. A thorough survey of castle sites was undertaken by A. H. A. Hogg and D. J. C. King and the following compilation is based on their lists. While some sites may still await identification, the following is a quite comprehensive listing of those locations which can properly be identified as castle sites.

Castles documented 1066—1215 and earthworks thought to date from that period

Grid Reference	Name	6 inch O.S.
SO217020	St. Illtyd, Twyn	17 S.E.
SO299139	Abergavenny	6 S.E.
SO310201	Pen y Clawdd motte	3 S.E.
SO320100	Castell Arnallt	12 S.E.
SO330218	Bwlch Trewen	4 S.W.
SO350069	St. Mary's Yard mound	19 N.W.
SO353233	Goytre Wood motte	4 N.W.
SO363096	Twyn y Cregen	13 S.W.
SO375000	Llanbadoc, Twyn Bell	24 N.E.
SO377010	Usk	19 S.E.
SO380168	White Castle	7 N.E.
SO394088	Wern y Cwrt	13 S.E.
SO405244	Grosmont	4 N.E.
SO410132	Coed y Mount, Penrhos	13 N.E.
SO415083	Raglan	13 S.E.
SO424011	Newhouse 'camp'	20 S.W.
SO448172	Newcastle	8 N.W.
SO452070	Trecastle	14 S.W.
SO455104	Dingestow	14 N.W.
SO457202	Skenfrith	5 S.W.
SO460104	Mill Wood mound	14 N.W.
SO483142	Rockfield	8 S.E.

SO500054	Trelech, Tump Terret	20 N.E.
SO507129	Monmouth	14 N.E.
SO518137	Dixton mound	8 S.E.
ST193938	Twyn Tudur	27 N.E.
ST210789	Rhymney	37 N.E.
ST227803	Cae Castell, St. Mellons	38 N.W.
ST243927	Twm Barlwm	28 N.W.
ST251835	Wentlwg Castle	33 S.W.
ST271878	Rogerstone Castle	33 N.W.
ST302858	Castell Glas	33 N.E.
ST311991	Panteg Rectory	23 N.E.
ST312884	Newport Castle	28 S.E.
ST319925	Graig Wood motte	28 N.E.
ST342905	Caerleon	29 S.W.
ST369973	Langibby 'bowling green'	24 S.W.
ST371895	Langstone Court mound	29 S.E.
ST389939	Kemeys inferior motte	29 N.E.
ST392880	Bishton, Castle Farm	29 S.E.
ST428998	Beiliau, Llangwm	25 N.W.
ST449998	Cwrt y Gaer	25 N.W.
ST470903	Caerwent motte	30 S.E.
ST480923	Dinham	30 N.E.
ST487885	Caldicot	30 S.E.
ST488895	Ballan Moor	30 S.E.
ST533941	Chepstow	26 S.W.

Possible Sites

SO359043	Trostrey	19 N.W.
ST330886	Maindee camp	29 S.W.

Late Sites (Sites widely held to be pre-1215, but regarded by Hogg and King as later)

ST226887	Machen, Castell Meredith	28 S.W.
ST415952	Cas Troggy	24 S.E.

Masonry Castles

SO218020	Llanhilleth	17 S.E.
SO299139	Abergavenny	6 S.E.

SO377010	Usk	19 S.E.
SO380168	White Castle	7 N.E.
SO405244	Grosmont	4 N.E.
SO415083	Raglan	13 S.E.
SO457202	Skenfrith	5 S.W.
SO507129	Monmouth	14 N.E.
ST226887	Machen	28 S.W.
ST312884	Newport	28 S.E.
ST342905	Caerleon	29 S.W.
ST364974	Llangibby	24 N.W.
ST371895	Langstone Court	29 S.E.
ST382926	Kemeys House	29 N.E.
ST406894	Pencoed	29 S.E.
ST415952	Troggy	24 S.E.
ST423908	Penhow	30 N.W.
ST433920	Llanfaches	30 N.W.
ST445924	Llanfair Discoed	30 N.W.
ST480923	Dinham	30 N.E.
ST487885	Caldicot	30 S.E.
ST533941	Chepstow	26 S.W.

Notes

There is repetition in the lists since many early castles were re-built in stone. All castle sites should appear on at least one list but remains such as Hen Gwrt, a moated site at Llantilio Crosenny (SO396151), do not since they were not technically castles.

The natural tendency is to associate all Gwent castles with the Marchers, but it should be remembered that several can be identified as 'Welsh' for at least a portion of their history. In addition to obvious examples such as Caerleon, Castell Arnallt and Raglan, there are others like Machen and possibly Llanhilleth (Castell Taliorum), the latter of which was probably associated with the demise of Gwynllwg.

See Hogg, A. H. A. and King, D. J. C., 'Early Castles in Wales and the Marches' in *Archaeologia Cambrensis*, vol. CXII (1963), pp. 77-124; 'Masonry Castles in Wales and the Marches' in *Archaeologia Cambrensis*, vol. CXVI (1967), pp. 71-132; and 'Castles in Wales and the Marches: Additions and Corrections' in *Archaeologia Cambrensis*, vol. CXIX (1970), pp. 119-124.

Seasonal Traditions

Survival of folk traditions offers an interesting demonstration of cultural continuity. There are many good examples from Gwent including a number of seasonal observances. One of the most notable of these was the Christmas season custom of the Mari Lwyd (grey mare, or perhaps more literally, grey Mary). The Mari Lwyd would be made from a horse's skull, or occasionally carved from a block of wood. The lower jaw would be hinged so that a man carrying it on a short pole could cause it to open and snap closed. The head would then be decorated with coloured ribbons and the man carrying it draped in a white sheet. Thus complete, the Mari Lwyd, accompanied by its companions, would form a procession ready to visit houses through the neighbourhood. When they arrived, the leader would tap on the door while the party sang traditional rhymes. A battle of wits would ensue with the householders singing verses in answer to those of the party outside. Traditionally, the Mari Lwyd would eventually be admitted for food and drink in return for entertaining those inside. Typical verses in the competition could include examples like:

Chwech o wŷr hawddgar	Six fine men
Rhai gorau ar y ddaear,	the best on earth
I ganu mewn gwir-air—	to sing truly—for beer.
am gwrw.	

A response might be:
Mi gwnnais o'r gwely	I rose from bed
Gan lwyr benderfynu	having firmly determined
Y gwnawn i dy faeddu—	to win against you. [1]
di'n foddau.	

The Mari Lwyd was once common throughout south Wales, but nowhere more than in Gwent. In the mid nineteenth century, in Gwent and Glamorgan the ceremony would usually begin on Christmas night and continue through the next fortnight or, in some regions, even a month. There are descriptions of the custom in the late 1830s in Pontypool, Govilon, Abergavenny and 'the mountainous district generally'.

The slow end of the tradition came in the late nineteenth century and went hand in hand with a decline in the language. The custom, as well as the language of the verses, was Welsh, and as men lost the required poetical skills, the Mari Lwyd disappeared. Still, it was a gradual process. The custom survived in Ebbw Vale, for example, through the 1870s and the Mari Lwyd appeared at public houses in Rassau in about 1880. Moreover, the custom also endured in the east with a modified ceremony in Monmouth and its environs until about 1913. The most remarkable survival, however, was in Caerleon where the Mari Lwyd was still seen in the 1930s. Men there had virtually lost their Welsh but could still sing the traditional rhymes and they persevered in the face of change. For example, when an English household moved into Glenusk, they tried to avoid the attentions of the Mari Lwyd by placing a fierce bulldog at their gate. The Mari Lwyd, however, had the last laugh. A few clacks of the horse's jaw was enough to send the terrified bulldog scurrying to safety. The highly insulted Mari Lwyd party, however, left, making straight for the Bull at Caerleon where they could expect a more friendly reception. [2]

Another Christmas custom which declined with the Welsh language was the plygain—an early morning carol service. A striking feature of the service was that the church would be impressively lit by candles. Sometimes each member of the congregation brought his own candle to add to those specially decorated by the women of the church. The hour for the service could vary from 3 a.m. to 6 a.m., although with the passage of time the later hour became more common. Sometimes, young parishioners would stay awake through the evening before the plygain, frequently decorating the houses or coming together to make cyflaith (treacle coffee). Interestingly, the plygain was one of the few traditional customs which bridged the divide between church and chapel. Many nonconformists also held plygain services. Once widespread in Gwent, the plygain disappeared at much the same time as the Mari Lwyd. The last services at Ebbw Vale, for example, were held in the 1870s. [3] Carol singing, however, continued. In Shirenewton, carolling took place not only on 25th December, but also on 1st January and 6th January—Old Christmas Day. The Gregorian calendar only became official in Britain in 1752 and some residents of Shirenewton clearly decided to continue to keep Christmas according to the old calendar—or, even better, celebrate it twice.

A wide range of these sorts of seasonal observances occurred throughout the year. For example, Mothering Sunday, the middle Sunday in Lent, was an important day in Chepstow and surrounding villages. *The Gentleman's Magazine* of 1784 reported that it was the practice for apprentices and servants in and around Chepstow 'to visit their parents and make them a present of money, a trinket, or some nice eatables'. The tradition was maintained and eventually the 'eatables' conventionally took the form of iced buns sprinkled with coloured sugar 'hundreds and thousands'.[5] In the same area, graves were decked with flowers on Palm Sunday into the 1880s.[6] In regions like Trelech, the Easter season was the time to prepare the fields symbolically. One custom was 'walking the wheat' which occurred on Easter Sunday. The farmer, his family, and the farm labourers would walk up and down the fields of young wheat, each carrying a small cake and some cider. They would eat a bit, bury a little, and throw a small piece to the wind. While doing this, they would repeat:

A bit for God, a bit for man,
And a bit for the fowls of the air.

Eggs also played an important role in Easter observances. On Easter Sunday in Pontypool, for example, hard boiled eggs which had been dyed different colours were rolled down a grassy slope. The owner of the last egg to break was the winner.[7] Gentle pursuits like Easter egg rolling, however, gave way to more boisterous celebrations at Whitsuntide. This was especially true in northwest Gwent where sporting competitions were held on Whit Sunday and Whit Monday and participants were refreshed with the specially brewed Whitsun ale. A variation on the theme was found in places including Bedwellty and Mynydd Islwyn where annual 'Lamb Ale' competitions were held. The competitors were women who had to chase and catch a fat lamb using only their teeth. To assure compliance with the rules, entrants had their hands tied behind their backs. The best strategy frequently proved to be attempting to coax the lambs to stay rather than chasing after them through the fields. The winner was proclaimed 'Lady of the Lamb' and she presided over the feast which followed the competition; her health was drunk repeatedly in 'Lamb Ale'. The people of Newport took a similar view of Whitsun through the annual Stow Fair held at Stow Hill during every

Whit Week until about 1860. During the fair, anyone was allowed to sell beer and people advertised their willingness to do so by hanging a bush or branch outside their house. A Lord Mayor was elected to preside over the raucous celebrations which became renowned — infamous is probably a more accurate description — throughout the county.[8] Oak Apple Day, 29th May, could also be quite rowdy in some parts of Gwent. Leaves or branches of oak were worn to commemorate the return of Charles II to London from exile in 1660. In some places, failure to wear the oak would result in attacks from small boys armed with stinging nettles. In Monmouth and Caerleon, regular combats would take place among boys armed with bunches of twigs tied up into 'muntles'. The Monmouth 'battle' took place on the Monnow bridge between boys from the town and from nearby Over Monnow. The custom of wearing the oak continued in Chepstow until after the First World War. Boys there wore oak apples to school until the 1920s.[9]

A particularly persistent tradition stemmed from the ancient Celtic festival of Samhain. The Celtic new year began on 1st November and it was thought that on the night before that day, which was also the anniversary of the creation of order out of chaos, barriers between man and the supernatural were lowered. As a consequence, precautions including bonfires, were needed to discourage visitations from the spirit world. Even after the church attempted to discourage observation of Samhain by incorporating the day into the church calendar as All Saints Day, to most minds the preceding evening remained an ysbrydnos (spirit night) which gave rise to the modern Hallowe'en.[10] In some regions during the last century, men would observe the night by dressing in sheepskins or old clothes, blackening or masking their faces and then going through the villages. These gwrachod (witches) would solicit coppers or apples from houses or passers by and drinks from public-houses. Another common practice was to make lighted Jack o' Lanterns by scooping out a swede or pumpkin before carving a face and placing a candle inside. At places like Griffithstown and Pontypool, these lanterns were placed on gateposts to ward off the bwci and other local spirits. Apples were used in Hallowe'en games for children. In Pontypool, cored apples would be hung on a nail over the doorway to houses. The object was to catch the spinning apples in the mouth and eat as large a piece as possible. A variation on the theme was found at Caerleon where shops would have tubs of water filled with apples which children would attempt to take out using only their mouths. The apple tradition is recalled in the popular old rhyme:

Nos g'langaea', twco 'fala',	Winter's eve, baiting of apples,
Pwy sy'n dod ma's i chwara?	who's coming out to play?
Ladi wen ar ben y pren	The White Lady on top of the tree
Yn naddu coes ymbrelo.	Whittling an umbrella stick. [11]

In recent years, one aspect of the Samhain tradition — bonfires — has been transferred to Guy Fawkes' Day. In some parts of Gwent, however, these observances sometimes got badly out of hand. This was nowhere more the case than in Chepstow where lighted barrels of tar were regularly rolled down the steep streets. The practice continued through the middle nineteenth century with, in 1863, a fireball set ablaze on top of the Beaufort Arms Assembly Rooms. At times full scale battles with the police ensued and in 1875 the practice became even more dangerous when local boys stole 24 pounds of blasting powder from a local contractor to ignite on Guy Fawkes' night. [12]

The persistence of seasonal observations like the Mari Lwyd and Samhain traditions confirms cultural continuity in Gwent. Most of these customs, however, had disappeared by the early decades of the present century. Still, some folk traditions have survived to more recent times. One is the custom of 'roping' the bride and groom at their wedding. There were variations in the practice, but at some stage — at the church porch, the church-yard, or in the road outside the church yard — the married couple would find their way blocked or 'roped'. In order to pass, they would have to distribute a small, symbolic sum of money to villagers. Sometimes flowers were attached to the rope and the bridal party, having 'paid' for them, were then given the flowers. In places, the custom has been preserved in recent times by couples trying to preserve old traditions. Brides and grooms in Devauden, for example, have been 'roped' for pennies right into the 1970s. [13]

An even more persistent folk custom is the calennig. The collection of this New Year's gift is an old one which was once common throughout Wales. Of particular interest, however, is the variation in the tradition found in Gwent, Glamorgan and old Carmarthenshire. In these regions, children made a symbolic calennig from an apple. Three short skewers were inserted into the apple making a tripod base and a longer skewer served as a handle. The apple would then be decorated with a variety of box, rosemary or other evergreens, or corn, stuck into the top of the apple. Sometimes, half-cracked hazel nuts would be attached as well. The apple itself was decorated with oats, raisins, cloves, etc. Village children would then carry the calennig from house to house and recite rhymes in return for small gifts of food or pennies. An example of the rhyme would be:

Mi godais heddiw ma's o'm tŷ	I came out of my house today
A'm cwd a'm pastwn gyda mi.	with a bag and sticks.
A dyma'm neges ar eich traws,	My errand here is to fill my
Sef llanw'm cwd a bara a chaws.	bag with bread and cheese. [14]

An English version from Chepstow, where the calennig was sometimes called a Monty, was:

Monty, Monty, Happy New Year,
a pocket full of money and a cellar full of beer! [15]

The most interesting feature about the calennig is that it survives to the present day in east Gwent villages near the Fedw Wood, including St. Arvans. While the recitations by groups of village children have largely disappeared, the calennig itself has not. Although not common today, some villagers continue to include the traditional calennig apple among their Christmas decorations. In some cases, the decorative design has been handed down within families making the colourful custom a remarkable unbroken folk tradition. [16]

NOTES

[1] Owen, Ifor, *Welsh Folk Customs* (Cardiff: 1978), pp. 49-54.

[2] Ibid.; and Roderick, Alan, *The Folklore of Gwent* (Cwmbran: 1983) pp. 102-105.

[3] Roderick, p. 107; and Owen, pp. 28-30.

[4] Roderick, p. 112.

[5] Waters, I., *Folklore and Dialect of the Lower Wye Valley* (Chepstow: 1973) p. 15; and Simpson, J., *The Folklore of the Welsh Border* (London: 1976) p. 140.

[6] Simpson, p. 142.

[7] Roderick, pp. 107-108.

[8] Ibid. pp. 109-110.

[9] Ibid. p. 110; and Waters, Folklore, p. 15.

[10] Chadwick, Nora, *The Celts* (London: 1970) p. 181; Owen, p. 97; and Norton-Taylor, D., *The Celts* (London: 1974) pp. 92-93.

[11] Owen, pp. 133-135; and Evans, John, *Llyfr Hwiangerddi* (Cardiff: 1981) p. 79.

[12] Waters, Folklore, p. 11.

[13] Howell, R., p. 81.

[14] Owen, pp. 43-46. In some places an orange was used instead of an apple. The custom spread into border regions like Herefordshire and Gloucestershire.

[15] Waters, Folklore, pp. 11-13.

[16] Howell, R., p. 81.

Index